PRACTICES FOR THE
REFOUNDING OF GOD'S PEOPLE

PRACTICES
FOR THE
REFOUNDING OF
GOD'S
PEOPLE

The Missional Challenge
of the West

ALAN J. ROXBURGH &
MARTIN ROBINSON

CHURCH
PUBLISHING
INCORPORATED

Unless otherwise noted, the Scripture quotations contained herein are from the New Revised Standard Version Bible, copyright © 1989 by the Division of Christian Education of the National Council of Churches of Christ in the U.S.A. Used by permission. All rights reserved.

Church Publishing
19 East 34th Street
New York, NY 10016
www.churchpublishing.org

Cover design by Jennifer Kopec, 2Pug Design
Typeset by Denise Hoff
Library of Congress Cataloging-in-Publication Data

Names: Roxburgh, Alan J., author.
Title: Practices for the refounding of God's people : the missional challenge
    of the west / Alan Roxburgh and Martin Robinson.
Description: New York : Church Publishing, 2018. | Includes bibliographical
    references and index.
Identifiers: LCCN 2017061192 (print) | LCCN 2018014344 (ebook) |
    ISBN 9780819233851 (ebook) | ISBN 9780819233844 (pbk. : alk. paper)
Subjects: LCSH: Christianity and culture. | Mission of the church. | Missions.
Classification: LCC BR115.C8 (ebook) | LCC BR115.C8 R668 2018 (print) |
    DDC 261--dc23
LC record available at https://lccn.loc.gov/2017061192

Printed in the United States of America

Contents

Introduction

This book addresses the nature of a missiological engagement with Western culture in all its paradoxical, conflicted complexity. What we call the West was formed out of Christian imagination. The modern West emerged from a trajectory that dispelled that imagination in what is called "modernity's wager,"[1] which consists of the belief that all life can be lived well without the need for God's agency. The practices and beliefs of the modern West were shaped by the conviction that the future lies in our own hands. Human agency became the primary driver of social, cultural, political, and economic life.

The West is like a child becoming independent of her parents. Imagine a parent teaching her daughter to ride a bike. At the beginning the parent reassures the daughter that she is (think—the Christian story) holding the bike solidly; she has no need to worry about falling and being hurt. For the daughter, it is a passage to adulthood, a step into maturity, a memory to look back on with the smiles of a grown-up. The parent's goal is straightforward: provide security as her self-confidence grows. Gradually the parent takes her hands off as the daughter joyously rides down the road with no assistance. The modern West has taken a similar view of its Christian past. We're all grown adults no longer in need of that kind of support. We're mature agents in control of our own destiny. For those who need it, there's still a religious tradition. God has not disappeared but become useful: a resource in our journey to independence. God, however, has nothing to do with the systems, structures, and operations of everyday life. Few foresaw this consequence as the modern West was forming out of its earlier Christian narrative, which is why Nietzsche has remained such a prescient voice. He declared that we killed God. For some, his language is too strong to accept. What we can say is that the West has transformed the God of the Christian tradition into a merely useful support or addendum to human action. God is still here, cheering in the stadium as we push ahead with our agendas.

We argue, in this book, that modernity's wager has been far more corrosive to human thriving than any of its architects would have imagined.

---

1. The term *modernity's wager* is taken from the book of that title by Adam Seligman (*Modernity's Wager* [Princeton, NJ: Princeton University Press, 2000]).

All of us in the West are part of the unraveling of this wager. Further, we propose that this unraveling is only part of the story. There is another story forming within the unraveling. It is about a ferment and bubbling happening across the West within which God is continuing to make all things new. The missiological challenge before the churches is to embrace this ferment in the confidence that God is the primary agent in the sea-change that is remaking the West. God is present in this disorienting change. Lesslie Newbigin asked, "Can the West be converted?" The response is "yes," but make no mistake: the missiological challenge is not to focus on fixing or reforming the churches but to participate with the Spirit in the refounding of an unmoored society.

The West and its Euro-tribal churches have entered a time of unraveling that questions the nature of Christian identity and the meaning of the West. This is more than a description of historical fact or a nostalgic longing for what once was. Far more is at stake. With the loss of the Christian narrative and the ascendance of modernity's wager, the West has lost its way to the extent that many of its citizens feel unmoored and cast adrift. Modernity's promises have lost their power to deliver. Questions of a missiological engagement with the West are not parochial; they are not primarily about the churches and their survival. The questions are about Christian vocation in the restoration and healing of all creation. This is the core vocational challenge confronting Christians. Larry Siedentop, Faculty Lecturer in Political Thought at Oxford, questions:

> Does it still make sense to talk about "the West"? People who live in nations once described as part of Christendom—what many would now call the post-Christian world—seem to have lost their moral bearings. We no longer have a persuasive story to tell ourselves about our origins and development.[2]

Niall Ferguson states it in these terms:

> I really got to the point about the first decade of the twenty-first century, just as it was drawing to a close: that we are living through the end of 500 years of Western ascendancy.[3]

---

2. Larry Siedentop, *Inventing the Individual: The Origins of Western Liberalism* (London: Penguin Books, 2014), 1.

3. Niall Ferguson, *Civilization: The West and the Rest* (Toronto: Penguin Books, 2011), xv.

Paul Weston, in reflecting on the intellectual work of Lesslie Newbigin comments:

> When Lesslie Newbigin returned from India in 1974 after 36 years of missionary experience, he was struck by what he came to describe as "the disappearance of hope" in the culture of the West. Always the missionary, Newbigin's quest to find out what had happened to produce such an effect propelled him into a program of study and reflection. As he would later describe it, this process led him to the judgement that the culture of the West was "the most challenging missionary frontier of our time."[4]

This book is not about how Christians might contribute to restoring the West. Our concern is about how God is calling the churches to participate in the healing of the world. In the West, too many of the children of modernity live without a narrative core that provides hope or direction. A widespread malaise, a disappearance of hope, has only deepened since Newbigin wrote. This book addresses ideas that might reorder Christian life in response to this challenge. The churches have little to say to the late modern culture of the West. They are little more than clubs where people gather for forms of personal reinforcement and are profoundly disconnected from the massive challenges of our culture. Christians in the West can discover ways to act in the conviction that God is the primary agent; only from this vantage point can we join God in the restoration of life in the West.

Throughout its history, the Church has faced crises of meaning and identity in all kinds of contexts. In the early 1950s, Newbigin presented the Kerr Lectures at Trinity College, Glasgow. In that time just after the end of World War II, there was a stark realization among Christian leaders that churches in the West had finally lost their identity as meaningful participants in the shaping of Western societies. They had become loosely compacted fellowships providing only a minimal, even token, part of the life of their members. They were mostly clubs with little to no effect on the wider society. Not much has changed. This loss of capacity for churches to influence and shape the lives of people in the West has, in fact, become more exacerbated. The societies of the West see churches as largely irrelevant to their search for a way out of the multiplying crises

---

4. Paul Weston, "Lesslie Newbigin: Looking Forward in Retrospect," *Journal of Missional Practice* (Winter 2015)

of Western life. Newbigin wrote of the need for Christian communities to be shaped around an eschatological and missionary imagination. The identity of churches cannot be formed around notions of religious clubs—even very useful clubs—but from the perspective of God's actions in the remaking of the world and the healing of life (eschatological). Such an orientation means that the Church's fundamental character is a community participating in the mission of God.[5] Newbigin's response to the crisis of the churches in the West remains before us. Augustine framed his great *City of God* in a similar situation. Benedict formed his order in another such context. Crisis is the soil in which God's healing, redemptive future flourishes through Christian life. The crises before the West are overwhelming. Christian vocation as a missionary people must be reframed for this context. At their best, churches have recognized their vocation is not fixing themselves or even calling for some kind of "new" reformation, but rather, joining with God in the transformation and refounding of society in the name of Christ. The distinction is key because reformation remains focused on the church, whereas refounding is focused on the missionary vocation of the church. This book explores how this vocation can be engaged in the West unfolding before us.

The dominance of those churches formed out of the European and English reformations of the fifteenth and sixteenth centuries is over. The churches that sprung from this five-hundred-year era in Western history became the dominant form of Christianity around the globe. That dominance lasted up to the end of World War I. These Euro-tribal churches now spread around the globe are in deep decline, especially in the places where they were formed—Europe and North America. They have lost their way. Turned in on themselves and the question of their own survival, they have become almost totally ecclesiocentric, preoccupied with trying to fix their structures and institutions in order to regain their place in Western societies. The result has been a profound loss of confidence that the God made known to us in Jesus Christ is the active agent in the world. There is a loss of confidence that God is out ahead, active in ordinary places in a dramatically changing West. These churches have failed to see this because they have been focused on fixing themselves.

In the midst of these realities, God is still up to what God has always been up to: the transformation, refounding, and reweaving of life across

---

5. Lesslie Newbigin, *The Household of God* (London: SCM, 1953), 9–13.

creation. The Church is continually being invited by the Spirit to join with God in this vast mission as a sign, witness, instrument, and fore-taste of what God is doing for the whole of creation. The unraveling of these Euro-tribal churches has not been primarily a result of socio-cultural factors (demographics, secularity, etc.) or economic, polit-ical, or ideological transformations in a networked, globalized world. While these are contributing factors, they are not the primary theolog-ical reason for the malaise of these churches and their vocation. In our view, it is the Spirit who is unraveling these Euro-tribal churches. We believe the Spirit is doing this so that they might come to their senses and embrace this gospel call to join with God in the refounding, the reweaving, the remaking of social life in an emerging West. The call and vocation of Euro-tribal churches has been lost in their anxieties around displacement and their obsession with trying to fix themselves and their institutions. It is time to heed the Spirit and go on a different journey out ahead where God is already at work.

This book addresses the questions of how Euro-tribal churches might engage the trajectory of the West inside modernity's wager in order to embrace the vocation to which God is calling them. For this to happen, these churches need an imagination that will move them away from agendas to fix the churches toward one of joining God in the transforma-tion of the postsecular societies of the West.[6] It is only from within this engagement that we will discern the practices for being God's people and, therefore, the shape of our churches.

There are many ways of framing the malaise preoccupying both these churches and the modern West. The English sociologist Elaine Graham describes our situation as "one of simultaneous religious decline, muta-tion and resurgence."[7] A massive de-institutionalization of religious life is occurring across almost all the Protestant denominations that are the heirs of the fifteenth- and sixteenth-century reformations. Euro-tribal churches were transported to the "new worlds" through conquest, com-merce, migration, and mission endeavors over the last five hundred years. Historian Susan Schreiner describes a situation where we are experiencing

> *"the inevitable response to the growing inability of an inherited culture to invest experience with meaning"*

---

6. For description and discussion of postsecularity, see Graham Ward, *The Politics of Discipleship* (Grand Rapids: Baker, 2009), chapter 3, and Elaine Graham, *Between a Rock and a Hard Place: Public Theology in a Post-Secular Age* (London: SCM Press, 2013), part 1. .

7. Graham, *Between a Rock and a Hard Place*, 3.

> . . . like early modernity, we, too, are consumed with
> the breakdown of traditionally certain beliefs. Like the
> early modern era, our own time is . . . a time of "great
> unmooring." . . . Every aspect of our culture reveals this
> anxiety that truth and reality are ephemeral. . . . The
> result is . . . a sense of vertigo and weariness.[8]

The sociologist Zygmunt Bauman characterizes the current situation of the West not just in terms of a liquid modernity but also as a state of crisis[9] that is not a short-term challenge soon to be fixed by tinkering with existing systems. This unravelling is about a passage wherein we have lost confidence in the primary institutions of the modern West (the state, economics, religious organizations, or a host of taken-for-granted ways of life)—particularly their capacity to address the deeply unsettling issues confronting life in our time. From financial crisis to massive increases in unemployment, from the loss of a sense that middle-class life is sustainable to the increasing fears of terrorism and extremism, people feel ever more vulnerable. They do not see existing institutions offering hope or ways forward.

One of the hard challenges is that the generation that has shaped the leadership of the Euro-tribal churches were raised during the heydays of economic progress and social development in the optimistic times of the sixties, seventies, and eighties when any downturn (for example, the economy) would be followed by an upturn and continuing progress. Crises were temporary. Things would always, eventually, right themselves and get better. Bred into the collective psyche of these leaders has been this presumption of progress and the capacity of human agency to develop strategies and programs to address any challenge. These convictions have guided leaders of the Euro-tribal churches for a half century of deepening crises. Up until very recently, the leaders of these churches continued to believe that some adjustments and well-designed strategies would result in a return to the upward curve of growth for their churches. All that was needed was the right leader, or the right key, to get the right adjustment. This perception lies shattered before us. The wreckage is profound; the disorientation extreme. The defaults of trying to fix must be replaced by a

---

8. Susan E. Schreiner, *Are You Alone Wise? The Search for Certainty in the Early Modern Era* (Oxford: Oxford University Press, 2011), xi–xiii (italics added).
9. Zygmunt Bauman, *Liquid Modernity* (Oxford: Polity Press, 2000); Zygmunt Bauman and Carlo Bordoni, *State of Crisis* (Malden, MA: Polity Press, 2013).

willingness to refound the life of these churches to be, again, a sign, witness, and foretaste of God's transformative kingdom.

The Euro-tribal churches have been living within a false consciousness for a long time. Collectively, their self-understanding and ways of engaging a changing West no longer have the capacity to explain or address the crises in ways that capture people's imagination. The arena of economics offers an illustration of what has happened to the Euro-tribal churches. Over the last decade the global economy has been confronted with shock-waves of upheaval. In addressing these disruptions, states and economic leaders have been guided by what might be called a fix assumption. This default assumption is manifest in the ways states developed legislation to govern banks and regulate the manipulation of the money supply. It is demonstrated in the attempts to fix national economies through massive infusions of money in the hope that this would result in a return to an expanding job market. Behind these, and other actions, stands the presumption that judicious fixes to the system would return the economic life of citizens to some form of normalcy—a resumption of life before the fall. What is settling into our general consciousness is that the upheavals manifest in 2008–2009 were not amenable to established assumptions and are not going to be fixed with established strategies. There is no returning to some pre-2008 normalcy.

Even the language that once seemed to make so much sense—for example, economic ups-and-downs—now seems archaic, incapable of making sense of what has happened. Economists and political leaders in Western nations assumed that standard explanations for economic challenges (embodied in such terms as *inflation, adjustment to globalization, recession, employment-unemployment projections from previous periods of downturn,* or *the application of financial stimuli* and so forth) would move economies back onto the path of expansion. But this is not happening. In plain terms, the presumed metrics are no longer usable. The assumption that if one can make adjustments using established metrics there will be a return to normal is dead. Economists are confounded with what is happening to the economies of nation-states and global markets. No matter how many buttons get pressed or levers moved, little changes a continuing malaise around a jobless economy, a constricting middle class, and an increasing sense of insecurity across the citizenries of the West. As this new, unanticipated reality sets in, there is a deepening fear that something has gone terribly wrong and that, whatever it is, it can't be fixed with established formulas or metrics. One can sense the panic rising in people. Citizens across Western nations are losing confidence in their political and economic establishments. The United States has become a polarized nation driven, to a large extent, by this underlying sense that the economic and political world that had given people confidence and stability has gone and that political leadership has no idea what to do.

This is also the story of the Euro-tribal churches. A fear has settled in among the people and leaders of these churches that one more attempt at renewal or restructure isn't going to get everything started again. When leaders feel this panic, their tendency is to work even harder at finding another fix, discovering one more new adjectival modifier to put in front of the word *church* (simple, natural, fresh, missional, and on and on and on) as if that will address what's happening. These churches are in a new land, a different kind of West from the one in which they were founded and flourished. The challenge can no longer be defined in terms of renewal or restructuring. But the loss of legitimacy across growing sectors of Western life (political, religious, economic) is sending leaders in a desperate search for strategies to fix and renew their systems.

This book argues that God is the primary active agent in the midst of all this and that God up to something different. The Spirit is inviting these once established churches to join with God in the remaking of Western societies, not in fixing themselves. The refounding vocation of this moment is to leave behind an ecclesiocentric imagination and embrace a missiological call to join with God, who is already out ahead seeking to form doxological communities of life and hope. This is not a new call. It has given purpose to God's people across the centuries. Its strangeness to us is testimony to our ecclesiocentric captivity. Growing numbers of Christians on both sides of the Atlantic sense the rightness of this description. They wrestle, however, with the question of what to do, of how to act. Over and over when we meet with church leaders, the fundamental question is "How? How do we go about such a process of refounding?" Hundreds of thousands are leaving their churches, tired of all the fix solutions.[10] They've come to the end of a well-worn road and have little interest in the vision statements of denominations or the latest metrics for making the church work again. They are fed up with churches talking about themselves in world facing such massive challenges.

---

10. In North America the varied groups of Christians leaving the churches are being designated as the "Dones." It is estimated that some 65 million such people have left North American churches over the past decade. They are not switching to another church but chosen to no longer attend or belong to a church. See, for example, Josh Packard, *Church Refugees* (Loveland, CO: Group Publishing, 2015).

What Are the Ways Forward?

How can the Euro-tribal churches be refounded? Catholic philosopher Louis Dupre describes our time as a passage.[11] We are in an unpredictable passage from one time to another. For the Euro-tribal churches, this passage must no longer be characterized by its own turning inward to describe itself with terms such as *loss* or *exile*. These metaphors of grief and loss are understandable, but they can only misdirect us in discerning the actions that need to be taken. Metaphors of loss and exile tend to focus on the inner feelings and experiences of those in the churches who feel that their world has been taken from them by forces they can't name. The terms *postmodern, secularization, liberal, fundamentalist* explain little except the sense of unmooring and disorientation. Such language tends to keeps us captive in our ecclesiocentrism—it's about our loss and what's happening to our churches.

The metaphors of journey and passage are far richer and evocative. They suggest invitation, discovery, discernment, and experimenting. They invite us to see that the location of hope is out on a road; it is neither predictable nor within our means to control. It is, however, in exactly this kind of place where we will see the work God has for us. Passage and journey are not about inner feelings. They are about actions: the decision and choice to go in a particular direction, to embrace a vocation that takes us beyond fixing. We live, to borrow George Steiner's memorable phrase, in the "age of the afterward."[12] It's the time after where we can't go back to what was. We are in the time after the domain of the Euro-tribal churches (of whatever color or shade, whether left or right, liberal or conservative, new evangelical or neoliberal). This is the time of the afterward in which nostalgia, yearning for a past or even the need to grieve is not the call of God, but rather a siren song that leads inexorably to death. Like Ulysses of old, church leaders need to tie themselves to the mast of God's future in order to resist the inexorable temptation of the sirens calling us back to ecclesiocentric fixes and the sad songs of false imagination around exile. The time of afterward requires different metaphors, an alternative imagination. Such imagination and metaphor were present in the ancient father

---

11. Louis Dupre, *A Passage to Modernity: An Essay in the Hermeneutics of Nature and Culture* (New Haven, CT: Yale University Press, 1993).
12. George Steiner, *After Babel* (New York: Oxford University Press, 1977).

and mother of our faith, Abram and Sarai. Here is the story of a worn-out, dried-up, dung-heap ancient couple, offering no hope or future. It is a picture that describes the Euro-tribal churches. From every reasonable perspective, Abram and Sara were finished. But God wasn't ready to leave them in grief, or allow them to feel that somehow they had been exiled. On the contrary, God called these ancient, finished old people onto a journey away from their self-oriented perception of the situation into a passage, a journey, to a place unnamed. They went in the confidence that the One who called was to be trusted. Metaphors of exile and loss pale compared to this couple, as described in the words of Hebrews:

> By faith Abraham, when he was called, obeyed by going out to a place which he was to receive for an inheritance; and he went out, not knowing where he was going. (11:8, NASB)

For some this imagination will miss the essential need of getting the church right: assuring that people truly understand its essence and nature in order to be the right kind of church in our time. If such an approach were to have worked, it would have already done so. Getting the right understanding of what Jesus meant by the kingdom of God or developing a new confession about the great ends of the church[13] sound like the right things to do, but we have now lived through decades and decades of this continual urging to get our thinking right and it has not resolved our crisis. There is no disagreement with the need for right thinking. Nevertheless, we could sink a ship with the books written with this aim of setting straight the way we ought to think about the church. Here's the problem: perhaps without intention, these moves are all focused on getting our understanding of church right. They are ecclesiocentric from top to bottom. Susan Schreiner writes of how "an age often talks most frequently and most stridently about that which it is already in the process of losing."[14] This fixation on getting the church right will not get the church right, yet it has been the only focus of the

---

13. The "great ends of the church" is a section in the first part of the PCUSA Book of Order. As such, it is a wonderful theological framing of Reformed theology. The point here is not to criticize this document but rather propose that more rounds of trying to clarify or explain more deeply what this means will not get at the more fundamental challenges before the Euro-tribal churches at this time.

14. Schreiner, *Are You Alone Wise?*, xii.

Euro-tribal churches for a very long time. In the age of afterward, we have become increasingly strident about getting an ecclesiocentric fix with ever more adjectival modifiers about the kind of church we need to be. These narratives have lost their capacity to provide reason or meaning to the experiences of a growing majority of the citizens of the West. The energies of the Euro-tribal churches are still being expended, like the flailing of beached whales, in desperate attempts to relocate and reestablish themselves in the West. In so doing, they continue to display their own enclosure with an ecclesiocentric ocean.

Ludwig Wittgenstein proposed that the challenge confronting people in times of transition was that they have a picture in their heads of what things ought to look like and how the world ought to behave. This picture is extremely hard to get outside of; it's like being held in a prison. Wittgenstein was saying that, after a time, one's habitual way of seeing and reading the world becomes so established that the picture becomes just the assumed way the world is. When this happens, the picture we have of the world ceases to be something we have to keep remembering and reminding ourselves of. It is fixed in our imagination. Most important of all for Wittgenstein, the main reason this picture holds us captive is because it has been embedded in our language, which means that every time we speak and use metaphors to explain ourselves, our language repeats to us our picture. Hence, the ways church leaders currently speak of exile or loss reflect a picture of the world inside them; they are trying to read what is happening in their changing contexts by looking in a mirror. Our seeing and interpreting the world can be like looking in a mirror. Our language, our speaking and explaining, repeats to us the image that is inside us. Wittgenstein puts it as follows: "A picture holds us captive and we couldn't get outside it, for it lay in our language, and language only seemed to repeat it to us inexorably"[15] All the efforts to reengineer, re-vision, renew, or plant over the past century as one long, desperate attempt to fix the church and stem its decline haven't and won't work. What is at stake is not amenable to adjustment of existing forms. Something far deeper is called for. Our situation is not exile. It is an invitation to a journey in the time that is the afterward. This is the context within which we must consider the question of the *refounding* of the Euro-tribal churches.

---

15. Ludwig Wittgenstein, *Philosophical Investigations* (Hoboken, NJ: n.p., 2009), 115.

The chapters that follow describe an alternative imagination. They paint the picture of the consequences of the modern West's choice to shape its life around modernity's wager. We will look at some of the primary sources of this wager, and then propose ways the churches can refound themselves to engage this changing West. Our ancient father and mother, Abram and Sarai suggest to us the way forward.

1

The Emergence of the Modern West

> Yet any history of the world's civilizations that underplays the degree of their gradual subordination to the West after 1500 is missing the essential point—the thing most in need of explanation. The rise of the West is, quite simply, the pre-eminent historical phenomenon of the second half of the second millennium after Christ. It is the story at the very heart of modern history. It is perhaps the most challenging riddle historians have to solve. . . . For it is only by identifying the true causes of Western ascendency that we can hope to estimate with any degree of accuracy the imminence of our decline and fall.[1]

The place of Christianity in the rise of Western modernity has been under discussion for more than a century. Those who are sympathetic to religion tend, these days, to give it an important place; those who are less so tend to minimize its role. Thinkers with a favorable stance toward modernity see it as the realizations of Christian ideals. Christian reactionaries who hate the modern world define Christianity as its antithesis. Ivan Illich changes the very terms of the debate. For him, modernity is neither the fulfillment nor the antithesis of Christianity, but its perversion.[2]

Modernity's Wager

The modern West is a construct, an idea, which has become the normative story of how we read and see our world. This chapter looks at

---

1. Niall Ferguson, *Civilization: The West and the Rest* (Toronto: Penguin Books, 2011), 18.
2. Charles Taylor, "Foreward," in David Cayley, *The Rivers North of the Future* (Toronto: Anansi, 2005), ix.

the development of this narrative. The modern West takes up elements of a prior Christian story (designated as Christendom) and reinterprets them in terms of modernity's wager.[3] That wager was the conviction that life could be lived well without God. It represented a conviction about the sufficiency of human agency that needed neither the sponsorship nor the undergirding of God. This huge change in the West's imagination did not occur overnight. It was the transition of some three centuries. It does not mean a majority of people in the West placed a bet, with all the concomitant risks, on living without God. Rather, there was a progression from the fourteenth through seventeenth centuries wherein leading thinkers and theorists came to believe that it was possible, reasonable, and desirable to reshape all aspects of life without reference to God. It is in this sense that modernity represented a massive wager never before attempted by any society or civilization. The institutions, habits, and practices that came to shape the West were born out of this wager. The question of a gospel engagement with this West must address this wager. Current forms of political (nation-states), economic (capitalism), and social life (the Self) in the West are all functions of this wager. At the beginning of our new millennium the modern West is experiencing its own disorienting transformations. These are, however, not moving away from the wager, but offering new proposals for making it work. The first half of this book looks at the emergence of the modern from this perspective.

The Idea of the *Modern*

The idea of the modern is not new. It emerged as the medieval synthesis broke apart starting in thirteenth-century Europe and into the fifteenth-century reformations. The notion of the West emerges in the nineteenth century. The word *modern* was part of a spiritual and intellectual struggle around the identity of Christendom that would, from the twelfth through the fifteenth centuries, change the very basis upon which the West had been formed. As such, it is a word that expresses the ending of the Christendom that began with the Germanic peoples and the formation of the Frankish kingdoms. The notion of the modern is formed around a conflict between the ancients and the moderns, and an intellectual movement known as nominalism. Only in the

---

3. This is a term first presented by Adam Seligman in his book *Modernity's Wager* (Princeton, NJ: Princeton University Press, 2000).

nineteenth century did the notions of the modern and the West came together to form the powerful, ideological imagination that has shaped our world over the last two centuries. Today, we take for granted the idea of the modern West. We assume a broad-based, common understanding of what it means. It is on this basis that many of us interpret and read our world. For some, there is the "West and the Rest."[4] Others wonder, "West of what?" The missiological challenges before the Euro-tribal churches must give attention to what happened in the formation of the modern West as a reigning narrative.

A Passage to Modernity[5]

> [M]odern civilization differs radically from other civilizations and cultures. The truth is that our culture is permeated by nominalism, which grants real existence only to individuals and not to relations. . . . Nominalism, in fact, is just another name for individualism, or rather one of its facets.[6]

Today people write about the modern West in terms of its transformation or decline, the end of an ideology, the end of history, or the renewal of the West.[7] While engaging these discussions, the intention here is to describe what is generally meant by the phrase *the modern West* today. The term means far more than a geography. It refers to ideas, institutions, values, and ways of seeing the world. The West came to view its social, political, economic, and religious forms as the apex of all civilizations. This viewpoint was then generalized into every society on earth. The idea of the modern West found its antecedents in European reformations and enlightenments that began in the late fifteenth century that would result in the end of Christendom. Those of us of European and North American descent have been inextricably born into a modern imagination, even as we participate in its continuing transformations. We take the modern as a given; we conceive of it as the normative way in which to see the world and, generally, have little awareness of the

---

4. See Ferguson, *Civilization,* and Roger Scruton, *The West and the Rest: Globalization and the Terrorist Threat* (New York: Intercollegiate Studies Institute, 2014).
5. See Louis Dupre's brilliant book by this title *Passage to Modernity* (New Haven, CT: Yale University Press, 1993).
6. Louis Dumont, *Essays on Individualism: Modern Ideology in Antropological Perspective* (Chicago: University of Chicago Press, 1986), 11.
7. See Ferguson's *Civilization.*

dynamics which brought it about. In its birth and the wager that it made are the clues for addressing Newbigin's question about a gospel engagement with the West. What was it about the birth of the modern that now raises for us questions about a gospel engagement? We must go back several centuries to understand.

The *Ancients* and the *Moderns*

From the thirteenth to the seventeenth century, Europe moved through a transformative social, political, economic, environmental, and religious upheaval that remade its basic animating ideas and institutions.[8] Over this period, Western assumptions about the nature of man, the world, and the universe were turned upside down. These were the centuries in which, for example, our understanding of the universe and our place in it underwent "one of the most dramatic changes in cosmology that the Western world had ever experienced."[9] Copernicus, Galileo, and a host of others upended a cosmology that had existed since the Greeks and had formed the basis of medieval theology. The established epistemologies (how we know) based on authority and revelation were also turned upside down. In the thirteenth century a theological and philosophical wrestling began between what would be labelled *the ancients* and *the moderns*. These debates signaled tectonic shifts in the Western imagination that led directly to the reformations and enlightenments.[10] By the seventeenth and eighteenth centuries, a different West had emerged wherein the modern was now its imagination.

Europe had moved through a series of transformations involving technological innovation, a fundamental philosophical reordering of the world, and an almost total social change. A new self-consciousness had emerged that demanded the name *modern*. These transformations hold

---

8. These transformations involved philosophical and political change as well as scientific revolutions, new technologies (the printing press), the end of a longer period of earth cooling that limited agriculture, and plagues, which cut European populations in half. It was only in the fifteenth century that the population curve began to reverse as a warmer climate provided longer growing seasons. See Stephen Toulmin, *Cosmopolis: The Hidden Agenda of Modernity* (Chicago: University of Chicago Press, 1992).

9. Oliver Davies, Paul D. Janz, and Clemens Sedmak, *Transformational Theology: Church in the World* (New York: T&T Clark, 2007), 25.

10. The authors argue that there never was a single "Reformation" or "Enlightenment" but, rather, a series of distinct movements in Europe that were then categorized into single movements. But there were significant distinctions in, for example, the ways in which "enlightenment" worked itself out in Scotland and Germany and France.

the clues to the shape of the modern West and its continuing effects on us today. An important term at the core of these transformations was *nominalism.*

Nominalism

What was the nature of the break that opened the way to the modern? The medieval notion of virtue helps to answer the question. Virtue meant something different from the modern idea of values. Virtue had to do with the source of authority ordering the universe. Authority was located in the two forms of God's law: nature and revelation. Nature was infused with God's laws in what were called universals. Being a virtuous person meant forming one's life in obedience to the laws set out in the universals. The virtuous life involved the schooling of one's desires around those laws. Virtue, therefore, directed one toward that which lay beyond the self and nature—toward God. The true end of life was found in the universals, the overarching laws given by God, which determined how the world operated.

The notion of universals is not easily translated into our time, but their meaning is important for understanding this passage to the modern. To the medieval mind there existed particular, concrete things: people, such as Mary, or Tom; a star cluster, such as Ursa Major; the actual chairs in an office; or the houses in which people lived. All of these objects and individuals were clearly present to people every day. At the same time, Mary and Tom, for example, belonged to a common species or group, along with millions of others, known as human beings. They existed in reality, and not just in categories we make up in our minds—a universal. It was on the basis of the laws within these universals that the particular Marys, Toms, chairs, and houses received their identity. In the thirteenth-century questions arose about this taken-for-granted perception of how things worked. The theologian and logician William of Ockham raised serious questions about the existence of universals. His reasons were based on his theological concern that the notion of universals undermined God's autonomy. For Ockham, if universals, with their laws, existed, then God could not be fully autonomous since God would also be bound and limited by these laws even if God had made them in the first place. Nominalism's critique of universals may seem abstract and esoteric to the modern imagination, but it was this debate that made the West modern.

Ockham made a sharp distinction between things as they existed in reality and the ideas, words, and signs we use to make connections between these real substances. To oversimplify, for Ockham, Mary and Tom really existed, whereas, human being was only a construct *in* our minds that people used to order the world. For Ockham and the nominalists, things in the world, to be real, had to be simple, unique, and distinct (there was only one Mary and no other Mary in the world). Neither man, woman, or human being were, therefore, a real thing in the world. Universals might be helpful generalizations, but they were not real. Today, his argument is reasonable because it is the way the modern mind understands the world. But in the medieval period the challenge to universals signaled something far more critical. It had to do with how God worked in the world. Furthermore, it represented a fundamental shift in the understanding of the sources of knowledge. Something was shifting in the established Western imagination. In one sense, the source of authority and meaning was moving from "out there" (external laws in the heavens) to "in here" (constructs of the mind), but that is getting ahead of the story.

For the medieval mind, universals carried within them God-given laws that shaped the particularities and determined their actions. Virtue was about aligning life with these laws. But if universals were merely the constructs of our minds, then there were no transcendent laws determining how the particularities behaved. The ontological, epistemological, and moral basis of the world had turned. The nominalists probably did not consider these unintended consequences; their concern was that universals presented a set of intermediary laws that undermined God's absolute power to act in any way God chose. Universals limited God's autonomous power, but God could be limited by nothing except God's self.

The rejection of universals meant that gradually the source of meaning in the shaping of the world moved from God to the individual. A new understanding of the individual set a path for it to be the source of authority in the world. This development took several centuries as it worked its way into the imagination, institutions, and social structures that would remake the West. In this are the seeds of the modern.

Because the medieval understanding of the relationship between God and the world was so radically different from the modern, it is challenging to grasp the radical nature of the changes involved in this passage. At the core of the transformation was nominalism. Catholic theorist Ivan Illich gave a significant portion of his life to understanding the twelfth century as a way of interpreting the modern West, offering important insight into how nominalism led to the modern.[11] Charles Taylor wrote the introduction to David Cayley's *The Rivers North of the Future,* a series of interviews with Illich near the end of his life. For Taylor, Illich's work demonstrated the ways the modern West was a mutation of Latin Christendom.[12] The medieval West was an ordered cosmos suffused with God's presence. The world was a living organism that did not get life from itself; it was, in every way, dependent upon God. The reasons for its existence did not come from within, but were given by God. God was not, however, some distant lawmaker who had wound up the universe like a clock, and then left it to run by its own mechanisms. Rather, the universe was a good, abundant, and gratuitous gift of an all-good and merciful God. God's brooding presence oversaw the unfolding of the created world as one filled with grace and abundance. According to Illich, the language used to describe God's engagement with the world "literally means womb, or more precisely the particular movements of the womb when it is inflamed with love."[13] In this sense, God is conceived as present in everything through God's goodness and love. The virtuous life was a participation with God who was the primary agent governing all of life. Nominalism undoes this imagination and offers a new sense that the universe was an undetermined and unpredictable place thrown on God's mercy.

The nominalist protest against universals was intended to protect the radical autonomy of God and ensure God's transcendence. The removal of universals as laws of nature and revelation created the sense that people now lived in an unpredictable world over which there was no control. How, then, could anyone know that the world he or she experienced one day might not be completely changed tomorrow by God's free and arbitrary choice? The answer that emerged was that human beings were freed with the power to shape the world through their own rational minds: the birth of the idea of the autonomous self. The medieval belief in a dependent, contingent world was ending. A world ordered by God's power was replaced by one with its own internal laws and rationality amenable to the human mind. The world now contained its own internal laws without reference to God. It was a revolution in understanding and human

---

11. The material that follows is based on Illich's multiple works but particularly two sets of interviews found in the following volumes: Cayley, *Rivers North of the Future,* and *Ivan Illich in Conversation* (Toronto: Anansi, 1992).
12. Cayley, *Rivers North of the Future,* x.
13. Cayley, *Rivers North of the Future,* 67.

self-identity. For the first time in human history, the connection between God and the world was severed. Creation became nature, which contained in itself all necessary laws. In this modern conception of the world, "each of us contains and possess our own *raison d'etre.*"[14]

The period from the thirteenth through to the seventeenth centuries was experienced as a radical overturning of people's belief about how the world worked and how God acted. Nominalism ended the established assumptions about an order given in God's law and fundamentally altered our perspective on the source of authority. In the absence of universals, virtue was no longer about discerning one's place in an established order. Rational agents had the power to decipher and control nature. Authority had become immanent. The world was under the control of human ends. There was no longer a need for transcendent explanations for why the world behaved as it did. Authority found its source in human experience and consciousness.

These are the sources of modernity's wager. The results were the disappearance of God as the active agent and the elevation of human agency as the primary authority in knowing and ordering the world. This transformation resulted in new structures and institutions designed to carry the weight of the modern imagination: the state, capitalism, and the Self.

God was relegated to a new category, the supernatural, which was beyond nature and material life. The supernatural was invented as a sphere separate from the natural world. The human mind was now free to compel nature to reveal its empirical secrets. There was less searching after the Good in a transcendent authority. The conviction that human agency was the authoritative maker of meaning took hold. External, mediating authorities, such as the Church, were deemed by individuals as unnecessary for comprehending the world. Certitude ceased to be located in God's authority or the Good beyond the self; certitude was gained through one's own direct experience. The implications were enormous. A new human self-consciousness entered the world stage. The cost was a world severed from God. For many, it was a terrible price. For others, it was the liberating experience of human freedom coming of age, a celebration of human autonomy. For Immanuel Kant, humanity had finally grown up.

---

14. Cayley, *Rivers North of the Future,* 68.

The new sovereign was the autonomous self. Notions of obedience to a Good beyond the self came to mean "an unnatural obedience to repressive rules."[15] In the place of revelation and natural order, Law emerged as the new virtue. Virtue was not something out there in nature or God's revelation; it was embedded in our own selves. We were our laws. This new, autonomous modern individual shaped the West from the eighteenth century forward.

The passage to modernity did not happen overnight, nor was it a simple, straight line of development. Not everyone embraced the modern just as, today, there are serious questions about its assumptions and agendas. But the emergence of the modern individual (the Self) was itself a development (some would say distortion) of the Christian imagination that had shaped the West for centuries.[16] It would be misleading to presume that the emergence of this self was some revolution over against the central Christian imagination. On the contrary, the Christian imagination of the medieval period, in its New Testament emphasis on human equality, established that all individuals were equal before God and were to be protected from the heteronomy of others. The medieval Christian imagination was the soil from which the modern individual formed. What was unforeseen was the aggressive removal of the conviction that human thriving lay in the agency of God. Modernity's wager was the new conviction that humankind could make a Jerusalem here on earth without need of God's agency. Separated from such agency, modern individuals would be left to themselves alone, self-authenticating agents with no reference point beyond the Self. The confidence of this new Self at the beginning of the modern became a deep anxiety by the end of the twentieth century. The modern self now entered the stage as the self-making, self-contained actor—the "director of his or her own passions and interests."[17]

---

15. Pierre Manent, *The City of Man* (Princeton, NJ: Princeton University Press, 2000), 35.
16. This is one of the important points Larry Siedentop makes in his book *Inventing the Individual: The Origins of Western Liberalism* (London: Allen Lane, 2014). Describing the role of the church in this process he states: "At the deepest level—the moral and intellectual levels—the church had won the struggle for the future of Europe. The church had projected the image of society as an association of individuals, an image, which unleashed the centralizing process in Europe.... More than anything else, I think, Christianity changed the ground of human identity.... By emphasizing the moral equality of humans, quite apart from any social roles they might occupy, Christianity changed the 'name of the game'" (347–53).
17. Seligman, *Modernity's Wager*, 35.

The European Reformations

> [T]he Western world today is an extraordinarily complex, tangled product of rejections, retentions, and transformations of medieval Western Christianity, in which the Reformation era constitutes the critical watershed.[18]

The fifteenth- and sixteenth-century reformations were the bridge between the Middle Ages and modernity—a period of transition from a time that acknowledged God's ordering of the world toward a normatively secular understanding of a world without need for such explanations. Charles Taylor described it as a transition from a "porous self" embedded in religious meaning to an autonomous "buffered self" in a disenchanted universe.[19] The undoing of the medieval understanding of authority, knowledge, and the individual was the context of the European reformations. The controversies precipitating the reformations were not just about the corruption of the Church. The fifteenth and sixteenth centuries were filled with anxiety about God's relationship to the creation and the extent to which human power interacted with God's works of grace and salvation. The reformations reacted to the medieval Church's sacramentalism around, for example, questions of God's presence in the Eucharist. An unintended consequence within Protestantism was the removal of the sacred as being present in and through the world.[20] The eucharistic controversies about how Christ was present at the table are an example of this larger dynamic. Such debates were part of this desire to safeguard God's means of grace and salvation, but such safeguarding contributed to the formation of an essentially desacralized world of God's absence rather than one filled with God's presence. The reformations contributed to the flowering of humanism and the Renaissance, with its celebration of a natural world filled with the potential for human creativity. But this sense of a world given to human beings to explore in art, politics, and vocations came with an awareness that God's presence was increasingly separated from that world. The reformations often concentrated their energies around questions of doctrinal truth, suggesting that they assessed the malaise of late medieval Christianity as being caused by doctrine and wrong thinking.

---

18. Brad S. Gregory, *The Unintended Reformation: How A Religious Revolution Secularized Society* (Cambridge, MA: Belknap Press, 2012), 3.
19. Charles Taylor, *A Secular Age* (Cambridge, MA: Belknap Press, 2007), 19–21 and 37–42.
20. Another element contributing to the secularization of the West.

[Doctrinal) controversy was literally endless, and religio-political conflicts between Catholics and the magisterial Protestants from the early sixteenth through the mid-seventeenth century were destructive and inconclusive. The undesired nonresolution of intra-Christian contention brought with it . . . (the question): How was human life among frequently antagonistic Christians to be rendered stable and secure? The solution eventually adopted in all modern, liberal Western states was to privatize religion. Not subjective faith but objective reason, in science and modern philosophy, would be the basis for public life.[21]

Sixteenth-century Europe overturned a world that had sustained a stable, long-established story about the agency of God and the place of human beings in God's universe. From the nominalists forward, questions about human identity, the sources of authority, and the place of certainty, had to be addressed in new ways. If not God's primary agency, what would be the basis of social and political life in the modern?

Remaking Political and Social Life

Medieval Europe, in the forms of the Church and feudalism, had emerged from the cataclysm of Rome's demise. This long, stable Christendom ended in the intellectual, religious, and violent transformations from the fifteenth to seventeenth centuries that shattered the hegemony of the Church and opened the way for the modern. Long-established institutions and social structures, as well as the natural world, were cut loose from their traditional foundations in God and the Church. The social, religious, and political fabrics of Europe were torn apart in turbulent wars and intellectual revolutions. The resulting anxiety manifested itself in a desperate search for a certainty to replace the certainty associated with God and the Church. The concrete particularity of experience became the new source of certainty and set in motion an era of radical intellectual search for ways to create philosophical underpinnings through the political, social, philosophical, religious, and economic systems. The outcome was not just a new understanding of the person but new social, political, and economic movements that converged to produce the modern West.

---

21. Gregory, *Unintended Reformation*, 21.

The breakdown of Christendom was slow, at first, but, by the end of the Thirty Years War in 1648, Christendom was structurally and functionally over. All that was left was to work through the time it would take for these implications to sink deeply into the Western imagination. This ending, with its deep sense of a loss, was hard to describe because so many of the architectural and linguistic forms of Christendom continued into the twentieth century. It took several centuries to see the ways in which modernity's wager had created a new world. The reformations, in their synthesis of doctrine and their own search for religious certainty, cannot address our question in the current West. The reformations were about a world that took for granted that everyone, in some form, was Christian. The churches the reformers developed were within that Christendom world. They still exist in the forms of denominations, but these very forms and identities belong to a time and place that cannot feed our own missiological questions. Lesslie Newbigin states it in these terms:

> Dissolution . . . of the synthesis between the Gospel and the culture of the western part of the European peninsula of Asia, by which Christianity had become almost the folk-religion of Western Europe. That synthesis was the work of the thousand-year period during which the peoples of Western Europe, hemmed in by the power of Islam to east and south, had the Gospel wrought into the very stuff of their social and personal life, so that the whole population could be conceived as the *corpus Christianum.* That conception is the background to the Reformation theologies. They take it for granted. They are not in a missionary situation but in this situation in which Christendom is taken for granted. This means that in their doctrines of the Church they are defining their positions over against one another *within* the context of the *corpus Christianum.* . . . It is not necessary to point out how profoundly this affects the structure of their thinking.[22]

The reformers were working out a new meaning for being the Church within a cultural world they took for granted. They had no expectation that the world would change. The reformations were largely theological conflicts around the nature of doctrine, rather than movements aware

---

22. Lesslie Newbigin, *The Household of God* (London: SCM Press, 1953), 11.

of the seismic shifts in the underlying imagination of the West. While standing at the end of a long transitional process from the medieval to the modern,[23] the reformers didn't see themselves as participating in the destruction of one kind of West and the birth of another. Their desire was to ensure that Christians had the certainty of salvation to undergird their faith as citizens in a Christian social and political world that did not distinguish the religious from the secular. With the upending of the penitential and sacramental systems of the Catholic Church, all bets were off in terms of the means of grace and the sources of certainty for salvation. The reformers provided a new basis for that certainty, rooted in God's grace through Jesus Christ and connected to the everyday life of the polis, the medieval order in which people lived. The ways the reformers shaped their doctrines had important implications for the emergence of modern social life.

A primary image of the Christian in the medieval period was that of pilgrim. Life was a pilgrimage toward the heavenly kingdom. Bunyan's *Pilgrim's Progress* is illustrative of this trajectory and illustrates that this was a corporate not individual journey. The pilgrim travelled with a community of others ensuring that each might reach the heavenly gates and pass the final judgement. The Church provided the guide for achieving the desired state of grace for this pilgrimage. In the forms of liturgies, indulgences, works, confession, and the Eucharist, the pilgrim traveled the way toward salvation. This image of journey to the heavenly realm directed the focus of medieval life beyond this world. Everyday life was not a sufficient explanation or goal of life. One was located in God's world by an outworldly perspective. A coherent world and way of life were shaped by reference to God's order, laws, and purposes, which lay outside the world itself. This outworldly perspective was given order, form, and meaning through the Church. One's life, therefore, made sense and found order within the Church's priestly orders, structures, and rhythms.

Both Luther and Calvin's reorientation of Christian theology left little place for salvation by works or through the proxy of priests. Justification by faith was undergirded by the convictions of human impotence in achieving salvation and God's omnipotence in giving us salvation. This reorientation resulted in fundamental changes to the imagination of the West. Four elements of this change are critical to the formation of the modern self:

---

23. See Dumont, *Essays on Individualism*, 52–59.

- **First,** the individual became the center of salvation and God's work of grace and salvation. Removed from the proxy relationship of church and priest, the sources of grace were directly accessible to individuals through their conscience.

- **Second,** the locus of salvation became less about a pilgrimage toward the heavenly city and more about the ways in which one lived in the present. People's attention was redirected into the world and away from a sense of participation in a life shaped by the church or a world filled with God's working. The doctrine of election, for example, meant the locus of one's salvation was worked out through his or her actions in the world. Here was the development of the modern individual: someone whose life was formed primarily in the world of everyday commerce rather than within the Church. The pilgrim's journey was relocated from the outworldly to the inner life of the individual. It can hardly be overstated how much of a transformation in imagination this was for the West.

- **Third,** the Church ceased to be the organic center, the womb, of social life. As the sources of grace and the means of salvation migrated to the individual, the Church became a container that individuals used for working out their salvation.

- **Fourth,** the community on pilgrimage turned into the individual working out his or her salvation; others might be helpful but were no longer essential. Herein lies the shift from a Western imagination rooted in the primacy of social community to a culture rooted in the primacy of the individual. The Church continued to function and, in certain ways, could be imagined to remain as a center in a community but it became a service agent for individuals.

In Louis Dumont's assessment:

What remained of the Church was an instrument of discipline acting on individuals (the elect as well as the reprobate, for they are practically indistinguishable). . . . [I]t had become, for all practical purposes, an association composed of individuals.[24]

The Enlightenments, the Secular, and the Self

The European enlightenments were pivotal to the formation of the modern. With the emergence of nominalism and the scientific revolutions (from Copernicus, through Galileo), a new cosmology—the understanding of the world and our relationship to it—ascended. The sensible, material world was increasingly understood to be outside God's direct agency and in the purview of human agency to analyze, control, and remake. Deism was an example of this shifting imagination. For the deist, God made the world, wound it up like a clock, and then left it to its own internal causality. God gave human beings all the rational capacity to engage the world, unfold its internal laws, and shape nature to human ends. The givenness of everyday life in work, politics, science, economics, law, and so forth was now separated and distinct from the work and actions of God.

Over time, all of this led to another quintessential characteristic of the modern West: the secular. Secularity did not mean the denial or absence of God, but the reduction of God's engagements within the private, inner world of the individual.[25] The outworldly perspective of the medieval gave way to an inworldly experience of God. The language of spirit, for example, remained central to Christian imagination, but its use now referred to the inwardness of the subjective self, not to the external secular world amenable to science and human technical skill. Religious life became reflexive, referring to the inner world of the individual. Such reflexivity had massive implications for how Euro-tribal churches addressed the challenge of the modern West.[26]

---

24. Dumont, *Essays on Individualism*, 58.
25. This was not the original meaning of the term *secular*, which is drawn from the Latin *saeculum*, meaning that period between the ascension of Christ and his return at the end of time. In this sense, in its medieval rendering, it simply means the temporal world that ended with death as compared with the sacred that continued beyond death.
26. This subjective turn into the self as the locus of God's agency has its parallel and mirror turn in the self-understanding and practices of the churches in their response to the modern West. There emerges a church-shaped reflexivity in which the churches turn into themselves to seek God's direction or frame their responses to an emerging modern West. There is an

The Emergence of the Modern State

The state is separated from society and church. Then the state is divided into separation of powers. Churches becomes sects. Society is fragmented into "an indefinite number of 'groups.' From now on life will be lived in the 'age of separations.'". . . . [T]his age of separations is also an age of agglomerations . . . the state grows ever more powerful as power drains from the peripheries to the center. . . . In the very midst of this radical depoliticization, we are called upon to affirm ourselves.[27]

The religious/secular distinction is a modern Western construction that arose as an adjunct to the rise of the modern state and the triumph of the civil over ecclesiastical authorities in early modern Europe. . . . It is only with the birth of the sovereign modern state that the concept of religion . . . was born. Over the course of the fifteenth through seventeenth centuries, religion came to be an essentially interior impulse, demarcated by sets of beliefs or propositions about reality, and essentially distinct from the "secular" pursuits such as politics, economics, and the like.[28]

The basic sociological fact . . . is that the nation . . . and nationalism . . . are historically conjoined with individualism as a value. The nation is precisely the type of global society which corresponds to the paramountcy of the individual as value. Not only does the one historically accompany the other, but the interdependence between them is clear, so that we may say that the nation is a global society composed of people who think of themselves as individuals.[29]

In the seventeenth century the nation-state emerged as the primary form of political and social life in Europe, marking the end of a Christendom

---

ecclesiocentric turn (see Alan J. Roxburgh, *Joining God* [New York: CPI Press, 2015]) which is deeply reflexive in that it is assumed that the missiological challenges posed by the modern West will be addressed by fixing, renewing, or transforming the church itself. There seems to be little awareness that such a reflexivity is rooted in a diseased cosmology that severed any sense of God's presence and agency in the world.

27. Manent, *City of Man*, x.
28. Cavanaugh, *Church as Field Hospital*, 181–82.
29. Dumont, *Essays in Individualism*, 10.

wherein a sacred order had shaped all of life in an interrelationship between the Church and the political orders. The religious had been inseparably bound to life as a whole; there was no conception of the one without the other. The coming apart of this overarching narrative created an urgent need to find new social and political structures. Human beings had finally taken their place as autonomous beings, free to order their lives within what Charles Taylor has called an immanent frame.[30] Following the Peace of Westphalia in 1648, the nation-state became that new form within which the rights of the individual took shape. New language emerged to express how people lived together. The idea of "society"—a taken-for-granted idea of the modern West—took center stage.

How individuals formed life together was the challenge for modern society. How did one create relationships and responsibilities between morally autonomous, individual agents? The answer was the modern state and the production of a new understanding of society around the idea of a social contract that self-regulating individuals negotiated with one another. The state arbitrated and regulated these new forms of society. The state's authority, however, was no longer derived from God, but its own sovereign power.

Language began to change, and with it the place of Christianity within the state. Christian life was placed in the generalized category of religion. Supernatural referred to an order outside the everyday, the political, and the economic. Christian life meant a private, inner, personal life. Society was no longer shaped around the rhythms of a Christian order, except for a remnant of holy days or holidays. Transcendence, the conviction that the creator God was actively present in the midst of life, no longer referred to the ordering of the universe within which God was the primary agent, but to a world beyond and unconnected to the material order of nature. Transcendence was all but irrelevant to everyday life.

To be modern was to live in a society that separated the material and spiritual worlds. The political and economic became public; the religious

---

30. Charles Taylor uses the term in his book *A Secular Age*. It refers to this overarching and all-pervasive sense for people living in the modern West that all of life is lived in and explainable in natural terms rather than supernatural causes and relationships. In this sense the term *immanent* can be used to differ from the idea of the transcendent. It means that we have all come to assume that our lives are lived within a self-contained, self-sufficient natural order. This immanent order is the primary narrative world in which we live. Everything else—belief in God, for example—is part of backdrop that doesn't affect or change this primary way in which we understand and live our lives. It is in this sense that we live in a world dominated by the immanent frame, but one that permits the transcendent in the sense, for example, that God is useful to our lives but not the primary agent in the living of our lives.

was about private life. The nation-state became the new center of power and authority, adjudicating how people formed and ordered their lives. Church and religious identity moved to the periphery. Nationalism replaced the experience of mystery and devotion toward God. Society operated with its own internal logic. Christian practice and order were limited to personal values that were not generalized beyond the private self. The modern state became the immanent replacement of the sacred ordering of Christendom. It is easy to lose sight of how massive and radical this shift to the modern imagination was.

A New Epoch—the Modern West

The modern nation-state embodied the migration of people's religious affections from the churches to the state itself. Religious language about identity and meaning moved from their center in the church to a new center in the nation-state. The sovereign state took the place of a sovereign God. The institutions of the state displaced those of the Church. None of this is new information.[31] What is critical for our argument is that the modern is not a radical rejection of the West's Christian past, but a transformation of the location of its meaning and identity. The modern West was a migration of the sacred from Christian structures into the state, the economy, and the Self. It represents the mutation of the Christian Trinity into the modern trinity of Self, state, and economy. The entire scope of public discourse and agency was redefined through the establishment of the modern. Within this framework, all other narratives (for example, the Christian) were to be judged.

Shifts in a culture's self-understanding, institutions, rituals, and practices are a complex mixture of events, actors, and interactions across a wide range of areas. Together, they forge a new epoch. The modern West was a new epoch, and did not come from the genius of personalities, or even from key events like the reformations. It required a whole complex of elements,[32]

---

31. William T. Cavanaugh, *Migrations of the Holy: God, State, and the Political Meaning of the Church* (Grand Rapids, MI: Eerdmans, 2011).
32. William T. Cavanaugh, *Church as Field Hospital: The Church's Engagement with a Wounded World* (Grand Rapids, MI: Eerdmans, 2016), 108.

- The immanent replaced the divine, or transcendent.[33]

- The individual, rather than God, became the primary agent in the world. "It is rather the condition of our freedom to become convinced that we are making it all up" for ourselves as the primary agents in the world.[34]

- As citizens of the state, people were sovereign, rational choosers.

- Independent individual choosers were in contract to each other for beneficial ends.

- Sovereign state and sovereign Self replaced a sovereign God.

- Personal identity and choice replaced calling and vocation as means of discerning a good beyond the Self, within a larger frame of meaning.

The people of the modern West came to believe they could write their story *ex nihilo*, as independent, self-making agents. The modern was not primarily about technology, economics, or even politics. It was a new story that settled into the bones, sinews, habits, perceptions, and ways of life: an epoch-changing consensus about how people saw and engaged one another and the world. Everything was filtered through the new story, and the Christian story was reread in the image of the West. In this epochal shift, the Euro-tribal churches were colonized, taking on the language, forms, and structures of the modern even in the midst of their traditional practices.[35]

Over time, nation-states institutionalized themselves as the central sources of authority in Europe and, then, in the colonized worlds of North

---

33. Language plays an important part in our understanding what was happening in this shift. In contemporary usage *transcendent* has come to mean that which is outside the order of the world. It now has reference to the belief in a God outside the world and is more related to other words such as *spiritual* that suggest polarities between the spiritual and the material. But this was not the understanding of the word *transcendent* at the beginning of the modern era. It referred to the commonly understood and culturally shared perspective that all of life was infused and governed by God's order. God was actively present in the created order and was the explanatory frame in making sense of the world. This notion of transcendence is no longer the case. As Cavanaugh states: "[N]ot until the dawn of the 17th century was *religio* identified with the *supernaturalis*" (*Church as Field Hospital*, 47, italics in original).

34. Cavanaugh, *Church as Field Hospital*, 107.

35. See, for example, the discussion of Ivan Illich's thought in Cayley, *Rivers North of the Future*, where Illich discusses the ways Eucharistic practice has been colonized and transformed.

America and elsewhere. As Cavanaugh points out, the modern state in its initial formation "was not the simple shedding of theological ways of handling the organization of society, but was rather marked by the migration of certain theological ideas from the church to the nascent state."[36] The modern state relegated theological and religious convictions to the private sphere. The nation-state, with its armies, bureaucratization, and national economies, transformed the locus of social and political life from traditional, small, local, autonomous groups into the state and its bureaucracies. The result was that a world in which political, social, and economic life had been formed in local contexts was transferred to the state that promised, in god-like fashion, to meet the needs of its citizenry so long as they gave it their loyalty.

Within the nation-state, people became citizens of a rational, bureaucratized order where the state provided the means whereby individuals came together in social contract to maximize their own needs and wants based on personal values or preferences. Within the state individuals could maximize these self-interests as long as they were loyal to the nation. The state's purpose was not to burden people with the restraints and controls of outmoded tradition, but to create the spaces in which the individual could maximize self-interest. The state embodied the material conviction that society was comprised of individuals who make their own meaning but required the ordering of the state to manage and order the ways in which that self-interest was balanced with the interests of other citizens. In the European enlightenments there was a flowering of confidence in the capacities of the human to flourish and make for itself a better world. This was linked to the emergence of a rationality and new science wherein the application of the experimental method compelled nature to reveal its secrets and create a more human-centered world. Less and less reason existed for religious explanations or institutions, unless those institutions and narratives were useful for the enhancement of the state, the Self, and the economy.

New Economic Forms

Entwined in these forces was a new form of economic life. Feudal Europe gave way to a nascent capitalism. As nation-states removed feudal structures, capitalism became a radically different and all-encompassing economic narrative that, together with technological innovation, led to the

---

36. Cavanaugh, *Church as Field Hospital*, 100.

Industrial Revolution. The state, the economic, the technological, the individual, and the rational method coalesced to establish an aggressive, expanding West confronting the rest of the world.

Contested in all these transformations was the source of agency, authority, and certainty. These contestations were about who and what were the primary agents shaping life in the world and providing the underpinnings of certainty. Luther's stand against the abuses of the Church placed the individual at the center of the question. Humanism placed the idea of human agency at the center of the conversation while the enlightenments provided the rationale. Throughout this passage to modernity, some argued strenuously that an autonomous, atomistic self was incapable of providing a satisfactory account of human thriving. However, arguments for the primacy of God's agency faded in the light of the modern story. Out of the reformations and enlightenments came the modern democratic ideal, with nation-states at its center and the autonomous individual as the primary agent in a world of social contract. The modern epoch was built on a set of convictions:

1. Authority was located in the self-constituting individual;
2. The state was the all-powerful source of social and cultural authority;
3. The "invisible" hand made capitalism the all-powerful source of economic authority;
4. The rational methods of the new science were the source of knowledge;
5. The form of relationality characteristic of this modern individual was contract rather than covenant.

Society was based on contract, exchange, and the rationality of natural law. God's agency in the lives of citizens evaporated with agency migrating to the state in the forms of bureaucracies that underwrote capitalism, raised armies, and made a new world. In modern democracies, the social contract and the autonomy of the individual become the loci of authority in a world of exchange rather than covenant.

The Idea of the West

The idea of the West developed within the emergence of the modern to produce what we call the modern West. The West is a nexus of ideas, ideals, and geography. One gets the sense of this by providing several antonyms. There is, for example, the West as opposite of the East, which was associated with Russia and Orthodoxy. Or, there is the West and the Sino world—China and the other Asian nations with their religious outlooks. Today, there is the West and the Middle East, shaped by Islam. Set within this ideal of the West are the characteristics of the modern such as democracy, the state, the rule of law, and the freedom of the individual. Thus, the modern West is an ideology and a geography.

In the eighteenth and nineteenth centuries, Europe and North America became the ascendant powers in the world, establishing colonies and empires across the globe. Driving this movement was the uniquely Western notion of progress. This quasi-religious idea, drawn from Christian eschatology, communicated that the West was the bearer of civilization to the rest of the world. It was the West's technological, scientific, social, cultural, religious, and political progress that made it the most advanced civilization in human history—the vanguard of a new world order. Here was a new mental map for reading and ordering the world. While notions of the modern West remained plastic, the term captured the conviction of the peoples of Europe and North America about the convulsive passage through which they had travelled over the previous four centuries.

2

The Ascent of the West: Nineteenth to Twentieth Centuries; Global Modernity and Contradiction

Introduction

Chapter 1 located the emergence of the modern West in the breakup of the medieval synthesis and the dual energies of the European reformations and enlightenments. The idea of the modern West came into its own in the nineteenth century. Even while core ideals that formed this West continue, it is now in the midst of its own unraveling. This chapter tracks some ways the West has been reshaped over the last two centuries, which will inform the question of a missiological engagement. The West in which church traditions were formed after the reformations isn't the West before the Church today.[1] To understand the current situation one must grasp the development of the West over the past several centuries. This chapter is not an exhaustive study of the political, sociocultural, economic, structural, or international relations that reshaped the West over this period; rather, it describes the ways in which elements must inform the missiological challenges facing the churches today.

Western narratives of progress (more recently expressed in the language of globalization) find their source in the residue of Christian eschatology.

---

1. From the perspective of addressing the question of a missiological engagement with the West, this is no small issue. The structures, habits, and practices of the Protestant churches were mostly formed in and for the context of a "West" that no longer exists in terms of social, political, and economic life. The implication is that these structures, habits, and practices make less and less sense in the unfolding shapes of Western societies. See Alan J. Roxburgh, *Structured for Mission: Renewing the Culture of the Church* (Downers Grove, IL: InterVarsity Press, 2015).

The trajectory of a modern, secular version of hope and progress is in a future discontinuous from a Christian past. The modern West involves a forgetting of the roots of Western hope in the Christian story of God's agency. Adam Smith's "invisible hand"[2] replaced God's agency. Hope has come to be rooted in futures made by human beings stepping fully into their adulthood as they trust in themselves and their powers to make a new world. The "invisible hand" takes individual economic self-interest and turns it to the good of all.

Adam Seligman analyzes the contestations that birthed the secular eschatology of the West in his book *Modernity's Wager: Authority, the Self, and Transcendence.*[3] He argues that the modern West is a civilizational experiment unlike any that has ever gone before it. This West bet the house on the conviction that life could be lived to the full through human autonomy and without God's agency. This wager remains its driver and dynamic. Its sources of identity, authority, and desire are the Self, the state, and economics. The result was a world evacuated of God's agency.

Global Modernity and Contradiction: The Ascent (Confidence and Contradiction)

In the nineteenth century, a disruptive, modern West emerged at the center of the world stage. It was a West of great self-confidence, privilege, power, and status. Its colonizations, conquests, politics, economics, laws, and technologies, read from the perspective of a social Darwinism, made it the center of new global order.[4] Inside this narrative, the West was confident that its future was the way the whole world ought to be.

No better example of that confidence exists than Kant's 1784 essay, "An Answer to the Question: What is the Enlightenment," where he declared,

---

2. Adam Smith, *The Theory of Moral Sentiments* (1756; Cambridge: Cambridge University Press, 2002), and *The Wealth of Nations* (1776; London: Wordsworth, 2012).
3. Adam B. Seligman, *Modernity's Wager: Authority, the Self, and Transcendence* (Princeton, NJ: Princeton University Press, 2000).
4. Social Darwinism was the application of Darwin's theories of species evolution to societies. This narrative took hold in the modern West in the later part of the nineteenth century, undergirding the already existing theories of progress. The result was the belief that some races (peoples or nations) had progressed further, or were move evolved, than others. This view became a powerful guiding principle across much of the West. Its effects, for example, can be observed in the Victorian period of British colonial expansion and empire building. Social Darwinism gave to this movement of colonization and empire a narrative that allowed British policy to enhance the expiration of the North American First Nations peoples as an older, weaker, declining race that could not survive. See, for example, John Ralston Saul's, *A Fair Country: Telling Truths About Canada* (Toronto: Viking, 2008).

"Sapere aude!" (dare to think)—a confident declaration of our release from self-incurred tutelage to external forces into the self's autonomous agency. In this context, a tiny peninsula of Asia,[5] comprised of tribal groups that had fought among themselves from time immemorial, became convinced they were the ascendant civilization of the world shaped by a destiny undergirded by a Christian story in which they had become the central actors in God's unfolding purposes for the world. The modern West was confident in its powers to remake and rule the world through its political institutions and economic power. Michael Steinberg puts it this way:

> Something terribly important happened in Europe some time between the sixteenth and nineteenth centuries. . . . From the European perspective these dizzying changes were proof of the superiority of the Western tradition. This was something new. It went beyond mere ethnocentrism, a bias to which nobody is immune. . . . European supremacy in arms, science, economic productivity, and cultural accomplishment became the touchstone for all nations. . . . [As] soon as Europeans decided they lived in the most advanced of societies they endowed history with a course and direction. This set up a race from the past to the present in which Europe came in first by definition. European history became universal history.[6]

In the midst of this self-confidence were self-doubt and anxiety. The French social philosopher Henri Lefebvre (1901–1991) saw these contradictions at work from the early 1900s up to the revolutionary events of the 1960s. He proposed that to understand our own time we had to recognize that these conflicting attitudes of confidence and anxiety continuously interacted with each other to shape the West. On the one side was a confident triumphalism, a certainty and arrogance about the role of the West in colonizing and subjecting the world to its social forms. This certainty came from its prodigious creativity in technology, science, the arts, medicine, and politics (the fact of democracy). The modern West was an immense achievement, but at such huge costs to so many peoples across the world. Conversely and at the same time, there was an undercurrent

---

5. The phrase "peninsula of Asia" is from Lesslie Newbigin, *Household of God* (London: SCM Press, 1953). In the introduction to that book he writes of the "synthesis between the Gospel and the culture of the western part of the European peninsula of Asia, by which Christianity had become almost the folk-religion of Western Europe" (11).

6. Michael Steinberg, *Fiction of a Thinkable World: Body, Meaning and the Culture of Capitalism* (New York: Monthly Review Press, 2005), 149–52.

of self-questioning, anxiety, fear, boredom, ennui—a search for certainty. Nietzsche expressed the ambivalence in his assertion that we had killed God. Lefebvre's quotation of Nietzsche captures the contradiction: "We are more free than ever before to look around in all directions; nowhere do we perceive any limits. We have the advantage of feeling an immense space around us—but also an immense void."[7]

These contradictions characterize modernity's wager.

The tension between confidence and anxiety has shaped the West for several centuries. The historian Susan Schreiner frames it by comparing our own time with that of modernity's beginnings in the sixteenth century:

> [L]ike early modernity, we, too, are consumed with the breakdown of traditional certain beliefs. Like the early modern era, our own time is . . . a time of "great unmooring." . . . Every aspect of our culture reveals this anxiety that truth and reality are ephemeral. . . . The result is not the sixteenth-century desire to "rise above ourselves" but, rather, a sense of vertigo and weariness.[8]

Within modernity's wager, confidence has been replaced by anxiety.

By the early decades of the twenty-first century, these forms of certainty are increasingly viewed as having failed to enact the promised future.[9] They have passed their use-by date, leaving most citizens with no sense of what will replace them. The growing sense is that there are no options beyond what Charles Taylor described as the "immanent frame."[10] In the West the search for an alternative future remains fixed in the conviction that only a self-sufficient, immanent order offers hope, even if we believe in God.[11] The West that stands before us remains embedded in modernity's wager. The picture holding its focus is one in which there are no ways out of the immanent frame. In its

---

7. Henry Lefebvre, *Introduction to Modernity* (London: Verso, 1995), 1–4.

8. Susan E. Schreiner, *Are You Alone Wise?: The Search for Certainty in the Early Modern Era* (Oxford: Oxford University Press, 2011), xi–xiii.

9. One can observe this, for example, in the writing of European social scientists such as Ulrich Beck in his last book, *The Metamorphosis of the World* (Cambridge: Polity Press, 2016) and Zygmunt Bauman's *State of Crisis* (Cambridge: Polity, 2014).

10. This phrase comes from Charles Taylor's *A Secular Age* (Cambridge, MA: Belknap Press, 2007), chapter 15.

11. For a helpful description of how Charles Taylor explains this process, see James Smith's *How (Not) to Be Secular: Reading Charles Taylor* (Grand Rapids, MI: Eerdmans, 2014). See especially chapter 5.

beginnings, confidence characterized the modern West like a young adult fully conscious of an open future and immense possibility; today, ennui and lost confidence pervade the modern West with the cynicism of an old man fearing the worst.

Hans Blumenberg described the initiating dynamic of the modern West as an unshakeable belief that all that was needed for human thriving was human self-assertion. Transcendence, God's agency, was not necessary in a world WE ordered. Experimentation and rationalized control would release the self into its full potential.[12] This conviction has eroded. People are experiencing rising anxiety and doubt about where to turn to find an alternative story to fund life, but there seems nowhere to turn except within the immanent frame, the wager.[13] Neither Disneyland, nor rising GDP, nor a more radical accounting of the self is able to suppress the anxiety. We inhabit a West where the grounds of our identity, and our framing stories are no longer clear. We are riddled with fear of the unknown and the other, whether those be unknown attacks from radicals, the incursion of some fearsome new diseases (real, as in Ebola, or created, as in the *Walking Dead*), or the return of a universe behind which lurks spirits and demons ready to undo us in unimaginable ways. We feel ourselves as a society at risk. Anxiety and doubt have won out over confidence and control.

Hub

Following Westphalia (1648), European nation states, energized by wealth and new technologies, set out on journeys of exploration, conquest, and colonization, with an awakening sense of control and dominance. The West increasingly saw itself at the center of a world birthed and maintained by military power, economic control, technological prowess, and an ideological base in both Christian and secular notions of progress. Initially, it believed this outburst of energy was part of its Christianized conviction of a West chosen to bear God's future to the rest of the world. The Church had a moral imperative at the center of God's world movement.

What made this narrative of ascent so reasonable was not just the West's economic and industrial prowess. Since the end of the Napoleonic Wars

---

12. Hans Blumenberg, *The Legitimacy of the Modern Age* (Cambridge, MA: MIT Press, 1985).
13. See Ian Kershaw, *To Hell and Back: Europe, 1914–1949* (New York: Penguin Books, 2015). In the opening pages he writes: "Europe's twentieth century was a century of war. Two world wars followed by over forty years of 'cold war'—itself the direct product of the Second World War—defined the age . . . . During the twentieth century, Europe went to hell and back" (1)

(1815), it had experienced a century of relative peace within which it came to see itself as the apogee of all civilization.[14] The structures of international order were remade as a

> complex configuration of industrialization, rational state-building and the ideologies of progress . . . changed the distribution of power by generating a shift from a "polycentric world with no dominant center" to a "core-periphery" order in which the centre of gravity resided in the West. . . . Although oscillations of power are nothing new in human history . . . , the global transformation opened up a vastly expanded pool of resources, making the power gap much bigger and much more difficult to emulate. In this sense, the global transformation also changed the basic source or *mode of power*, stimulating the emergence of global modernity.[15]

Europe had been innovating and expanding its sea power across the world. Driven by the Industrial Revolution's expanding demand for resources and markets, this sea power transformed global power relationships. Up to that point, Islamic countries had controlled global trade routes over which they levied taxes on Western trade and travel. Wealth accumulated in the Islamic Middle East. The ascent of Western sea power opened alternative sea routes and ended the tax system to the extent that a reversal of imagination took place—the West no longer felt encircled. It was now the Islamic world that felt surrounded by the West.

The West had become the hub of a center-periphery world, resourced, from the late nineteenth into the early twentieth century, by social Darwinism. The forces making this global modernity were industrialization, rational state building, and ideologies of progress. Each illustrated Western confidence and authority. The Western story was to become everyone else's story, as if the modern West had discovered its own immanent missiology—the modernization and westernization of all the world with the West at the beneficent center. The industrial revolutions gave the West a huge advantage over the rest of the world. It was now positioned at the center of a new world order (retrospectively labelled imperialism and colonialism) through their respective Empires.

---

14. Kershaw, *To Hell and Back*. See also Barry Buzan and George Lawson, *The Global Transformation: History, Modernity and the Making of International Relations* (Cambridge, UK: Cambridge University Press, 2015), 56–57.
15. Buzan and Lawson, *Global Transformation*, 1, italics in original.

This modern Western identity became normative in the nineteenth century.[16] Nation-states formed new social institutions and bureaucracies to manage and order their industrialized societies. The distinctly secularized ideal of progress was expressed in the narratives of liberalism, social Darwinism, and nationalism. A mixture of Christian and secular beliefs congealed in the nineteenth century, solidifying a sense of the West's vocation and carrying forward the unstoppable work of progress (whether in the form of God's kingdom or theories of the individual and survival of the fittest). This West became civilization: the legitimating narrative for the rest of the world. It was natural, therefore, that Western Christianity would follow the same pattern. This hegemonic, core-periphery world would last right up to the end of World War I, underwritten uniquely by the child of the modern West—capitalism.

Capitalism[17]

> [N]ascent capitalism has a religious dynamic that, over the years, has been secularized. Frequently, in secularization . . . religious aspiration still remains—for infinite freedom, infinite choice, total immersing satisfaction, and so forth. The power of wealth can seem deifying. It runs absolutely counter to the Christian conception of salvation as *theōsis* in that it sets up a false god, an idol, a fetish.[18]

The new controlling narrative of the modern West, capitalism, meant that for the first time in history, the market determined everything. Western identity was shaped by the overarching ideologies of a free market and invisible hand, both secular forms of transcendence.[19] As

---

16. See Philip Bobbitt, *The Shield of Achilles: War, Peace and the Course of History* (New York: Anchor, 2002).

17. The authors understand that capitalism has its own history and that it has taken multiple forms over the last several centuries. The point of this section is not to provide that history or to describe its forms but to offer a reading of how it was an essential part of the formation of the modern West and its identity. For a recent, helpful assessment of capitalism and the question of its place now, see Paul Mason, *Postcapitalism: A Guide to Our Future* (New York: Farrar, Straus and Giroux, 2014). Also, for a helpful reading of capitalism from a very different (Latin American liberationist) perspective, see Daniel M. Bell Jr., *Liberation Theology After the End of History* (New York: Routledge, 2001).

18. Graham Ward, *The Politics of Discipleship: Becoming Postmaterial Citizens* (Grand Rapids, MI: Baker, 2009), 267.

19. See Karl Polanyi, *The Great Transformation* (Boston, MA: Beacon Press, 1957); Giorgio Resta and Mariavittoria Catanzariti, eds., *Karl Polanyi: For a New West* (Cambridge: Polity Press, 2014); Bob Goudzwaard, *Capitalism and Progress: A Diagnosis of Western Society* (Grand Rapids, MI: Eerdmans, 1978); Wendell Berry, *What Matters: Economics for a Renewed*

Karl Polanyi demonstrated, in capitalism everything else came to be defined in terms of exchange value—not just commodities (goods produced) or money (the means of exchange), but human beings (wage labor) and the land (real estate). Everything was rationalized and commodified by capital. The market defined the meaning and value of all elements of society. Nation-states made laws conforming their societies around the free market. Money became the measure of social meaning and political identity. Even though at the beginning of the nineteenth century this state-supported capitalism represented a radical, destructive departure from all previous forms of social and political life, that fact is hardly understood today. Capitalism became the hegemonic ideology of the West.

As the West expanded globally, capitalism became the norm of the new global world order. Societies became subsets of the market. Maurice Glasman suggests that the

> emerging nation-state subordinates the existing institutions of social organization, such as the cities, guilds, corporations, churches, unions, parishes, municipalities . . . by establishing unmediated sovereignty, a national currency and uniformity of tariffs within its borders. The market, in its turn, opens up the substance of society for sale on the open market. . . . Society, understood as a stable network of self-governing institutions as well as self-regulating systems, disintegrates.[20]

Glasman, Polanyi, Cavanaugh, and a host of others argue that those mediating institutions that had formed the substance of social life (guilds, clubs, neighborhoods, churches, social groupings of all kinds) that had preceded modern forms of the West (the state, its bureaucracies, and capitalism) were subordinated to the primacy of the nation-state and the dominance of the market. The norms of social life became calculation and exchange. The result was the evisceration of a local, social life that had been the generator of human flourishing.[21] The implications of these transformations for Christian life today will be the focus of later chapters.

Commonwealth (Berkeley, CA: Counterpoint, 2010); Daniel M. Bell Jr., *The Economy of Desire: Christianity and Capitalism in a Postmodern World* (Grand Rapids, MI: Baker Academic, 2012).

20. Maurice Glasman, *Unnecessary Suffering: Managing Market Utopias* (London: Verso, 1996), 7.

21. See Marc Dunkelman, *The Vanishing Neighbor* (New York: W. W. Norton, 2014).

The structures of life were transformed as the sources of agency shifted to the impersonal state and the market. For Polanyi:

> Both the sovereign agent of rational choice and the sovereign state of politics view dependency as a weakness, a denial of autonomy, and are constantly resisting the demands of social and economic co-operation. . . . Those autonomous societal institutions which organize the satisfaction of need and the preservation of a practical culture are considered a constraint on the individual freedoms of the person and the political will of the state. Squeezed between the individual maximize and the collective aggregator, society as a functional moral entity disappears.[22]

Economies ceased to be about things made and traded (commodities) or the exchange of money within local societal rules. The market redefined the meaning of persons and land (labor and real estate). Set free from social constraint, individuals became self-made agents in a free market. This coalescing of state, economy, and Self embodied a deep-seated contempt for and desire to root out social institutions formed around local community and social integration because such social forms were direct competitors to the state, the market, and the autonomous self. Ways of life, therefore, that had shaped humanity through history were dissolved in the blink of an historical eye. Economy had normatively been understood as a subset of social life. The social traditions of a group had determined the ways the exchange of goods and services took place. In the nineteenth century, this narrative was swept away. The modern West is discontinuous from all previous forms of social and political life. Its confidence is sourced from an entirely new imagination about the nature of social life. People's work and the land within which they had dwelt were disconnected from located narratives of place and tradition to be reconfigured as commodities of the rational state and the free market. The global hegemony of the West made this imagination global as everything became reconfigured around the market. Even the church and trade unions became colonized by the market and redefined in terms of the consumer: does this entertain me, or meet my need in some other way?

In the twenty-first century, the West has lived within this narrative for so long it is difficult to appreciate what a radical shift it was, or how

---

22. Glasman, *Unnecessary Suffering*, 7.

devastating it has been for human belonging. It now seems impossible to imagine any other form of social or economic life. A state-sponsored market society is simply assumed as the normative way the world works. At the heart of this narrative lies the enlightened self-interest of the individual—the modern West's core definition of what it means to be human. We are now all self-defining individuals with our own inherent rights; we are free to pursue our self-interest.

The Individual Self

The individual became the agent and meaning maker of the modern West. Personal identity is now about individual rights and freedoms paralleling a laissez-faire, market economy. The one begets and needs the other. Both required the disembedding of people from forms of social life built around common belonging and shared identity in order to thrive. Loyalty migrated from small, locally based social groupings and institutions to the impersonal nation-state (nationalism), the calculation of the market, and individual rights. Citizens were remade as individual wageworkers.[23] Work moved out of the home, where extended families had been local economic communities of women, men, and children. Work moved into factories; people became hands and wage earners, elements in the machinery of calculation and production. Local economies and the social life they formed were relegated to the peripheral.

This Western project was not without its challenges. Western capitalism across the globe had produced a world of winners and losers. Modern, industrial societies were deeply stratified, and far from egalitarian despite the pretensions to freedom and individual rights. Social stratification, illustrated in the contemporary British series *Downton Abbey*, was widespread.[24] While the West was achieving great things (Ferguson's argument in *Civilization*), the results were unevenly distributed across society. The greatest benefits went to a small, privileged class in a bourgeois society.[25]

---

23. For example, advertising shifted from hiring "people" to the abstract, impersonal, and interchangeable language of "hands."
24. The series demonstrates how modernity remakes history in its own imagination. Practically all signs of religious life were airbrushed from the drama. It was a secular rendering with no accounting for undergirding narratives that had shaped people in the midst of empire or war.
25. Part of Thomas Piketty's argument in his book *Capital in the Twenty-First Century* (Cambridge, MA: Harvard University Press, 2014) is that the West is returning to this

Downton Abbey also illustrated that while the Christian story that had shaped the West, with its morals, folkways, and language, remained formally at the center, it had become a privatized religion in a pubic-private world with a religious-secular divide.[26] It had been relegated to a matter of personal, inner life (the moral support for the nation and the new self-making individual), where it functioned as a subset of the dominant market-nation narrative. By the beginning of the twentieth century, the idea of a Christian West remained as the formal narrative, but Western democracies had entered a space of neutrality toward religious belief. The role of religion in the market state was to supply moral and ethical succor. God was useful to the market in terms of private, individual sustenance, but, beyond that, religion was of little import except in sustaining the legitimacy of nation-states to send their citizens to war and death. The Christian story was effectively neutered. In its place was the trinity of market, state, and Self, each functioning independently of any grounding other than itself. By the end of the twentieth century, this confidence in the secular structures of social, political, and economic life began to come apart in what some describe as a postsecular West.[27]

Implications for Christian Imagination[28]

These tectonic shifts didn't happen overnight. Christian institutions continued to function, sometimes as if nothing had changed, but the idea of a Christian society became increasingly ancillary, a background

---

upstairs/downstairs world. The challenge of such a transformation is that the social contract upon which the modern state has built its legitimacy with its citizens is fundamentally undermined. The prospects for social destabilization are massive.

26. In so many ways the churches have remained captive within these profoundly modern and troubling categories with little capacity to imagine themselves outside these immensely false polarities. The source and role of these modern polarities deserve much attention that cannot be offered in this book. But the secular-religious polarity, for example, is an illustration of how false and unhelpful these taken for granted descriptors are. The political, for example, is run-through with religious imagery, claims, and structures. The claims of nationalism are little more than replacements for the Christian confession of God's sovereignty. See Cavanaugh, *Church as Field Hospital*, 99–105.

27. See, for example, Ward, *Politics of Discipleship*, 117–58, and Ulrich Beck, *Risk Society: Toward a New Modernity* (London: Sage, 1992).

28. This heading is taken from the title of a series of lectures given by T. S. Elliot in 1939 at Corpus Christi College that was published as the book *The Idea of a Christian Society* (London: Faber and Faber, 1982). It illustrates the ways in which there had set in a loss of clarity about what had been taken for granted (a Christian society) and an attempt to rehabituate this idea at the center of British society on the eve of the second great cataclysm of the twentieth century to descend on the "Christian" West.

to the primary story. The modern West remained nominally Christian. While Christendom had long been demolished,[29] the marriage of Christianity, empire, and progress undergirded the West. The churches hooked a ride on national expressions of global power and the ideologies of God's choosing the West to bear the civilizing work of progress and Christianity around the world. The Christian story had become a fundamentally white, Western narrative.[30] Notions of leadership and formation within these churches were increasingly shaped around narratives of power, control, and management within an ecclesiocentric core.[31] The answer of the churches to marginalization was, more often than not, to turn inward. They became preoccupied with their own inner life. As tribal enclaves, they focused their energies on questions of ecclesiological identity, while directing their resources to mission activity in colonies and across empires. The notion that the churches continued to be in control of their cultures remained a powerful myth. The churches were granted privilege but not power. Christianity ceased to be the driver of social change, becoming, rather, the safeguard of national morals and codes of business and the inner life of individuals. In return, they had the sop of privilege. Christianity had been a primary reforming movement of society in the early industrial age: spearheading laws to ameliorate the worst of industrialization, and leading abolitionist movements, the emancipation of women, and the control of alcohol as it destabilized family finances and, therefore, affected women's and children's lives. This activism became, largely, a memory. Protestant denominations were busy creating denominational organizations that mirrored the center-periphery nature of Western power. Narratives of progress and control were theologized into convictions about the Western churches being the center and vanguard of God's future. Christianity meant the West and that translated into being the center, in control, and in the driver's seat.

---

29. This occurred much earlier with the Peace of Westphalia in 1648 that initiated the process whereby nation-states displaced the Christendom that had existed for more than a millennia. Formal Christendom would rapidly disappear, to be replaced by a functional Christendom that increasingly lost its capacities to shape the narratives of growing numbers of people in the West. Christianity had place and form, but it no longer shaped the legitimating narratives of citizens of the state.
30. For a full description of this movement, see Willie James Jennings, *The Christian Imagination: Theology and the Origins of Race* (New Haven, CT: Yale University Press, 2010).
31. See Alan J. Roxburgh, *Joining God* (New York: CPI, 2015).

In his study of these developments, *The Christian Imagination*, Willy Jennings explored how successive European colonizations shaped missionary expansion from the fifteenth century forward. A metaphor he uses to describe the effects of these developments is displacement. When the European explorers and colonizers entered what they viewed as new worlds, they did so with a distorted imagination that failed to see the other except in terms of their own Western cultural center. As had happened in Europe, these colonizing and missionizing movements saw the local, everyday life of different places as problems to be overcome in the spread of the Western ideals of God, church, state, and market. Europeans "establish a new organizing reality for the world— themselves."[32] Western technological, social, political, scientific, and economic transformations were self-authenticating evidence that God had given the world a new center. As Israel had once been the center of God's unfolding story, the modern West was now the new people of God. This Christian West saw the rest of the world in the light of its own shadow.[33] This was something new. The global future and the kingdom of God (secular or religious) had a new still point in a turning world—the West. All the principles of society—understanding nature, shaping religious life, and forming an economic or political culture— were based on the intellectual groundings of the West. Everything outside this imagination was displaced. The process of becoming a Christian took on new markers defined by the West. The primary marker of Christian identity became race:

> This effect begins with positioning Christian identity fully within European (white) identity and fully outside the identities of (sic. Others/non-Europeans). . . . Here was a process of discerning Christian identity that, because it had jettisoned Israel from the calculus of the formation of Christian life, created a conceptual vacuum that was filled by the European. But not simply qua European; rather the very process of becoming Christian took on new ontic markers. . . . If Israel had been visibly elect of God, then that visibility in the European imagination had migrated without return to a new home

---

32. Jennings, *Christian Imagination*, 58.
33. Jennings describes this critical move as supersessionist, wherein the church replaced Israel in the mind and heart of God. He describes this imagination as a decisive distortion that has had awesome effects on Christian thinking (*Christian Imagination*, 32–33).

shaped now by new visual markers. If Israel's election had been the compass around which Christian identity gained its bearings and found its trajectory, now with this reconfiguration the body of the European would be the compass marking divine election. More importantly, that newly elected body, the white body, would be a discerning body, able to detect holy effects and saving grace.[34]

To be fully human was to be white. "Christianity in the Western world lives and moves with a diseased social imagination."[35] Jennings says, a "theological mistake so wide, so comprehensive that it has disappeared, having expanded to cover the horizon of modernity itself."[36] There was now a "deep theological architecture that patterned early modern visions of people, places and societies."[37] European churches were caught in the tension of confident expansion across the globe and a growing insecurity about their own place in West itself. At the same time, the churches in North America thrived as they received European immigrants and expanded their footprint across the New World.

Missionizing across the globe was such an all-encompassing, absorbing focus that the Western churches largely missed the effects of modernity's wager. The triumph of the nation-state, capitalism, and the Self made the churches peripheral, or, at best, confined to offering moral support. From the perspective of the late nineteenth century, however, the churches saw themselves as the center hub of a world order that God had called into existence.[38] Few could have imagined that this established sense of center, destiny, and power would soon be seriously questioned. Some artists and writers, like Blake and Dickens, were signaling that something had gone terribly wrong. There were warnings that the trajectory of the West was deeply troublesome.[39] Doubt and

---

34. Jennings, *Christian Imagination*, 33–34.
35. Jennings, *Christian Imagination*, 6.
36. Jennings, *Christian Imagination*, 38.
37. Jennings, *Christian Imagination*, 6–7.
38. See, for example, the 1910 Edinburgh World Missionary Conference, where the watchword "the evangelization of the world in this generation" captured this sense of a centered Western movement toward the rest of the world.
39. See, for example, William R. Everdell, *The First Moderns* (Chicago: University of Chicago Press, 1997). Blake's image of the *Land of Ulro* expresses these deep concerns about the trajectory of the West (see Czeslaw Milosz and Louis Iribane, *Land Of Ulro* [London: Farrar, Straus and Giroux, 2000]). These were also the concerns that occupied Marx and Engels in their early writings.

anxiety were just under the surface. The next chapter considers the West in crisis in an era of self-destruction (1918–1945) and remaking (1946–1960).

3

From Self-Confidence to Doubt: Western Modernity in Crisis (1918–1946)

> We British pray that God will help Britain, not because she is Britain, but because she is righteous . . . [1]

> We are on the side of Christianity against the anti-Christ.[2]

The late nineteenth and early twentieth centuries witnessed new levels of transformation in the modern Western imagination. By the turn of the twentieth century, movements in physics, electricity, painting, and music were again changing the way people understood the world. Some in the West had become aware that the rock-solid world of Newtonian physics had questionable foundations. While the world had again entered uncharted waters, the period leading up to 1914 was viewed as a continuation of the present order. The cataclysms that were about to erupt were out of the purview of most. The world wars between 1918 and 1945 represented a second Thirty Years war, separated by some three hundred years. The first signaled the confidence of a newly emerging modernity. The second shook this confidence to the ground, propelling the West into a series of crises that continue into the present. In its two world wars, the West implicated the rest of the world through its empires, trade treaties, and colonizations. Some framing of this period is important to our story.

---

1. Quoted from Christ Church Cannon in A. J. Hoover, *God, Germany, and Britain in the Great War: A Study in Clerical Nationalism* (London: Praeger, 1989), 6.
2. Quoted from the Lord Bishop of London in Hoover, *God, Germany, and Britain*, 24.

World War 1

World War I was a massive shock to Europeans in particular but also to the many other nations around the world who were drawn into the conflict. It was expected by the original combatant nations to be short-lived: a cleansing, purifying experience (the flushing of a system, or a ritualistic bloodletting) producing even greater opportunities for European nations to demonstrate their ascendant power across the world. It drew the world into their vortex, wrapping the war in terms of a holy Christian battle with God on the side of their nations. In this first modern, technological war (machine guns, gas, tanks, planes, and trenches), the Christian narrative was put at the service of nationalism. By its end, the Great War had shattered the confidence of the West, setting the stage for an era of contradiction and a crisis of identity that continues to this day. That so many were slaughtered in the name of God and country undermined what had been the unshakable confidence of the West. The fabric of family and society was torn apart. Killing, maiming, and destruction were out of proportion to anything people had up until then imagined or experienced. Multitudes of the injured were not capable of work. Soldiers returned home numbed by the carnage and emptied of the confidence with which they had bravely gone to the front. In North America, however, there blossomed a growing confidence and sense of righteous power.

The postwar period continued the contrast between Europe and North America. Europe's doubt and questioning were addressed, to some extent, by the extremes of left and right, Fascism and Communism. In America, an era of optimism and confidence emerged in the form of immigration, a growing industrial base, and expanding churches filled with hope about their place in the world.[3] The center-periphery, dominance-control story described above came apart in Europe even as it solidified in North America. The conviction that the West was the controlling center of the world continued in the emergence of America as a world power and the vain attempts of European powers to reestablish colonial rule. Ennui characterized one part of the West while confidence and destiny flourished in the other.

Just as America confidently emerged as a superpower, cataclysmic destruction made it impossible for many Europeans to imagine the

---

3. It is in this period, for example, that a magazine such as *The Christian Century* could be introduced in the USA and make perfect sense to people.

West as the apogee of civilization. There, a period of dark self-examination ensued. The conditions upon which a nineteenth-century liberal society had been built were unraveling. Karl Barth's *The Epistle to the Romans*[4] laid down a devastating critique of the optimistic liberalism that had pervaded pre–1914 Europe and its Protestant churches. The Great War unhinged people, yet the memory of what had preceded it was mostly lost. "Nineteenth-century society was based upon the two pillars of liberal capitalism and representative democracy,"[5] and both were under severe stress in the intrawar years. Across the Atlantic, a very different story unfolded as the United States geared up to take on the Western mantle of a global world order and mainstream churches were forming themselves as the moral and spiritual foundation for this new role.

Between World Wars: The 1920s and 1930s

The 1920s and 1930s were an extended period of crisis and disorientation, and were experienced differently on each side of the Atlantic. In Europe the question was: how could so much that was so clear and unassailable come apart so quickly? In the twenties, Europe was rebuilding its shattered prewar world and reestablishing hegemony through military power and political organization across its colonies. The expectation of Europe was continuity and restoration—a return to the world that existed before the cataclysm. From the twenties to the Great Depression, multiple efforts were made to return the West to its immediate past. The center-periphery world was to be restored with grand alliances, a redrawing of the global political map, and the spread of Western institutions. The Treaty of Versailles exemplified the drive to restore the imperial balance of power among victorious European and North American nations and restore liberal capitalism through international agreements.

The impulse was to return a world that had been lost. This was to be expected. The majority of Western leaders immediately following the Great War were the products of the nineteenth century. Their actions were framed by that period. Even in the context of revolutions like the Russian Revolution, the imagination of these leaders was that of nineteenth-century global modernity. Because so few realized there could be no return, their energies were bent toward a restoration of the previous

---

4. Karl Barth, *The Epistle to the Romans* (Oxford: Oxford University Press, 1963).
5. Georgio Resta and Mariavittoria Catanzariti, *Karl Polanyi: For A New West* (Cambridge: Polity, 2014), 214.

century's order and its religious life. Church leaders were not different. They hoped that a reestablishment of the previous period was not only possible, but that it would fix the growing anxieties about their place of the Church in a postwar West. The conditions that had made the nineteenth-century global world work and the belief systems that had undergirded it had, however, been swept away. Few grasped this situation in the rush to return the West to its prewar status.

North America had little doubt about its new role. Its social and economic transformations were characterized by hope. There was growth in national wealth, military power, and personal income as a middle class began to develop within a nascent consumer society. The Roaring Twenties and the Jazz Age made some feel an unbridled loss of moral and spiritual direction. Prohibition attempted to impose moral rectitude on society. Unions sought to secure the American dream for working people in the midst of laissez-faire capitalism. The push for women's suffrage and a nascent civil rights movement shaped the twenties. Waves of immigrants from Europe responded to the American invitation to start over again by working hard and believing in God's destiny for the nation.

Churches thrived as birth rates grew. Christianity remained at the center of American life, and the dominant Protestant establishment expanded to include Catholic and Jewish traditions to share in the mainstream of public life. Commentators of the time wondered how this idealistic nation would come to terms with social and economic inequality in the midst of unrestrained wealth. Some struggled with what felt like the loss of a moral compass in an America that had become a global superpower. Such questions, however, received scant attention amid growing populations and a growing capacity to produce goods and services for all its citizens.

If the 1920s were characterized by attempts at return and reestablishment in Europe and self-confident expansion in North America, the 1930s witnessed another upheaval of everything across the Western world. In the disruption of the Great Depression, the appeal of Communism, and the rise of Fascism, the economic basis of global modernity grew tenuous. The democratic ideal upon which the West had been built came under severe threat. The "international system upon which our civilization had unconsciously depended for its life and growth" dissolved.[6] The Great Depression raised questions about

---

6. Resta and Catanzariti, *Karl Polanyi*, 211. Polanyi provides an extensive explanation for this dramatic change that cannot be addressed in the scope of this chapter.

the underlying basis of the modern West. Global modernity had been built around the ideology of the market and made possible through the military power of the state. For Polanyi the crises of the 1920s and 1930s was that European leaders continued trying to return their economic and political realities back to the prewar situation. They did not grasp that the issue was more than making adjustments but dealing with the collapse of the liberal economic order.

The onset of the Great Depression led to a sense that the liberal, market-driven, democratic era of Western dominance had lost its way. Europe's upstairs-downstairs society, seen by some as a God-given order, came apart. The resulting anxiety left a despairing sense of another impending cataclysm. People searched for ways to stop a possible slide into war. In England, Christian leaders brought eminent thinkers together to ask how Christianity could fix social, economic, and political life. The Christian academic and statesman J. H. Oldham formed the *Moot* (with members such as John Baillie, Karl Mannheim, J. R. R. Tolkien, Michael Polanyi, Eric Vidler, and T. S. Eliot) to think about a Christian response to the crisis of the West. In 1937, Oldham convened the Oxford Conference. It assembled the best Christian minds from across multiple disciplines to provide Christian solutions. The goal was nothing less than the remaking of the social order, thus averting another possible catastrophe. Knowing that the Christian narrative was unraveling, the participants made recommendations for its restoration to the center of the West. There was little engagement with the underlying assumptions about the state, the economy, and the Self as primary agents. The instinctive response was to reestablish a Christian basis for the social order, but there was little ability to see alternatives beyond support for the existing order within which God had been rendered nothing more than a useful support. On the other side of the Atlantic, a young Harold J. Ockenga's address at the founding of the National Association of Evangelicals set out the urgent need for the "rescue of Western civilization by a re-emphasis on and revival of Evangelical Christianity."[7] In both settings the foundations of the modern West—the state, capitalism and the Self—were not called into question, but assumed as normative. Christian responses remained locked within modernity's wager.

---

7. See Molley Worthen, *Apostles of Reason: The Crisis of Authority in American Evangelicals* (Oxford: Oxford University Press, 2014), Kindle Edition, Loc. 243 of 8371.

World War II

The doubts and questions about Christian identity and the future of the West were gathered up and thrown into the maelstrom of World War II. Ian Kershaw states:

> The devastation of the Second World War plumbed new depths. The moral consequences of such a profound collapse of civilization would be felt for the rest of the century, and beyond. . . . Where the First World War had left behind a legacy of heightened ethnic, border and class conflict together with a deep and prolonged crisis of capitalism, the Second swept away this concatenation in its very maelstrom of destruction.[8]

The end of World War I solidified doubts about the viability of the modern Western project while the end of World War II was characterized by the conviction that traditional morals were disappearing. The moral basis of the West, centered in Christian identity, had come off its moorings. Society was adrift. During the wars, men were absent for a long time. When they returned, they often found it difficult to fit back into assumed social norms. The wars tore apart the fabric of traditional moral life, leaving people with little sense of what might take its place. Historically, war had been limited to professional soldiers in some exotic place. It had been a patriotic moment for young men but had not, for more than a hundred years, involved Western societies directly. That all shifted in the twentieth century. Whole societies were implicated in the devastation. For Europe, there was no separation between combatants and society. All were devastated. Women were involved in factories, building bombs, and putting out fires from incendiaries. Populations were bombed on a horrific scale. Populations had been sold on war as an act of religious conviction. The Great War was to be a holy and righteous war prayed over by bishops and church leaders. The unimagined devastation introduced growing questions about the religious basis of society. If these wars were God's, then there was no longer a moral order. Life could not go on as it had, but what would it look like?

---

8. Ian Kershaw, *To Hell and Back: Europe 1914–1949* (New York: Penguin Books, 2015), 6.

Economic Security and Social Upheaval (1946–1960)

For some historians the two conflicts of the First and Second World Wars were really a single conflict separated only by an uneasy cessation of conflict accompanied by intensive rearmament. So the end of the war was an indescribable relief for the citizens of the West. Thirty years of conflict had resulted in the death of tens of millions, and the destruction of cities, infrastructures, and landmarks that had stood for centuries. Unsettling questions about the identity and direction of the West following a period of such destruction were inevitable. The seeds for the revolts of the 1960s were sown amidst the intimations of what some were beginning to call a postmodern world. The energies of nations and citizens were directed toward returning a shattered world to some kind of normalcy. In the midst of crisis, the hope for return to family and community life was uppermost in people's minds. For most, this involved a doubling down of loyalty to established norms and the need to reestablish patterns of life shattered by the long years of war. For others, it was impossible to fix or make well again the West that had caused these wars. An experimenting with alternative forms of identity and social life began. Was there any normalcy to which one could return after Auschwitz and Hiroshima? While the question lurked under the surface, a new economic golden age moved across the West, bringing about forgetfulness and filling its churches with a new kind of social form: the middle-class family.

Reconstruction and Economic Growth

The postwar era was consumed by the need for both reconstruction and expansion as soldiers returned home and a baby boom arrived. Bretton Woods[9] played a major part in this reconstruction. It was an agreement to reconstruct the monetary order of the West, its allies, and

---

9. Bretton Woods was a conference formally sponsored by the United Nations just at the end of World War II in 1944 to address the challenge of remaking and reforming the global monetary system following the hostilities and in the light of the emergence of the Soviet Union. It was a meeting between the United Kingdom and the United States that established the International Bank and the International Monetary Fund. The primary figures shaping this new international monetary order were John Maynard Keynes (UK) and Harry Dexter White (USA). In many ways this agreement laid out a means by which the nation-states of the West could manage capitalism in ways that protected their citizens from the worst of its fluctuations. These agreements came to be known as an economic policy called Keynesianism, which shaped the Western nation-states up until the mid-1970s. See Benn Steil, *The Battle of Bretton Woods* (Princeton, NJ: Princeton University Press, 2013).

colonies.[10] It framed the role of the state in terms of the management of national economies. There would be no repeating the mistakes of Versailles by punishing losing nations. Measures were set in place to manage the ups-and-downs of market cycles. Out of this context, the welfare state emerged as a combination of Christian moral practice and liberal socialism. By the postwar period, large proportions of the elite and intellectual classes in Europe and North America had rejected Christianity. The welfare state, while rooted in Christian imagination, illustrated how the secular state had taken the place of church and local communities to become the primary space for the care and support of citizens. Care became managed and bureaucratized through state legislation and public policy. By means of taxation, state-run safety nets protected citizens from the worst effects of the invisible hand. Churches were increasingly relegated to the care of the private, inner lives of those citizens who chose spiritual succor. From the perspective of 2017, this story now seems to describe a strange, alien world, but it was the one that shaped the stories of success, class, and economic progress that still infuse our imagination. Within this story, it would be the state that stepped in to provide the support systems for social life. The primary unit of social life shifted from the neighborhood to that of the state and its apparatus for looking after people.

In this period Protestant denominations fully structured themselves around the hub-spoke organization that ran the dominant business organizations of the day. These organizations were run by centralized managers and professionals resourcing local congregations. As managed care through professionals became the norm, churches followed suit in the training of the clergy and denominational leadership. While churches were invited to provide ameliorating programs for people in need, their base purpose was clear. Their role in the postwar era had radically changed. Churches were now useful adjuncts to the liberal state and the capitalist economy. The state and the market were the overarching framers and sponsors of social life. The market provided a brief golden age of goods-and-services and full employment. It offered the means for individuals to make their own private lives. It was as if, with the end of war, that the promise of modernity's wager had finally

---

10. The postwar era saw the emergence of the binary situation of the Communist world and the West. Most nations of the world aligned themselves with one or the other, though there were some nations that chose a third way of being non-aligned.

become available for everyone as the new middle class took its place at the center of this society.

As Maurice Glasman points out, the patterns of social life and work once formed by localized groups (societies, churches, clubs) had been starkly diminished as the primary agents of social formation. State and market now assumed these roles. The "breaking of society, its patterns of work and local modes of association leads to . . . the dominance of the state and the market" in the postwar years.[11] The local had alway been the basis for support, sociality, and the sustenance of life together. As the state and the market grew, the bonds of a local life, once so essential for human thriving, were diminished. For the state and the economy to have that hegemony over the lives of citizens, these older forms of social identity, located in small, idiosyncratic local groups, had to be removed as primary shapers of people's lives. The modern secular state and consumer capitalism became the primary shapers of society.

Huge demographic shifts in North America were inculcated by the Baby Boom, the flight from cities into the new suburbs, and the development of interstate highway systems. State-sponsored projects undermined local forms of social life.[12] Burgeoning populations of youth entered a world less and less connected with the local. The state and the invisible hand promised a new kind of future. A radical experiment in individualism, unlike anything experienced previously, was about to begin. It would be an experiment in which the state and the economy underwrote the full development of what Charles Taylor describes as the "buffered Self." The West entered a postwar world disengaged from the local and focused on manufacturing a new kind of agent—the unfettered, self-expressive individual. The development of the white, suburban church was the perfect fit for this new kind of person.

With growing employment, working-class populations entering educational systems as never before, new suburban housing developments, and the Baby Boom, a new era was emerging. Churches filled up. New ones were planted and denominations experienced an era of unimagined corporate expansion. It seemed as though a golden era had emerged after the horrors of the first half of the century. The West's global dominance was solidly in place again, thanks to America, an emerging middle class, and

---

11. Maurice Glasman, *Unnecessary Suffering: Managing Market Utopias* (London: Verso, 1996), 8.

12. See Marc Dunkelman, *Vanishing Neighborhood* (New York: Norton, 2014), whose book makes this argument.

the expansion of the manufacturing and corporate world. Even though the Communist threat was emerging and the nuclear race was beginning, there was a sense that a new age now promised a new self within a continued economic growth. The West was still Christian, but superficially so. In the face of the Soviet Union, the Cold War, and threats of a nuclear winter, the churches remained the bulwark of democracy and private succor.

In Europe, reconstruction was initially difficult but, eventually, economies picked up steam. Returning soldiers returned to the workplace, working with a deep loyalty to their country's rebuilding efforts. Factories turned out immense quantities of goods and services for the new families fueled by a baby boom and growing financial security. Conforming to the organizational and institutional traditions of marketplace individualism seemed to offer the way toward a hopeful future.[13] Affluence, coupled with the technologies of travel and communications, set the stage for an unparalleled transformation of society. Commitments to place and tradition broke down as people embraced a new era of prosperity and freedom.[14]

The New Self

Economic expansion brought the promise of freedom. A consumer-oriented market economy made it possible for younger generations to disconnect from place, authority, and traditions. The states' engagement in society made local forms of social life less and less attractive to the new individual. Another transformation of the West was underway as a radically new independent, self-making "I" came into full bloom in the 1960s. Europe already had harbingers of this transformation. Abraham Maslow's *A Theory of Human Motivation* and his hierarchy of needs suggested that the highest end of human life was self-actualization. Written in 1943, the paper indicated that the seeds of this huge generational transformation had been long gestating beneath the surface of social life in the West. Society had previously been built around an understanding of a self who was part of and responsible to a circle of others within local familial and economic units seeking to guarantee life's basics for one another. The shift to self-actualization suggested that something deep in the identity

---

13. William Whyte, *The Organization Man* (New York: Simon & Schuster, 1956).
14. See Robert Nisbet's classic 1952 study *The Quest for Community* (San Francisco, CA: ICS Press, 1990 edition) as well as Maurice Stern's 1959 study, *The Eclipse of Community* (New York: Harper, 1960).

of the West was changing. Carl Rogers (1902–1987) brought these ideas into mainstream America. His books, *Client-Centered Therapy* (1951), *Psychology and Personal Change* (1954), and *On Becoming a Person* (1961), elaborated the core element of this shift in Western imagination. The self as the center of meaning and purpose would enter powerfully onto the stage in the 1960s. Within this new affluence and consumerism came an unprecedented environment of experimentation across all layers of society, opening the floodgates to individualism.

Urbanization, Anti-Colonialism, and a Changing West

Another factor contributing to the West's transformation was the growth of cities with their new middle-class populations seeking new social structures. The children of the older, immigrant, urban working classes received the benefits of affluence and formed the seedbed for the cultural revolutions of the 1960s. Churches, by contrast, did not understand or adjust to these new middle-class movements. These newer classes were already alienated from Christian life. Cities, where the social revolutions were generated, were being effectively de-Christianized.[15] In North America, traditional forms of Christianity flourished in the suburbs and the mind-numbing conformity of middle-class enclaves of individualism and affluence.[16] As economies were able to create a thriving middle class, the suburbs grew and the churches followed, planting and growing in order to produce busy programs for consuming selves eager to be self-actualized.

The Complexities of a Changing West—toward the 1960s

Complex elements catalyzing in the postwar West ignited the explosive, transformative 1960s. The 1950s were neither dull nor conformist. The 1950s were a decade of stark fears and new hope that laid the groundwork for even greater social change. While the upheavals were enormous, the underlying elements shaping the modern West were not fundamentally changed by of 1960s. The primacy of the state, the overarching control of consumer capitalism, and the ascent of the Self remained the driving forces. In this sense, the movement of the 1960s was not new. The Euro-tribal churches on both sides of the Atlantic had been displaced as the

---

15. See, for example, Harvey Cox, *The Secular City* (New York: Collier, 1965) and J. A. T. Robinson, *Honest to God* (Louisville, KY: Westminster John Knox Press, 1963).
16. See Gibson Winter, *The Suburban Captivity of the Churches* (New York: Macmillan, 1962).

centers of social, political, economic, and personal meaning, albeit in different ways. Modernity had begun as a grand experiment that, by the midpoint of the twentieth century, seemed to confirm that life could be lived well without God, and that God could, indeed, be made useful to the new, self-actualizing individual.

This Golden Age, this Aquarian time, did not need God, but it was certainly okay if people needed a bit of God for their personal experience. By the midpoint of the twentieth century, the state, the economy, and the Self had fully displaced God's agency in the narrative of the West. God didn't disappear or cease to be the subject of multiple debates. It was, rather, that God had become simply useful for the autonomous self's personal development and the state's need for religious legitimization when required. Consumer capitalism and the autonomous self now overrode all else.

4

Hope for Transformation within the Wager: The Sixties

For the next generation, the events of May 1968 were their decisive experience. Both its partisans and critics agree that after May '68 we became a society that undoes its bonds. France was no longer seen as a distinctive nation that strives for unity and independence. Collective rules, both political and social, were delegitimized. The citizen of action was succeeded by the individual of enjoyment. This movement appeared to be very political, even revolutionary, with its various groups competing to be the most radical ideologically. In reality, political differences were levelled in a flood of slogans, and the scene was prepared for the great withdrawal of loyalty from the community, a withdrawal that would take place over the years to follow. . . . After '68, relaxation became the law of the land. Every constraint appeared to be useless and arbitrary, whether in civic or in private life. Now, as each letting go justifies and calls forth the next, successive governments tout themselves, no longer because of the guidance and the energy they give to common life, but because of the "new rights" they grant to individuals and groups. Underlying the ostentatious solicitude for the wishes of society and the desires of individuals, there is a growing incapacity to propose goals for common action. . . . Neither the institutions of Europe . . . nor what is called civil society have enough strength or credibility to claim the attention or fix the hopes of citizens. . . . Nothing seems to have the power to gather us toward the common action.

> . . . Real political leadership of the kind that calls on our deepest loyalties and highest capacities is nowhere to be seen.[1]

The Western imagination was a convergence of Greek, early Christian, and Roman stories into an overarching narrative called Christendom. With the ending of Christendom, another West was birthed. While recognizing important differences across the West, this chapter looks at common elements shaping it today. The story moves from the nineteenth into the transformations of the twentieth century. The hinge is the 1960s. That decade distilled and coalesced reactions that had been gestating in the previous decade as people came to terms with a half-century in which the West took the rest of the world to the hell of war and back. The 1960s launched what many people then believed to be a new Aquarian moment presaging a break with a blood-soaked past, and promising a new future. Something deep inside people hoped for a future that would break from what the modern West had bequeathed to them. People began using the term *postmodern*, a phrase that expressed the struggle to name the changes occurring and signal that something was terribly amiss about the modern West with its wars and political ideologies.

The Tipping Point of the 1960s

For David Cayley, "Many layers of nostalgic legend now encrust the period from the early 1960s to the mid-1970s."[2] Something remarkable took place in the 1960s as people became aware that something was wrong with the way the modern West had remade the world. With huge doses of idealism, people believed transformation was possible. This optimism peaked on the streets of Paris and Berlin in the spring and summer of 1968 and spread to other urban centers across the West. For many people, the sources of society's crisis were not always clear. Generally, people had little memory of the antecedent forces that had formed the modern West. People blamed abstractions: the system, hierarchy, government, and capitalism. It was fashionable for them to blame the ambiguous notions of institutions and structures and demonize them as being the primary inhibitors of individual freedom. If the individual could

---

1. Pierre Manent, "Repurposing Europe," *First Things* (April 2016), https://www.firstthings.com/article/2016/04/repurposing-europe.
2. David Cayley, *The Rivers North of the Future* (Toronto: Anansi, 2005), 16.

be freed from the constraints of the existing systems of social, governmental, and economic life, then the Aquarian Age would dawn as bright and full as John's imagination of the kingdom of God on Patmos. The failure of the 1960s was not in its idealism or the sense that the West had become destructive, but in its commitment to the ideal of the autonomous individual as the primary, ontological reality of the world. Hope for a new world amounted to one more form of the Self as the independent, free agent who makes its own world. The 1960s may have wanted to form an alternative society, but, in the end, it accelerated consumer capitalism and the primacy of the Self.

The Demographic Transformation

The Baby Boom that defined the 1960s has redefined every decade since.[3] Even in their seventies, some of the leading musicians of the 1960s (McCartney, Dylan, Baez, and Jagger) continue to shape culture. The Baby Boom Generation created a huge demographic spike right in the midst of attempts to build a new and better world. The Boomers remained attached to this myth of building a new world right up to very recent times when it lost this force in society. The Boomer Generation bequeathed to us the idea of a youth culture. This idea flowed from the emergence of the teenager in the 1950s and the extension of education across all strata of society. Prior to World War II, education for the vast majority of people in Europe ended at fourteen. There did not exist this time between childhood and adulthood that came to be described as that of the teenager. Employment often meant doing the same job as one's parents with a single employer for one's entire working life. One participated in a common culture, be it working class or middle class. Life was predictable, and choices were rare and, possibly, unwelcome. The arrival of education extended childhood without introducing the responsibilities of adulthood.

Another key to the creation of a youth culture was the growing wealth of the postwar West. Harold McMillan's famous adage in the late 1950s, "You've never had it so good," was true. Newly affluent parents could make unprecedented resources available to their high school and university children in the form of money and consumer goods. Future employment

---

3. "The truth is that we have never really left the Sixties. We have simply repeated them, and that goes for those who were only born later. Sixties music, shopping, and celebrity culture have been spread far beyond their first makers and participants, to almost everybody in the land," Andrew Marr, *A History of Modern Britain* (London: Macmillan, 2007), 263.

would not be a problem. Saving didn't seem to be necessary. For young people, the future seemed assured, including the idea that when adulthood arrived, it would include a higher living standard than one's parents had enjoyed. There was no need to worry; a Golden Age had been born. Teenagers had disposable income to be spent purely on their own pleasure. Nothing like this had happened before across so broad a swath of society. Consumer capitalism contributed to the continuing transformations of society.

Advertising became a new industry.[4] Consumer goods were manufactured in ever-larger numbers for a society shifting from depression, war, and scarcity to one in which there was renewed economic growth, peace, and a new abundance of consumer goods.. What would ad-men now sell to this new, expanding demographic called the teenager? Not fridges, sewing machines or vacuum cleaners, but entertainment and clothing. Hollywood recognized the value of this new audience, manufacturing actors or heroes, like James Dean, to form a new consumer youth audience. The development of television in the 1950s paralleled this move. The vinyl record industry became the locus where huge amounts of creative energy were released. The music industry, which became one of the ways youth were forming their identity, was a new fusion of older African American traditions along with country and western traditions that came from the white and poor southern states in the United States. This combination produced a new, highly marketable product—rock and roll. Rock, together with folk, represented a generation making a fundamental break with its parents' politics, social mores, and hopes for the future. A new force was set in motion as the youth cultures on both sides of the Atlantic reshaped their tastes and experiences through this music, their fashion, and their new freedom from traditional work roles. The fashion industry quickly recognized the money to be made as a new generation styled itself differently from its parents' generation of conforming, stuffy, and limiting dress codes. Teenage fashion created a whole new industry that overturned established codes of conduct.

The postwar consumer society enabled this youth culture to break from its parents' traditional forms of life and values—especially traditional, class-based structures—to embrace new, self-constructed identities. The Self was given the economic base and freedom to come fully into its own. This was not a break with the story of the modern West, but the

---

4. The "hidden persuaders" was the title of Vance Packard's book *Hidden Persuaders* (New York: Ig Publishing, 1959).

acceleration of its deepest instincts in a Boomer Generation that thought it was changing the world. The hopeful desire to remake the world was subsumed beneath the full-blown emergence of the Self. In this economized freedom of the unfettered Self the dream was that the world could be remade. With the throwing off of convention, duty, and responsibility, the new world was born.

The Swinging Sixties

The myth of the Swinging Sixties was created by a relatively small number of people who inhabited the world of pop music, advertising, television, film, fashion, and even architecture. In the UK, many of them came from the emerging world of art and design. John Lennon, Ray Davies, Keith Richards, Pete Townsend, and Eric Clapton, to name a few, received some education in art schools. What you put inside buildings became as important, or possibly even more important, than the buildings themselves. As Richard Weight notes:

> More than in America, art schools were an engine room of youth culture. "During the 1960s British art colleges acquired a reputation for being the most experimental public-funded educational institutes in the world," wrote the critic Nigel Whiteley in this study, *Pop Design: Modernism to Mod.* "They became the focal points for those who sought change, excitement and an alternative culture."[5]

The idea of the modern, whether it be the modern architecture of Le Corbusier, the Bauhaus school, or other related movements in modern art, fed the most important elements in creating British youth culture in the 1960s.

The Ordinary Sixties

In practice, not a great deal had changed for most young people by the middle of the 1960s. Most still lived fairly conventional lives with their parents. They were a generation that enjoyed full employment. The workplace remained hierarchical and workers behaved deferentially toward

---

5. Richard Weight, *MOD: from Bebop to Britpop, Britain's Biggest Youth Movement* (London: Vintage, 2015), 120

managers. Many teenagers aspired to be married at an early age, have children while still young, and perhaps live near where they had grown up. For most young people the 1960s were a weekend phenomenon and usually ended by Monday morning. For many of them, this youth culture was conducted during leisure hours.

And yet something had shifted. There was an unmistakable sense that youth were living a different life from their parents—a modern life. There was a break with tradition in terms of aspirations about careers, possessions, and social attitudes. The arrival of the pill produced different attitudes toward sex before marriage. The end of censorship in the theatre had a knock-on effect on what was available on television, film, and literature. All this contributed to a feeling of a brave new world that radically broke with the traditions of the past. These feelings were both true and deeply false. The biggest shifts from previous generations were economic transformations that freed a new generation from the constraints of the local, opening them to a wide vista of consumer goods, travel, and the narrative of the Self set free to be whom and whatever they chose. This emerging youth culture tended to derided the immediate past as being Victorian or, dismissively, as just nineteenth-century ideas. The *ad hominem* was the youth's response to everything that failed to match the emotions and expectations for personal freedom and experimentation. Almost everything that came before, they regarded as outdated, worthless, and, therefore, to be rejected. Social relationships, in terms of the role of women and the shape of family life, were re-evaluated. Homosexuality and abortion were legalized in Britain in 1967.

North America and the Psychedelic Sixties

Developments in North America were striking similar chords with the emergence of a "beat" generation. A similar mix of jazz and blues coalesced with writers and poets who, in the late 1950s, were the Beatnik and Beat poets. Allen Ginsberg's writing mixed with the protest singers in Greenwich Village. Joan Baez represented a generation of folk singers connected with older performers like Pete Seeger and Woody Guthrie. The Newport Folk and Jazz Festivals, held in the 1960s in Rhode Island, catalyzed a variety of traditions from both African American and European American folk traditions. Such festivals gave impetus to an emerging protest movement that involved the

Civil Rights Movement and the Vietnam protests. These movements grew even as earlier idealisms about America as a moral champion in the world faded in the light of the John Kennedy, Martin Luther King Jr., and Robert Kennedy assassinations. The violence attached to the struggle for civil rights combined with the return of conscripts from Vietnam brought a degree of vitriol to the previous idealism that had fueled earlier nonviolent protest. As some young people began to turn against the culture, values, religion, and economy that had nurtured them, a feeling grew that the society that had been bequeathed to them was fundamentally broken and required radical change.[6]

Searching for Something Spiritual

One response to this sense of something being profoundly wrong with Western society was the cultivation of alternative lifestyles. Those alternatives were debated, for example, at the Human Be-In festival at Golden Gate Park in 1967. Reportedly, the musical *Hair* was an attempt to replicate the feeling present at the event. Thirty thousand people attended what was billed as a gathering of tribes. Timothy Leary voiced his mantra, "Turn on, tune in, drop out."[7] Following the success of the Human Be-In, another festival was planned for later that year, the Council for the Summer of Love. In excess of 100,000 young people turned up and the "Hippie" entered the consciousness of Western youth. Two years later, 400,000 attended the Woodstock Music Festival. The festival had many of the markings of the American religious revival movements, but this time, reference to the Christian God was absent This revival did not draw on the older Christian traditions; it was a generation looking for spiritual inspiration from Eastern thought, from pantheism, and from Native American spirituality.

---

6. See Nancy Fraser, "Progressive Neoliberalism versus Reactionary Populism," in *The Great Regression,* ed. Heinrich Geiselberger (Maldon, MA: Polity Press, 2017), 40–48. Fraser's reflection on this period is that the developing "liberal-individualist views of progress gradually replaced the more expansive, anti-hierarchical, egalitarian, class-sensitive understandings of emancipation that flourished in the 1960s and 1970s. As the New Left waned, its structural critique of capitalist society faded, and the country's characteristic liberal-individualist mindset reasserted itself, imperceptivity shrinking the aspirations of 'progressives' and self-proclaimed leftists" (42).
7. Some authors claim that Leary was not primarily advocating taking drugs so much as protesting against modernity and pointing to "a meaningful spiritual path out of modernity's misery factory." Richard Weight, *Mod: A Very British Style* (London: Bodley Head, 2013), 231.

Beyond Style—the Sixties Substantive Break with Tradition

The expansion in education during the 1950s and 1960s provided the ground for a break with tradition. As an increasing percentage of young people went to universities and colleges, they delayed their entrance into the customary workforce. These schools shaped the imaginations, changed the horizons, and transformed the assumptions of the Baby Boomers more substantially than the gyrations of the Summer of Love ever did. For the Boomers, education involved experimenting with drugs, attending pop festivals, protesting, turning toward Eastern religions, and, often, rejecting those Western traditions that had created these seats of learning. An unintended consequence of the opening up of education to large numbers of the younger generations was this encouragement to experiment in ways that represented a rejection of the norms and values of their parents. It was in the 1960s, with a democratization of curriculum and a push against educational methods framed around the West's great code, that a shift occurred from a teacher-oriented curriculum in the Western tradition to a student-demanded curriculum that educators determined appropriate for the new order.

Something happened in these processes that undermined continuity with the past not only in intellectual, social, and cultural ways, but also in a very physical way. Heidegger, for example, notes that the Old English and High German word *bauen* used for building, originally meant "to dwell," which suggests to remain, or to stay in place. He noted that a trace of *bauen* is to be found in the word for neighbor, which implies to cherish, protect, preserve, and care for.[8] The word carries a sense of rootedness that connects with continuity, community, and home. It is precisely these forms of life that were eviscerated from the 1960s forward. What was celebrated as the coming of a New Age was the ending of rootedness and connectedness. The conviction that feeling at home was essential to human thriving was lost. All this formed part of the angst of modern times. It became the raw material for playwrights, novelists, and movie producers.

In the 1960s, particularly in Europe, the sense that "we're all secular now" indicated that a radical detachment from organized religion was occuring. This happened at different speeds in various parts of Europe. Its dramatic impact on church attendance and church membership in

---

8. John Inge, *A Christian Theology of Place* (Farnham: Ashgate Publishing, 2003), 19.

England was first documented during this period. The sociologist Callum Brown made the case for a broad shift of the place of religion in British and then Western European society in the 1960s:

> What happened in the late twentieth century has been unique and epoch-forming. Since around 1963, Britain has been in the brave new world of secular secularization—that is, the permanent decline of religion. This decline takes two main observable forms. It is the terminal decline of virtually all of the large, organized conventional Christian churches in Britain; and it is the permanent decline of the common and pervasive Christian culture to which most Britons has adhered most of the time to greater or lesser extents for centuries (and arguably since the start of the second millennium CE). For the historian of religious decline, there is no period in history as important as the 1960s. What was different about the 1960s in the history of religion was not just the scale and suddenness of religious decline. The uniqueness of the Sixties was, first, that for the first time Christian religiosity underwent a common and virtually simultaneous change within nearly all countries in Western Europe.[9]

He suggested that

> the religious change that occurred was one of profound secularization of—or decline in—"conventional" religion which opened up British popular access to previously exotic, bohemian or socially circumscribed religious/ spiritual movements, and allowed for the lowering, at the point of consumption, of barriers between religious and spiritual movements. . . . [T]he 1960s was and remains unique because it marked the beginning in many countries of the collapse of religious culture as a whole: the religious value-system which, embedded through complex cultural formations in the family, community and state, had stewarded European civilization for a millennium (under Christianity), and possibly longer (under pre-Christian religions).[10]

---

9. Callum G. Brown, *The Death of Christian Britain* (London: Routledge, 2000), 29.
10. Brown, *Death of Christian Britain*, 30.

Assessing the Sixties

The myth of the 1960s went something like this: it was a decade of liberation, freedom, increased opportunity, and a break with a traditional and confining past that opened the door to an entrancing world of new possibilities and horizons. The 1960s produced liberal values that ushered in a more humanitarian view of society—a caring and compassionate society. It heralded a concern for the environment and the needs of the global poor. The reality, however, is more complex. Arguably, the 1960s produced freedom for the privileged few, but the majority experienced it as a time when the removal of traditional frameworks of obligation did not increase the sum total of human happiness so much as signal a time of increased anxiety about the future. For some, the felt realities were more frightening, whether it was unemployment, the collapse of key manufacturing industries, an increase in divorce, the collapse of stable families and communities, the growth of violent crime, increased drug abuse, the creation of an unemployable underclass with little stake in society, a growing fear about immigration, and a sense that a liberal elite was dramatically out of touch with the social classes that elected them. For a significant minority, access to the privileged world of the wealthy was never a possibility. It took until the present moment for these underlying experiences to erupt in a new age of anger.

The sixties were a watershed moment of massive social and cultural change across Europe and many parts of North America. The modern narrative of individualism came to the center of the West. Ulrich Beck explores the extent to which individualization now determines every kind of social institution, creating what he calls "the risk society."[11] All forms of institutions are now suspected of confining the Self. The small, mediating institutions that had formed the basis of society are, therefore, always suspect. Whether trade unions, political parties, Scouts, or the church, the idea of "belonging"—of being part of a group identity or a social class— has become much more challenging to sustain since the 1960s. Institutions that thrive are those that proffer individual freedom and offer consumer products to accent the Self, rather than those that invite belonging. The Euro-tribal churches on both sides of the Atlantic have been shaped by this new reality.

---

11. Ulrich Beck, *The Risk Society: Towards a New Modernity* (London: Sage Publications, 1992).

5

Where Were the Churches?

Introduction

The story of the modern West is rooted in the image of *Modernity's Wager*. Within this wager the Western narrative comes to be characterized by the forces of the state, consumer capitalism, and the Self. What emerges is a new ideal of cosmopolitan liberalism transferred across the planet through colonialism and globalization. Its creed lies in the belief that when a society is shaped by rational, self-interested individuals in a global market, all benefit. Where were the Euro-tribal churches in these transformations? This question can be addressed by looking at two historical periods: first, the period before the cultural upheavals of the 1960s and, second, the period since the end of the 1960s.

1900–1960: Restore and Repair

Prior to World War I, church leaders in both Britain and the North America were confident about the progress of Christianity in their own lands and the likelihood of its continual worldwide expansion through their missionary efforts. This confidence was demonstrated in the way that the Euro-tribal churches were being exported by missionaries as normative forms of church across the globe. The New York Ecumenical Conference of 1900 expressed this spirit. Honorary speakers included such political figures as Benjamin Harrison, William McKinley, and Theodore Roosevelt. As one writer reported,

> The opening hymn, "Jesus Shall Reign," unleashed a wave
> of emotion that would reverberate through the entire ten
> days of the conference. . . . New York 1900. . . resonated
> with the popular assumption that Western Christendom

and the church were agents of progress for the world's peoples. All the speeches by public dignitaries reflected this confidence. President McKinley said of the missionaries, "Who can estimate their value to the progress of nations? Their contribution to the onward and upwards march of humanity is beyond all calculation." Expounding a branch of "muscular Christianity," Governor Roosevelt echoed similar thoughts. . . . This emphasis on the unity of humankind and the gradual redemptive and civilizing power of the Gospel confirmed a confidence that the native populations of the globe could be elevated by embracing Christianity.[1]

It is difficult to find these sentiments being expressed in the second half of the twentieth century and impossible to imagine them in a European context after World War I. On the European side of the Atlantic, secularizing tendencies were well advanced, and were accelerated by the impact on church attendance of so many men who did not return from the war (750,000 Britons died in the conflict).[2] Many of those who did return could no longer attend the churches that had sent them out with the belief that God was on their side. Church attendance declined. Churches were in crisis because they were being marginalized. Church leaders attempted to reassert the position of the church in society, presenting it as a bulwark against Fascism and Communism, but the voice of the Church had been weakened in the midst of scandal, war, and secularization.

The Edinburgh Missionary Conference of 1910 attempted to extend the popular enthusiasm of the 1900 New York conference. Edinburgh created several permanent structures, the most important being: (1) the Faith and Order group which tried to bring the churches closer to one another; (2) the Life and Work group whose brief was to examine a Christian voice in the world; and, (3) the International Missionary Council (IMC) which continued the missionary agenda. These streams eventually coalesced

---

1. Thomas Askew, "The New York 1900 Ecumenical Conference: A Centennial Reflection," *International Bulletin of Missionary Research* 24, no. 4 (October 2000): 148.
2. The population of the UK at that time was close to 42 million people. Because so many of those who died were in their late teens and twenties, 750,000 deaths, combined with those who suffered lifelong disabilities, from a single generation had a significant impact. The numbers were even more severe in Germany, France, and Russia. It is therefore not surprising that the impact of the war on the population of Europe was different from the impact of the war on the United States.

into the World Council of Churches in 1948. The thinking behind these developments is well-expressed by the historian Adrian Hastings:

> What had hardly existed at the beginning of the century and seemed still in the 1920s something new, marginal and fluctuating came suddenly in the thirties to capture, almost for good, the centre of the stage. The young SCM pioneers of the pre-1914 period—Oldham, William Paton, William Temple—were now the ecclesiastical statesmen of Protestant Europe, dexterously creating the structures for the Church of the future. . . . Faced with the fearful challenges of the time, the need to provide a Christian leadership which somehow answered the taunts of Fascism and Nazism and which might in some way assist Christians in Europe to withstand the totalitarian assault, the captains of ecumenism were emboldened to press ahead more than might otherwise have been the case and to put through a plan for a single unified international body which could represent the churches, hopefully all but the Roman Catholic, throughout the world.[3]

One of the most significant events prior to World War II was the 1937 Oxford Conference on Life and Work on the theme Church, Community, and State:

> Its thinking represents the most mature ecclesiastical approach to social and political problems of the inter-war years—an approach immensely sobered by the gravity of the international situation around them. . . . Faced with the challenge of Nazism and stiffened by the revival of a more conservative theology the churches of the thirties and still more the ecumenical movement of the thirties saw themselves as Church over and against the world, in a near Barthian way, different from that of the theologically rose-tinted spectacles and natural/supernatural assimilationism of earlier years. Let the Church be the Church.[4]

This conference attempted to place Christianity firmly back in a place of relevance amidst a secularizing twentieth century but, like many other

---

3. Adrian Hastings, *A History of English Christianity (1920–1990)* (London: SCM Press, 1991), 302f.
4. Hastings, *History of English Christianity*, 304f.

initiatives of that period, its imagination remained that of Christendom. The Oxford Conference was the best known and most significant of a whole series of meetings and conferences and represented attempts to unite and restore some kind of Christendom by equipping it intellectually for an increasingly secular context. The hope was that by ending the scandal of division, pooling the efforts of the various branches of Christendom, and offering an intellectual critique of society, the cause of the gospel would be advanced. Evangelicals, while helping to birth the modern ecumenical movement, grew deeply suspicious of its agenda and moved apart from it. This marginalization of the evangelical movement led it to emphasize the preaching of the gospel over and against social action and to become perceived as against the world in contrast to an ecumenical movement attempting a conversation with the world.[5] This dichotomy and suspicion shaped the Protestant churches of the UK and North America in the twentieth century.

Immediately following World War II, there was much to encourage the church. The defeat of Fascism and the holding at bay of the specter of Communism seemed to offer the chance for a recovery of a Christian civilization. The Queen of England, who took faith seriously, and the crusades of Billy Graham were illustrations of a new moment for the churches with the suggestion that more traditional family values were shaping society again. Stability, well-being, and rebuilding led many church leaders to think that the first half of the twentieth century had been an unfortunate, atypical blip. The fortunes of Christendom were about to be restored.

In the United States church attendance was decidedly not in decline. The historic denominations grew significantly right into the 1970s. Even so, divisions between fundamentalists, evangelicals, and mainline Protestants continued. These divisions damaged older Protestant denominations and led to the energizing of more conservative groups. Mark Noll describes the situation:

> The 1930s proved to be a difficult decade for the older Protestant denominations. With the traumas of the fundamentalist-modernist debate behind them, these groups did display a measure of bureaucratic unity. But they also suffered from the difficulties of the era, especially economic uncertainty. Theological uncertainty was almost

---

5. For a summary of the flavor of these developments from an Anglican point of view, see Perry Butler in *The Study of Anglicanism*, ed. Stephen Sykes, John Booty, and Douglas A. Knight (Minneapolis: Fortress Press, 1998).

as pronounced. The older mainline churches struggled, and often failed, to maintain numbers and contributions on a par with the 1920s. They were the groups who experienced an institutional "religious depression" to match the nation's economic depression. . . . Yet other, more sectarian Protestant bodies knew better how to redeem the times. The fundamentalists, while vanquished in the old denominations, sustained a thriving variety of evangelistic, educational, and missionary activities. . . . Some of the traditionally more sectarian denominations also prospered throughout the decade by providing a religious home for ordinary people and by offering a convincing Christian interpretation of daily life. . . . What were hard times for the mainline Protestants turned out to be good times for others.[6]

In North America and Europe, mission remained that which took place outside the West. Within Europe and North America the task remained repairing, strengthening, and making more effective the structures of Christendom.

1960s Forward: Unraveling Sets In—React, Repair, Retrench

Something decisive and convulsive happened to the relationship between the Euro-tribal churches and the emerging culture after the 1960s. The historian Hugh McLeod, a significant contributor to the debate on secularization, suggested that through the first part of the twentieth century there was a fine balance in the relationship between religion and secularity, but after the 1960s the balance shifted decisively in a secular direction.[7] Callum Brown expresses that shift more dramatically as *The Death of Christian Britain*, in a book about the demise of the nation's core religious and moral identity. "As historical changes go, this has been no lingering and drawn-out affair. It took several centuries (in what historians used to call the Dark Ages) to convert Britain to Christianity, but it has taken less than forty years for the country to forsake it. . . . [Q]uite suddenly in 1963, something very profound ruptured the character of the

---

6. Mark Noll, *A History of Christianity in the United States and Canada* (London: SPCK, 1992), 431f.

7. Hugh McLeod, *Secularization in Western Europe, 1848–1914* (New York: MacMillan Press, 2000), 289.

nation and its people, sending organised Christianity on a downward spiral to the margins of social significance."[8]

North America was different. There was no immediate rapid decline of the liberal mainstream Protestant denominations until after the 1960s were over. Noll points out that the mainline churches attempted to accommodate themselves to the times in marked contrast to the more conservative churches who saw themselves attempting to hold back a tide of moral and social decay:

> In the churches, efforts to respond to the crisis of the times led to deep intramural divisions. While the relative importance of the denominations had been declining throughout the century, they were moved further to the sidelines by the controversies of the 1960s and following years.[9]

In Europe, the idea of recovering Christendom was over. At the time—the 1960s—it was not obvious to the churches why this was so. A variety of responses followed this realization from the call to embrace secularism (Harvey Cox's *Secular City*) to liberationist movements to church renewal and evangelism programs. Characteristic of most of these responses was an anxious search for ways to fix the churches and make them relevant again. Some secular theologies deemed the churches irrelevant as God's agency now transcended the need for the Church in a secular culture that now carried the immanent presence of God. Lesslie Newbigin recounted this atmosphere at a conference in 1960:

> The new vision was of the world, not the Church, as the place where God is to be found. Consequently "the mission and renewal of the Church in our day depends on acceptance and affirmation of the secular world in place of traditional Christian tendencies to reject it." The most articulate exponent of the dominant mood was Hans Hoekendijk whose address called us "to begin radically to desacralize the Church" and to recognize that "Christianity is a secular movement—this is basic for an understanding of it." . . . I had to recognize the big element of truth in what was being said, but I was acutely aware at the same time of what was being ignored or denied. . . . It

---

8. Callum G. Brown, *The Death of Christian Britain* (London: Routledge, 2000), 1.
9. Noll, *History of Christianity*, 442.

was painful to experience the contempt with which missions were held."[10]

By the end of the decade, Newbigin was even more shattered: "The scars left on the body of the Church by that traumatic decade will take a long time to heal."[11] He saw modernity as a new faith that had evangelized and undermined Christianity in the West.

Alongside this unraveling of established denominations, two new movements grew in the 1970s. The first was the reemergence of conservative evangelicals as a force to be reckoned with. Evangelicalism had been an ecclesial and societal force in the nineteenth century.[12] On both sides of the Atlantic the movement had declined in the early years of the century, but experienced a renewal of life in the post-1960s era. Attendance at evangelical churches grew as people left older, mainline churches. In the UK, the new Evangelical Alliance, representing one million evangelicals, quickly realized that such numbers carried political influence. After years in the wilderness, evangelicals reacquainted themselves with their own history, which included a social activism dating back to Wilberforce and the Clapham Sect. This reconnection with their early social reforming past was illustrated by a growing influence within national and international charities, such as the Tear Fund, the Bible Society, and the implementation of thousands of local and regional initiatives. But, on balance, evangelicalism's notions of God's agency remained limited to overseas mission, church planting, domestic evangelism, and some social action. The focus of its congregations was primarily on numerical growth within monocultural suburban populations where the expressive individuals of modernity's wager now lived.

The second movement, the charismatic movement, was related to, but initially distinct from, evangelicalism. In North America, the UK, and Europe, Pentecostalism had operated on the periphery of broader holiness movements. The arrival of the charismatic movement changed people's perception. From the late 1960s forward, it became a vibrant form of church renewal for many in Boomer, middle-class, Euro-tribal churches. It seemed to promise the end of crisis and the start of a new movement

---

10. Quoted in Geoffrey Wainwright, *Lesslie Newbigin: A Theological Life* (Oxford: Oxford University Press, 2000), 11.

11. Wainwright, *Lesslie Newbigin*, 12.

12. The story of this movement's growth in the latter half of the twentieth century in the UK is well documented in Rob Warner, *Reinventing English Evangelicalism 1966–2001: A Theological and Sociological Study* (Eugene, OR: Wipf and Stock, 2007).

of God in such organizations as the Fountain Trust (UK), House Church movements on both sides of the Atlantic, and John Wimber's Vineyard Movement in the United States. By and large, the charismatic movement continued to see God's mission in more or less the same way as the evangelicals though emphasizing the idea of the kingdom of God within the frame of signs and wonders.

The charismatic movement, like the post-1960s evangelicals, were centered on notions of church renewal. Practically all Protestant denominations and movements on both sides of the Atlantic remained fixated on finding some form of renewal, some way of fixing themselves. The hope was that a renewed church would be better able to be involved in mission. The leaders of the charismatic movement promulgated the idea that spiritual power was needed to affect/change/influence society, which usually translated into a focus on dynamic worship or varied forms of self-development for the Christian individual. A new emphasis, for example, on discovering one's spiritual or charismatic gifts came into play. Movements developed around liberating the laity from the dominance of the clergy or giving the laity guidelines for working as Christians in their jobs. These movements were illustrative of anxious churches, who felt increasingly marginalized, and were looking for ways to become relevant again. Reality on the ground did not match the expectations of these renewal movements. The decline and loss of place of the Euro-tribal churches accelerated even while many European church leaders looked at the small sampling of American megachurches for help.

The energies of evangelical leaders were directed toward finding programs for fixing or renewing their churches. Most of these programs originated in North America and were exported to Europe. They came in the forms of the Church Growth movement, the Purpose-Driven Church, the Seeker-Targeted Church, Cell Church, and the Emerging Church, and so forth. All offered pragmatic, programmed solutions to the problems of church decline. While some of their insights were helpful, their approach was deeply flawed. They were preoccupied with making the churches work again rather than engaging the deeper questions of God's agency in a world that had left behind the narratives of the Euro-tribal churches. They were focused on the consumer self who was seeking new forms of personal identity through spiritual experiences. There seemed little capacity to imagine God at work beyond fixing the existing forms of church life or resourcing the individual.

The Gospel and Our Culture Movement

Newbigin's sense of shock in 1968 was compounded in 1974 when he returned to Europe, following his retirement. His initial reflection on the situation of the churches led to the publication of *The Other Side of 1984*[13] where he raised, for the first time, a key dilemma. His contention was that the crisis facing the church was not the absence of faith but the full-frontal attack of another faith: the secular Enlightenment project. Newbigin's argument and subsequent publications created the Gospel and Our Culture Project in the UK and the Gospel and Our Culture Movement in North America. Both liberals and evangelicals embraced Newbigin's assessment and a new alliance coalesced around these Gospel and Culture initiatives. The Gospel and Our Culture project in the UK ran out of direction in the 1990s; though the Gospel and Our Culture Movement in North America continued into the new millennium, it, too, sputtered out, limiting itself to occasional publications. The language of "missional" entered the vocabulary of Euro-tribal churches to describe the mission of God and its meaning for reengaging the West. The great sadness is that, certainly in North America, this missional language quickly focused itself on ecclesiocentric questions about the churches and how to make them work again. Ecclesiology eclipsed the mission of God.

Fresh Expressions of Church

Another form for engaging the challenges before the Euro-tribal churches was called Fresh Expressions, launched in 2004 by the then Archbishop of Canterbury, Rowan Williams. An early task was to change legislation within the Church of England to create a "mixed economy" designed to invite missional experiments across parishes. The Anglican Church sought to create a new kind of ministry, Pioneer Ministry, that allowed individuals to experiment with new forms of church. Fresh Expressions raised questions and challenges for the churches. A primary question raised by the term *Fresh Expression of Church* is whether the emphasis on church causes missiology to collapse into ecclesiology. To some extent this seems to be the case with the Fresh Expressions movement, especially in North America, where it has reverted into a church renewal movement.

---

13. Lesslie Newbigin, *The Other Side of 1984* (Geneva: World Council of Churches Risk Book Series, 1983).

The challenge for Protestant denominations is that, despite theological claims about their specific identities following the European reformations, their actual embodied forms of life as institutional and organizational systems[14] emerge out of the nineteenth and early twentieth centuries as accommodations to modernity's wager. Their modern ways of being church were formed in the eras of imperial sovereignty, the structuring of bureaucratic systems of experts, the overarching centrality of the state, the hegemony of capitalist systems, and the ascent of the rational individual.

Their current forms of life and their operating narratives, irrespective of theological and ecclesial claims around uniqueness and identity, have been colonized by this modernity so that, in almost all the situations described in this chapter, their underlying drive has been ecclesiocentric—continuing attempts to reinstate their place in the culture through varied means of renewal, restructuring, and fixing their existent forms of life. But these forms of life and organization have unraveled.

These Protestant heirs of the European reformations are in liminal space with little sense of what this might mean, how they might connect with traditions, or how they might go about the transformations required to connect with the communities they seek to serve. What's at stake here is not abstract definitions of some ideal nature or purpose of the Church. Will these churches be able to turn their attentions from their ecclesiastical survival to discern what God is already doing ahead of them in multiple contexts? What will be involved in forming common life together in an age of consumer individualism? What are the practices of a people shaped by a marginal narrative? What kind of common life invites a different imagination than a feral capitalism, or the unfettered individual whose needs are at the center of all life? These are questions the Eurotribal denominations have consistently failed to ask throughout the twentieth century. Part two of this book examines these questions in terms of how the churches address the challenge of modernity's wager and of the liminal space in which they now find themselves.

---

14. See Alan J. Roxburgh, *Structured for Mission* (Downers Grove, IL: InterVarsity Press, 2015).

6

The Nature of the Challenge

We have entered an age of fear. Insecurity is once again an active ingredient of political life in Western democracies. Insecurity born of terrorism, of course; but also, fear of the uncontrollable speed of change, fear of the loss of employment, fear of losing ground to others in an increasingly unequal distribution of resources, fear of losing control of the circumstances and routines of daily life. And, perhaps, above all, fear that it is not just *we* who can no longer shape our lives but those in authority have also lost control, to forces beyond their reach.[1]

As Susan Schreiner stated so well, the contemporary loss of transcendence carries in its wake an exhaustion of all confidence in anything beyond ourselves.[2]

Introduction: A World Unhinged

Modernity's wager came with an eschatological promise—a secular salvation in which the future would be materially superior for everyone. This central promise has failed. The wager is a religion that has not just disappointed. What is now being birthed across the populations of Western democracies is a depth of resentment not experienced before.[3] The promise that if we followed its core values all the good things in life would come to us is increasingly seen as empty by growing numbers of citizens across the West. The finely woven cloth of state, market, and Self

---

1. Tony Judt, *Ill Fares the Land* (New York: Penguin Books, 2010), 217.
2. Susan E. Schreiner, *Are You Alone Wise?: The Search for Certainty in the Early Modern Era* (Oxford: Oxford University Press, 2011), xiii.
3. See, for example, such recent books in North America as Yuval Levin's *The Fractured Republic* (New York: Basic Books, 2016) and Patrick J. Deneen's *Why Liberalism Failed* (New Haven, CT: Yale University Press, 2018).

is now producing a bifurcated society of the few who have the benefits and the majority who are losing their place in a race to the bottom.

The late German sociologist Ulrich Beck was wrestling with the question of what had happened to the modern project when he died in 2015. His posthumous *The Metamorphosis of the World* begins with the declaration: "The world is unhinged."[4] The book describes the inchoate sense of people living in a world out of joint; we find ourselves in a collective space where we wander aimlessly and confused in the midst of a failed story. We have become aware of living in a West we no longer understand without a story that can make sense of the times and places in which we live. The missiological challenge is to address a time and place where we no longer have confidence in the stories that, until so recently, undergirded our shared lives.

Modernity's wager has replaced the Christian conviction of a world shaped by its Creator. God, however, has not disappeared but been rendered useful for the states' need to manufacture consent, for capitalism as a private source of sustenance, and for the Self in confirming the individual as the center of the universe's purpose. All this change seemed to be confirmed by a postwar "Golden Age." As economists and social historians recognize that this period of economic expansion was an aberration,[5] an exceptional time whose "repetition should absolutely not be expected."[6] It has been torn asunder in the endless crises of both capitalism and the state. It was an unprecedented moment that is over and cannot be repeated. It was a euphoric period as an emerging generation drank deeply of modernity's wager before the darkening shadows of crisis, doubt, confusion, and resentment reappeared at the edges of an all-too-brief Aquarian age. Few in the late 1960s could have imagined the upending of their confidence. But it was upended as the contemporary West entered the "risk society" described by Ulrich Beck.[7]

---

4. Ulrich Beck, *The Metamorphosis of the World* (Malden, MA: Polity Press, 2016), xi.
5. This is part of the argument made by Thomas Piketty (*Capital in the Twenty-First Century*). Following the Great Depression and the devastations of World War II, a combination of public infrastructure building (example: highways) and massive birth rates (Baby Boom) created a situation in which Western nations could, through taxation and public spending, bring into being some level of economic redistribution across populations as well as provide a broadening of the middle classes. But this up-curve in the development of the middle class with the broad sense of security it produced came to an end in the 1980s so that, today, we are witnessing the hollowing out of the middle class and the return of anxiety. See also Jennifer Welsh, *The Return of History: Conflict, Migration, and Geopolitics in the Twenty-First Century* (Toronto: House of Anansi, 2016), especially chapter 6, "The Return of Inequality."
6. Wolfgang Streeck, *How Will Capitalism End?* (London: Verso, 2016), xiii.
7. Ulrich Beck, *Risk Society* (London: Sage Publications, 1992).

Modernity's wager remains the creed of the West even as its pillars collapse. Its birth was characterized by an optimism that propelled the West to the center of a global hegemony. At the beginning of the twenty-first century, that confidence is severely shaken. We are confronted with the unraveling of the West's primary narratives because they no longer invest citizens with hope.[8] Increasingly, citizens experience anxiety, vertigo, resentment, and weariness. Our cultures are characterized by a rising xenophobia and an irrational search for the strongman who will make one's country "great again," promising the hope of recreating some mythical past.[9] For many, the promises of consumer capitalism have failed. Nation-states are unable to fix their globalized economies or stop the wars of terror threatening their once-secure lives. The Self is left exposed, fragile, and vulnerable to forces that cannot be named or controlled. Economic security has disappeared for many.[10] The West is now an economized society wherein people are objects of economic ends as producers and consumers. Societies, individuals, and creation cannot thrive in such a situation. Most people now recognize their plight, but have few options for alternative stories. Something must give, for good or ill.[11]

Winter Is Coming

Thriving societies are predicated on trust and hope. The modern West is now shaped by a pervasive loss of both. This loss is not only felt in the macro mechanisms of social, economic, and political life but, more critically, at the micro level, by the people who live around us, especially those who look or sound different from us. What are the sources that might reshape our communities? We have entered a precarious place that has not come by chance or fate; it is the outcome of modernity's wager. The Euro-tribal churches have been deeply complicit in creating our situation. The symptoms of this loss of hope and trust are everywhere. Politics, education, law, and religion are increasingly incapable of addressing the

---

8. Schreiner, *Are You Alone Wise?*, xi–xiii.
9. See Heinrich Geiselberger, ed., *The Great Regression* (Maldon, MA: Polity Press, 2017).
10. Neal Gabler, "The Secret Shame of the Middle Class," *Atlantic Magazine,* May 2016.
11. Dunkelman argues that more and more Americans are responding to this insecurity and polarization by embracing built environments where increasing numbers choose to live in neighborhoods with others of like values, economics, and demographics. "Over the course of several decades, the nation's social architecture has been upended. . . . American community is undergoing a transformation at its very core. . . . Our sense today that the American dream is slipping away—that the legacy of American exceptionalism is newly imperilled—Is more intertwined with the structure of American society than we tend to appreciate" (Marc J. Dunkleman, *The Vanishing Neighbor* [New York: W. W. Norton, 2014], xii–xiv).

crises. This is evident in low voter turnout in elections, the incapacity of governments to solve issues across party divisions, the belief that political and economic institutions are controlled by elites out of touch with people who are struggling with economic downturn and the loss of social traditions, the fear of the stranger in the form of refugees, the failure of movements like Occupy, the environmental movement, and the Trump election of 2016. All of these indicate a turning away from once trusted institutions in search of alternatives to the political, social, and economic order. When none are found, buried anger and resentment erupt. People turn to guns, or gurus, or strongmen who promise to stop the turmoil and return them to a time when life seemed to work. Participation in the public sphere has become a media spectacle that exacerbates disengagement from one another. Participation in public and social organizations for the common good has declined dramatically. Identity politics has displaced dialogue across difference.[12] We are witnessing a widespread obsession with the apocalyptic as seen in TV shows like the *Walking Dead, The Handmaid's Tale,* and the endless stream of zombie movies. TV shows about the dead or a world behind the world of secular reality have caught the fascination of people. It is as if the Western imagination has embraced the siren voice of the *Game of Thrones*: winter is coming.

People are searching for alternative stories that will orient them in this unraveling. We are at the front end of difficult questions: What has gone wrong? What are the forces that stand behind this time of insecurity and fear? How can life be ordered in ways that bring hope and thriving to all? How do we find ways to rebuild the common good? There is a desire to reestablish a "commons," to find safe spaces for dialogue across differences and the alienation of constant change.[13] An instinctive conviction

---

12. Judt expresses it in these terms: "The politics of the '60s thus devolved into an aggregation of individual claims upon society and the state. 'Identity' began to colonize public discourse: private identity, sexual identity, cultural identity. From here it was but a short step to the fragmentation of radical politics, its metamorphosis into multiculturalism. . . . Back home, the individual reigned supreme. However legitimate the claims of individuals and the importance of their rights, emphasizing these carries an unavoidable cost: the decline of a shared sense of purpose. Once upon a time one looked to society—or class, or community—for one's normative vocabulary: what was good for everyone was by definition good for anyone. But the converse does not hold. What is good for one person may or may not be of value or interest to another. Conservative philosophers of an earlier age understood this well, which was why they resorted to *religious* language and imagery to justify traditional authority and its claim on each individual" (Judt, *Ill Fares the Land*, 88–89).

13. See Nicholas Sagovsky and Peter McGrail, eds., *Together for the Common Good: Towards a National Conversation* (London: SCM Press, 2015); Peter Block, *The Abundant Community* (San Francisco, CA: Berrett-Koehler, 2012); Bruce Fuller, *Organizing Locally* (Chicago: University of Chicago Press, 2015).

that the local and everyday are places that can generate hope and over-come the fear of the other is a part of this desire. Local spaces, like neigh-borhoods, have been emptied of the moral and communal dimensions that once made them givers and sustainers of common life and sacrifice for one another.[14] Practices of care for the other have been attenuated; people are seeking ways to reengage such habits.[15] For Luke Bretherton, the institutional, structural, and imaginative narratives of the West cre-ated a context in which we conform "to the spirit of capitalism that pre-cisely demands the dissolution of particularity and the formation of liquid identities in order to aid capital flows," so that civil society serves the sov-ereign state and capitalism.[16]

We propose that in tentative experiments in the local lie the hints of where God is inviting Christians to reimagine engagement with our troubled West. Modernity's wager cannot be addressed through pro-grammatic engagements, the restructuring of organizations, or even the reformation of the churches that came out of the European refor-mations. The situation we face cannot be addressed by these defaults. The missiological challenge lies much deeper than proposals for turning affinity-based congregations into neighborhood churches. It is far dif-ferent from planting hundreds, or even thousands, of new congrega-tions, and far bigger than rejigging denominations with Reformation frameworks. Another list of five or ten ways to do church differently is out of touch with the missiological challenge before us. The peoples of the modern West struggle to imagine alternative stories to the one in which they currently live and the churches continue to provide hollow solutions that no one believes anymore.

Why Is It So Difficult to Imagine an Alternative Story?

The Protestant churches have proven themselves unable to address the challenge of modernity's wager because they themselves are colonized by its power and have little sense of an alternative imagination, as illustrated by their fixation on themselves and ways to fix their churches. They have focused their energies on reorganizing or restructuring their institutions,

---

14. See, for example, Dunkelman, *Vanishing Neighborhood*.
15. See the helpful theological engagements in such books as Elaine Graham, *Between a Rock and a Hard Place: Public Theology in a Post-Secular Age* (London: SCM Press, 2013) and Luke Bretherton, *Christianity and Contemporary Politics* (Chichester, West Sussex: Willey-Blackwell, 2010).
16. Bretherton, *Christianity and Contemporary Politics*, 87.

as if these reforming activities will make any material difference to the missiological challenge before them. The wager's narrative has gone deep. At the same time, across the West, there is an increasingly urgent search for replacement narratives to those of state, capitalism, and Self. There seems to be a healthier desire among citizens-at-large to discover alternatives to the challenges confronting late modern societies than there is in the churches. Some of the contending replacement narratives are environmentalism, globalism, equality of various kinds, racial reconciliation, and reconnection with the local.[17] From a missiological perspective, even these important narratives are still continuations of the wager. As levels of anxiety, dis-ease, and resentment grow,[18] the underlying conviction that our world can be remade without God remains embedded in our collective imagination. This missiological challenge is being drowned in a deluge of new techniques for discipleship, neighborhood engagement, fresh expressions, new forms of pastoral leadership, and church planting. It is the retreading of old tires.

A helpful guide in understanding what has happened is the work of the American sociologist Philip Rieff (1922–2006), who examined the underlying shape of late modernity.[19] His language and style were never easy to understand, but his thinking raises important perspectives. For Rieff, culture is the process whereby a people create a world that gives shape to their beliefs and provides the rituals with which they can collectively live out those beliefs. Culture is about the "creation of a world in which its inhabitants may find themselves at home and yet accommodate strangers without yielding their *habitus* to him."[20] The word *habitus* refers to the habits and dispositions a people develop over time to organize their world and respond to those from outside.[21] We become aware of *habitus* when

---

17. See, for example, Peter Block, Walter Brueggemann, and John McKnight's *Another Kingdom: Departing the Consumer Culture* (Hoboken, NJ: Wiley & Sons, 2016). It presents an alternative proposal to consumer capitalism rooted in neighborhood community. As laudable as this proposal is, it artfully presents an imagination in which God is not the primary agent but a useful force in this greater end. Hence, the book remains firmly embedded in modernity's wager.

18. Few have chronicled these fears better than Zygmunt Bauman. Several of his more recent books examine the counters of these fears: *State of Crisis* (Cambridge, MA: Polity, 2014), *Strangers at Our Door* (Cambridge, MA: Polity, 2016), and *Liquid Fear* (Cambridge, MA: Polity, 2006).

19. Some of his best-known and most influential books were *Freud: The Mind of a Moralist* (Chicago: University of Chicago Press, 1959), *The Triumph of the Therapeutic* (Chicago: University of Chicago Press, 1966), and *My Life Among the Deathworks*, Volume 1: *Sacred Order/Social Order* (Charlottesville: University of Virginia Press, 2006).

20. Rieff, *My Life Among the Deathworks*, 14.

21. A humorous example of this is found in Canadian culture. For those who have grown

visiting a different culture. Even inside the same country differing habits and dispositions can be found. An American in the South can distinguish different habits of life from a friend living in the Northeast or Southwest. In the UK, travelling from the south to the industrial belt of Scotland or the valleys of Wales makes clear noticeably different ways of life. Nations are created, and worlds brought into being, by a series of common practices, stories, and perceptions.[22]

Rieff argues that until the modern West, cultures were formed out of the ways groups translated a sacred order into social forms, roles, and structures. Culture was the expression of the sacred translated into the *habitus* of a people. This was true throughout human history, until the emergence of the modern West. Prior to that, all cultures were shaped by some source of authority outside of, or beyond, themselves. They were constituted by systems of moral demands whose authority came from outside in some form of transcendent order. Rieff described this as a "vertical structure" and, as we shall see, it correlates with Micah White's evaluation of how we structure ourselves in modern societies. The norms and habits shaping a culture were not just a set of agreed upon rules individuals contracted to live by. On the contrary, these norms were rooted in truths that, objectively, resided in the sacred. These moral obligations were institutionalized in social organizations whose source of the authority was the sacred.

For Rieff, the modern West is a radical break with this story. Modernity removed the sacred as the primary basis of culture. It institutionalized an asacred order that replaced God with new loci of authority and agency: the Self, the state, and a capitalist economic imagination. As this narrative unravels, citizens have no other *habitus*, no other practices or habits,

---

up in Canada, is it a normative social response to engage people with the word *sorry*. Alan, for example, was standing in line at the payout desk of a bookstore. The woman in front was asking questions of the cashier about a title she couldn't find. In the midst of conversation, she turned to Alan and said, "Sorry, I'll just be a moment." Once the woman had got the information she needed and paid her bill, the cashier then turned to Alan and said, "Sorry, how can I help you?" This is a classically embedded Canadian habit, a way of engaging each other. We will tend to say we are "sorry" to someone irrespective of needing to be sorry. Our *habitus* is to be as polite as possible and to do that by presuming some level of responsibility. Alan saw this kind of established pattern of relationality at work the first time he went to Korea. It was a strange moment when everyone stood up when he entered a room and wouldn't sit down at a meal table until he sat down. Age has its benefits in some societies and their *habitus*.

22. For an important and extremely helpful assessment of nations and nationalism as creations of worlds, see Benedict Anderson's *Imagined Communities* (London: Verso, 2006 edition).

other than the wager. They have no alternative to what Charles Taylor calls the "secular frame."[23] The Euro-tribal churches are practically useless in addressing this massive cultural upheaval because they have turned the sacred, the primacy of God's agency, into useful memes for supporting self-oriented individuals in a globalized capitalism. Rieff presents three types of historical cultures:

First World Cultures—a World Governed by Fate

When describing First World cultures, Rieff is typically identifying what we would call pagan cultures that understood themselves as living in an enchanted world populated by mythical creatures. Nature is made up of myriad of gods and primordial powers. The primary relationship of peoples with this divine order is that of a fate; this is a world governed by fate. While this ancient world might be viewed as historically old and characteristically nonmodern, it is a resurgent imagination in the modern West. TV series and recent movies indicate the extent to which a reenchanted world of god-like creatures with superhuman powers of good and evil has reemerged across Western societies. It's also present in the reemergence of pantheism where "god" is immanently present in and through all things. Such pantheism runs counter to the great monotheisms that presume the particularity of God's presence in terms of specific revelations. The modern twist of this emergent "first world" pantheism is in its dismissiveness of the particularity of monotheistic faiths and the elevation of the notion that it is within the Self that some sort of divine or supernatural powers are located.

In this context, the great monotheisms, such as Christianity, are simply specific, contextual expressions of innate experiences within the Self. In the modern West, this resurgence of Rieff's First World culture gets its own peculiar twist wherein it is turned into another means of making the Self the center of all meaning; fate is seemingly discarded while, in fact, this Self feels increasingly abandoned to an amorphous series of powers over which it has no control. In an age of anxiety, fear, and resentment, these suprahuman powers have great appeal. But what can't be missed, even if it is blanched out of the media's presentations, is this overarching sense of a world driven by a fate beyond our control. In an amazing

---

23. See Charles Taylor, *Modern Social Imaginaries* (Durham, NC: Duke University Press, 2004).

reversal of the hope that initiated modernity's wager, fate and karma have returned with a vengeance. The loss of nerve is profound.

Second World Cultures—a World Shaped by Faith

Rieff's Second World culture is sourced by the great monotheisms of Christianity, Islam, and Judaism. At its center is a self-revealed Creator from whom every living creature derives its being and identity. Truth about the world and how to act in the world are grounded in revelation. Truth is creedal in character, as, for example, one can still observe in the recitation of the Nicene Creed or the Lord's Prayer within Christian liturgies. Faith, rather than fate, is the dominant cultural motif. It is a faith that God is active in history. God's order undergirds all social life and human beings are not left to a lurking fate. Ascent in the vertical is possible through trust and obedience in the guidance of teaching authorities. Some of the key words in this Second World culture are truth, authority, and faith.

Third World—Late Modern

For Rieff, Third World cultures are negations of Second World cultures. They are the active negation of the sacred. In Third World cultures, social order has no sacred basis. There is no truth that is not socially constructed, no sacred order shaping meaning, no transcendent authority. The reality is that human beings make their own rules and habits of social life. The idea of social contract, when disconnected from a sense of God's agency, moves toward Foucault's dark conclusion of "power over" as the primary form of any society. The individual is the source of social order and authority. We choose to contract with other human beings to form associative societies. The sacred—or any other external authorities—are convenient, fictional creations used by those in power for their own self-interest. Third World cultures remove all vertical authority from the field of consideration. Inherited moral constraints are social constructions with no status beyond that of the individual who might choose to use them for her or his own support.

Rieff's framing lifts up the radical difference between Second and Third World cultures. All three worlds are simultaneously present today, but our overarching narrative is the overarching presence of the third. The tension in trying to navigate these contrary narratives within modernity's wager is that it feels as if there is no other means for determining

anything other than the internalized authority of the Self and its experience. For Rieff, Third World culture is unprecedented in human history. It is what makes the modern West such a fundamental break with
inherited systems of moral and social life. Its habits and beliefs are now
institutionalized in the structures and *habitus* of everyday life: the political liberalism of the social contract, the economic myth of the invisible
hand, and the inviolable autonomy of the individual. Life is effectively
lived without a transcendent reference. While still present in the language
of everyday life and the rituals of the state, God has been rendered but a
useful assistant for the Self. In this sense, the modern West is a negation
of all sacred orders. "Third worlds exist only as a negation of sacred orders
in seconds."[24] It is "directed against the verticals in authority that mediate
sacred order in the social world."[25]

Authority and tradition are replaced by values whose sources are individual autonomy and self-making. This culture is open-ended. We can be
who and what we choose to be as makers of our own truth and identities.[26] Values are not attached to anything other than the particular ways
groups happen to form their personal and social relationships at a particular moment in a particular historical context. Values fluctuate like
commodities in the marketplace. Late modernity creates a world in which
there is religious belief, but it no longer has any need for God's revelation or authority. There is no human thriving within any heteronomous
regime. There is no sense that God is the primary agent shaping our social
systems. "Little is left of second world cultures except their aesthetics and
persistent but enfeebled and often compromised institutions."[27] A social
world is created that is self-referential and self-legitimating—a world
unprecedented in human history. For Rieff, it is an "anticulture" that only
leads to the negation of all that is human.

This is why it is so hard for most of us in late modern Western societies
to imagine an alternative narrative. The transcendent has been thrown on
the dust heap of history, and turned into an aesthetic, an appreciation for
the past, an emotional undergirding, a beautiful "spiritual" experience for

---

24. Taylor, *Modern Social Imaginaries,* 6.
25. See James Davidson Hunter's description of Rieff's argument in Rieff, *My Life Among the
Deathworks,* xxiii.
26. See Cavanaugh's brilliant deconstruction of this primary myth in chapter 4, "Actually,
You *Can't* Be Anything You Want (and It's a Good Thing, Too)" in William T. Cavanaugh,
Church as Field Hospital: The Church's Engagement with a Wounded World (Grand Rapids,
MI: Eerdmans, 2016), 74–95, where he concludes: "We are not sovereign rational choosers but
fragmented selves."
27. Rieff, *My Life Among the Deathworks,* xxiv.

those who need such things. "Religion, then, provides a convenient way of fulfilling certain emotional needs. It can inculcate moral discipline, strengthen the social order and provide a degree of ceremonial form, aesthetic resonance and spiritual depth to otherwise shallow lives."[28] But, as Terry Eagleton aptly points out, the fly in the ointment of this reigning elitism is that the "Christian faith, however, is not about moral uplift, political unity or aesthetic charm. Nor does it start from the portentous vagueness of some 'infinite responsibility.' It starts from a crucified body."[29] This is why renewed pantheisms ring tragically hollow. They can never become an apologetic for Christian imagination as if the divine is just some way in which we all feel the world. Christian imagination has to do with another order, an authority and tradition, a way of life rooted in God's own presence in the world. The difficult vocation before the churches is not in a focus on its own reforming or renewing, but on a refounding.

---

28. See Terry Eagleton's masterful analysis of this modern sense among elites that faith in God has some kind of useful, aesthetic attribute for those who need it in *Culture and the Death of God* (New Haven, CT: Yale University Press, 2014), 205.
29. Eagleton, *Culture*, 206

7

Refounding in Liminal Spaces

Introduction

The Euro-tribal churches' entanglement in modernity's wager has made them increasingly irrelevant in the face of an unraveling that involves both the modern West's trust in the state, its economic systems, and the Self. At the same time, this broader unraveling of modernity's primary structural systems is reflected in the concomitant unraveling of the Euro-tribal churches. Their story and tradition are seen, by an increasing majority of people across the West, as irrelevant to the challenges now confronting it. This later unraveling is largely due to the reality that these churches responded to the challenge of modernity by accepting modernity's wager and making God a useful adjunct to the systems of modernity. Rieff described Christian leaders "as pessimists with dog collars, who in their despair welcome our third culture as if it would save second from itself."[1] The unraveling is witnessed, for example, in the precipitous decline of church attendance with the attendant rise of the so-called "Nones" and "Dones."[2] In this unravelling is the collapse of confidence that these churches can address the crises of late modernity. They confront not a hostile culture over against which they need to form their own "culture" (a false Benedict option), but the failure to recognize that they offer no real alternative to the wager.

---

1. Philip Rieff, *The Crisis of the Officer Class* (Charlottesville: University of Virginia Press, 2008), 96.
2. These two terms have recently become popular ways to characterize various ways people describe themselves in terms of religious affiliation. The "Nones" refers to the increasing percentage of people who, when asked their religious affiliation, describe themselves as having no religion or religious affiliation. The "Dones" refers to a broad category of people who would identify themselves, for example, as Christian but are finished with attending any church.

Something is happening to Western societies which is beyond the control of managing elites. Under the surface is a bubbling and fermenting that can't be pressed back into the current forms of either church or society. Such ferment is taking many divergent forms. It drives some to try and recapture something they sense has been lost (the early Church, the essence of the Reformers, a Benedictine "option," making America great again, France for the French, and so on). It is expressed in both the xenophobic fear of the other and the desire to recapture some romantic past. At the same time, however, there is also bubbling up all kinds of hopeful experimenting. Around the edges of the dominant culture and its denominations, ordinary people seek alternative forms of life.[3] This chapter argues that we are far beyond any kind of reformation. We must enter the ferment and bubbling of a refounding.

Lessons from Occupy

Rieff's Third Culture of the modern West, unprecedented in human history, is the default out of which we operate. In his arguments concerning the crisis of Third Cultures, Rieff calls for the reappropriation of what he describes as "the vertical in authority."[4] By this he means that Western societies must now be refounded within the Christian understanding of a world shaped and ordered by God's transcendent authority. That may initially sound like an unrealistic desire, but there are intimations that it is, in fact, the kind of ferment that is already happening out of sight of the official Euro-tribal churches and out in places in which these churches hardly ever imagined to find God. Here, Rieff's notions connect with the recent work of a young social activist, Micah White. White has participated in recent movements seeking to foment nothing less than a revolution against neo-liberalism.[5] He was one of the animators of the Occupy Movement that began in September 2011 in Zuccotti Park, New York. Occupy quickly went viral as a global protest against the 1 percent. The rapidity with which it spread was not just about the power of social media to diffuse ideas but, more importantly, about the extent of resentment felt

---

3. See, for example, such diverse illustrations as: sara arthur & erin f. wasinger, *the year of small things: radical faith for the rest of us* (Grand Rapids, MI: Brazos, 2017); Tom Rinaldi, *The Red Bandanna* (New York: Penguin Books, 2016); and Rebecca Solnit, *Hope in the Dark: Untold Histories, Wild Possibilities* (Chicago: Haymarket Books, 2016).

4. Rieff, *Crisis of the Officer Class*, xiii–xvi.

5 See Micah White, *The End of Protest: A New Playbook for Revolution* (Toronto: Alfred A. Knopf, 2016).

by millions of people globally. After a brief flowering, Occupy failed. It stands, however, as a testimony to two things. First, it points to the depth of disillusionment and anger across the modern West and the bubbling and fermenting that is occurring just beneath the surface. But, second, Occupy also demonstrated how difficult it is to cultivate cultural change. Whatever else may be said about Occupy, it, along with refugee movements and anarchic forces at work around the world, dispelled the myth promulgated by nation-states and corporations that everything is OK and in good hands. The truth is, nothing is unfolding as promised.

For a time Occupy looked as if it was a movement of social transformation, even revolution, had broken out in response to the unraveling of the West's narratives that the state and neo-liberalism would create the good life for all. A bottom-up movement, not led by elites or gurus, fermented and broke out amid unprecedented social, political, and economic unraveling. But it wasn't to be. Occupy failed despite, White argues,[6] the presence of all the elements required for social change. Why? How could such an auspicious moment be lost in such a brief period? White has given that question a great deal of thought.[7] How can you foment alternative practices of hope in the unraveling of the wager? This is a focal missional challenge for the churches of the West. It places the missiological challenges far beyond questions of reforming or fixing institutions. If Euro-tribal churches cannot be a sign, witness, and foretaste of another hope in this unraveling, they have nothing to say and deserve to die.

The first part of White's book offers a good bit of analysis about the nature of revolutions, their sources, and the theories driving them. His theorizing comes out of his own grounded practice in Occupy and other movements.[8] He wrestles with the question of why the apparatus of

---

6. White, *End of Protest*, 34–43.

7. Pankaj Mishra's *Age of Anger* (New York: Farrar, Straus and Giroux, 2017) makes an argument like White's about the deeper sources of our own tumultuous times in terms of the failure of the modern Western narrative to address the needs of its people. He points out that the anarchism that emerges in the nineteenth century through the likes of Bakunin became the texts that still provide the resources for revolutionary movements today. Mishra is clear that the resentment that is being experienced across the world and the reactive actions of radical Islam or new nationalists are not about clashes of civilizations but the abject failure of the modern narrative to fulfill the promises and longings it created. Michael Ignatieff in the *New York Review of Books* 64, no. 6 (April 6, 2017): 4–6, provides a critical review of Mishra's thesis in which he proposes that the author overstates his case and fails to express a sufficient appreciation of the Western liberal tradition. While there is a level of truth to this critique, Mishra's broader argument about the levels of resentment toward the neo-liberal, globalized world birthed by this West remains convincing.

8. See Mark Lau Branson and Juan Martinez, *Churches, Cultures and Leadership* (Downers Grove, IL: InterVarsity Press, 2011).

modern Western states so easily absorbs movements of change, neutralizing the possibility of fundamental change. Modernity takes movements that challenge its hegemony and turns them into new forms of itself. Why is this so? What do we have to learn from White's experience to embark on a long journey of refounding? He proposes a theory about the sources of agency in Rieff's Third Culture. This "unified theory of revolution"[9] relates to Rieff's work by proposing that Third Culture modernity eradicates the possibility of agency outside itself. While somewhat oversimplified, White's theory points to why the Euro-tribal churches are so colonized and where we need to go to engage in refounding.

White's Unified Theory of Revolution

Why is a fundamental refounding so difficult within modernity's wager? Refounding doesn't necessarily mean revolution. Rather than the language of revolution, we propose the language of/the images of ferment and bubbling. The idea of ferment is more aligned with the work of the late Alan Kreider, whose book, *The Patient Ferment of the Early Church*,[10] analyzes how early Christian communities transformed their times. Its emphasis on patience offers a different kind of revolution from those of the bloody, brutal nineteenth and twentieth centuries. But we are getting ahead of our story. In asking why the Euro-tribal churches have failed to address modernity's wager, both Rieff and White are guides to places we have not gone as God's people.

Occupy was started by a small number of people who identified themselves as revolutionary anarchists seeking to change society through consensus-building assemblies. Such assemblies would, potentially, become the basis of a government by and for the people. It was no small undertaking! Occupy, however, was a failure of its most basic imagination. Leaderless revolutions are difficult. In the context of that failure, White frames a theory of revolution. The theory proposes two axes, one vertical and one horizontal, along which are located the forces shaping modernity. Diagram 1 is a modified summary of White's framework.

---

9. White, *End of Protest*, 73.
10. Alan Kreider, *The Patient Ferment of the Early Church* (Grand Rapids, MI: Baker, 2016).

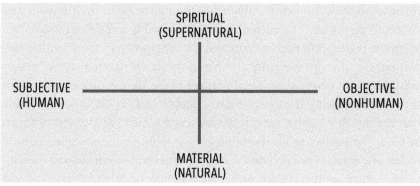

Diagram 1

The Vertical Axis

The vertical axis proposes two sources, or causes, of change. The forces of change are immanent; all meaning, values, and action are located in what we call the material or *natural* world. This is Rieff's Third Culture. The modern imagination is effectively closed to what we would call the vertical, or transcendent, in terms of valid explanatory frameworks. Functionally, all action and agency are restricted to the immanent, material, and natural.

What White identifies as the supernatural end of the axis proposes that the causes of change cannot be explained only from within a materialist frame. They require what he describes as a Theurgist, or supernatural, event. In White's usage, this notion of theurgism reads like a muddled amalgam of neo-pagan and other forms of spiritualist beliefs from Rieff's First Culture. They aren't particularly convincing. White encourages those seeking to embark on revolutionary change to read sacred texts so that they can recognize that without reconnecting to forces of life that lie outside the so-called natural world, there will be no change. While White's instincts are right, the list of options offered muddle his underlying point: there must be a reengagement with the transcendent before there can be any fundamental transformation of culture. White is questioning the occlusion and limitation of all explanatory frameworks to the material. He concludes that there can be no fundamental transformation without the conviction that agency must have some vertical, or transcendent, basis.

In this context, it is important to touch on the sources of the word *supernatural* (and hence *spiritual*) in the modern West. The language of the *spiritual* has entered our common vocabulary. We need to ask, as Christians, whether we want to work within the modern usage of the terms *spiritual* and *supernatural*. The idea of the supernatural as a separate realm outside of the world only came into existence in the fifteenth and sixteenth centuries. The current use of the word is a child of modernity.[11] With the triumph of nominalism and the emergence of the scientific revolution, the idea of supernatural came to mean a separate realm of reality totally outside what we now call nature. There were multiple reasons for this, not least being the discoveries of people such as Galileo, who found that the sky above (what we call the universe) wasn't the location of angels or God, but subject to all the same laws at work in the so-called natural order. The result was the creation of a supernatural realm beyond the universe, nature, or the created order. In this new understanding, God was separated from the natural world.

God was no longer required as agent, or explanation, for how the world worked, and was effectively removed from any connection with the natural order, except as a vague deistic guarantee of its existence. Enlightenment philosophers easily discounted these deistic notions once the idea of the supernatural became the norm. That modernity did not need divine causality except in the superstitions of simple people became an unquestioned norm of modernity's wager. What is effectively absent from the Western imagination, within and without the churches, is a sense of God as agent active in the world. We don't look to the upper, vertical axis when asking questions about change or the reordering of social life. It's all up to us. The only exception is the private individual's desire to appropriate some inner, personal spiritual experience to guide her or his life. In the place of language that describes God as the primary agent among us, we use abstract signifiers such as love, peace, justice, righteousness, reconciliation. The point isn't that these are bad words; they aren't at all. The point is these abstractions replace any real sense of God's agency.

In both Rieff's vertical structure and White's stretching for the supernatural, what is at stake is the fundamental question of agency. In modernity's wager, the question of agency gets settled in terms of the autonomous individual and its concomitant fixation on rights that protect that autonomy. The identity of the individual is set up over against any form of vertical or theonomous agency. The language of virtue is replaced with the language of values. What gets connected to this strong sense of human agency is modernity's primary methods of management

11. For an excellent discussion of a whole series of transformations in our understanding of God and God's relationship to the created order, see Louis Dupre in his brief book *Religion and the Rise of Modern Culture* (Notre Dame, IN: University of Notre Dame Press, 2008). Its final chapter, "Conclusion: Religion at the End of the Modern Age," provides an important summary of the book and some of the issues discussed in this chapter.

and control. These methods tend to objectify everything outside the self—everything outside the self becomes an object of the self's management and control. The twin factors of the primacy of human agency and its method of control and management codetermine the shape of life in the West, and will, without attention to their iniquitousness, always predetermine how decisions are made.

This immanent, materialist narrative cannot render a way of life any different from the one that has plunged the West into crisis. What is called for is a Christian imagination that can build life no longer around the self as an autonomous agent but upon the heteronomous agency of the God who calls us to a life of virtue. Without such a refounding of Christian life, moves to the local or the neighborhood, for example, are limited in their impact because they cannot, of themselves, change the form of the Third Culture. Examples of this are fermenting in numerous ways. The new monasticism that has sprung up across the West over the past decade provides examples of Christians gathering in the local around specific practices of Christian life (see chapter 10 below) that are focused on learning how to ask the question of where they discern God at work ahead of them in their local communities.

The Horizontal Axis

The horizontal axis has objective and the subjective poles representing differing naturalistic explanations for why and how change takes place. The former understands the causes of change to be in objective social structures; the latter sees change as generated within the subjective actions of individuals. Using this framework of a vertical and horizontal axis, White proposes four quadrants to explain the sources of cultural change: voluntarism, structuralism, subjectivism, and theurgism.

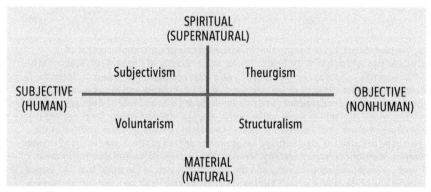

Diagram 2

Voluntarism

Voluntarists presume that human actions change the world. Transformation comes from movements of people who act together to effect some change. Their conviction can be recognized in the myriad of calls to action based on the view that within every individual are the sources for world transformation. This can be as crass as the advice or actions of self-growth gurus, or as elevated as the vision of Obama's "Yes we can!" For voluntarism, when we truly act out of our inner selves, world transformation occurs. It is captured in the slogan: "You are the solution!"

Structuralism[12]

Structuralism is the opposite belief. It sees the sources of change rooted in the objective structures and systems that shape human actions but are not directly under the control of human action. It is this underlying conviction of structuralism that drives so many of the attempts across all kinds of church systems to change or reorganize their structures. The power of structuralism as an overarching narrative in modernity is illustrated by the innumerable attempts of leaders to restructure their systems in the belief that that will bring about some desired cultural change. Any social change is the result of complex interactions across a myriad of social, hereditary, and natural forces that simply can't be managed. Human agency is not the primary factor in social change; rather, systemic structures built into the ways human societies live and interact are the sources. Structured forces act independently of human subjects. On balance, the root causes of change lie outside the influence of people. Fundamental change is dependent on a randomness that cannot be managed or controlled by human actions.

---

12. We realize that this is a vastly simplified description of the complex notion of structuralism, which had its genesis in France in the writing of Claude Levi-Strauss (1908–2009), who was influenced by the earlier French anthropologist, Ferdinand de Saussure. Structuralism certainly does engage the question of what shapes and forms societies. It is also based in more fundamental questions about the sources and role of language in forming cultures with a rejection of some realist, one-to-one correlation between language and reality (see George Steiner, *Real Presences* [Chicago: University of Chicago Press, 1989]) that the came to be described as logocentrism. Lying underneath all of this, however, are even more complex questions of human identity. Structuralism is responding and reacting to these deeper conversations about identity and the sources of action in the world that had shaped the disputes and philosophies of such luminaries as Sartre and Heidegger. For further reading, see the excellent, brief framing of structuralism provided by Mark Lilla in *The Reckless Mind* (New York: New York Review Books, 2001), 164–84.

Segue

In reference to diagram 2, we can make two observations. First, there are lots of admixtures between voluntarism and structuralism. What is presented here are the sides of White's axis without discussion of the multiple variants. Second, within modernity's wager both the voluntarist and the structuralist positions function within the materialist[13] belief that all change is generated from within the natural plane. Explanations for change from within the upper two quadrants are considered, more or less, as illusions in that they tend toward nonmaterial explanations for change by referencing some kind of spiritual or supernatural source. This particular use of the term *materialism* is quite a limited one. The word has a far wider meaning. Much about materialism travels well within the Christian narrative. Christianity is a materialist faith. Christians confess that this is God's creation. God made the material world, declaring it all very good. God made us fully embodied beings that can only know and experience life as material beings. In this sense, Christians are materialists.

We are not materialists if it means only the natural world can explain itself. In the act of creation and in the Incarnation, God participates in this material world. Indeed, God can only be known within this materiality. The modern use of the word *spiritual* has produced an antimaterialist bias in many of the Euro-tribal churches. *Spiritual* has come to mean nonmaterial, which was never the meaning of the word prior to the modern era. Such oppositional language is contrary to the Christian imagination. For Christian life, spiritual means engaging with God in God's world—in the ordinary, sensual order of everyday life. In the context of White's framework, however, materialist refers to the overarching narrative of modernity's wager that excludes the notion of a world infused with God's agency (what he names a theurgism). It is important to be clear that there are two different comprehensions of both material and spiritual at work here. Those understandings framed within modernity's wager have colonized the others, which leads White to describe the two other quadrants.

Subjectivism

Subjectivism has affinities with voluntarism and the supernatural. The subjectivist believes there are spiritual, not material, sources that are resources for human action. These spiritual resources provide persons

---

13. See Terry Eagleton, *Materialism* (New Haven, CT: Yale University Press, 2016).

with the inner power to change the world. For White, "Subjectivism is the intersection of spirituality with the primacy of the internal world. The subjectivist activist sees social networks as the channels of emotional contagion . . . the primary work is to produce and transmit emotions."[14] Subjectivism is a step away from an overarching materialism toward some form of spiritual imagination that shapes an individual's inner experiences. In this description, the primary locus of action is the inner self, but it is resourced by the spiritual. This now tends to be the ways the churches resource people in modernity—they offer spiritual goods and services as resources to the autonomous self. The problem is that spiritual then means whatever an individual wants it to mean; it is a resource for an inner decision to act.

The subjectivist believes that if his or her inner spiritual dispositions can be transferred to others, transformation will happen. But make no mistake—the source of transformation remains firmly materialist. The individual is primary and the spiritual is a useful resource in self-expression. Rather than using the language of God's agency, for example, there is the tendency in Christian discourse to use abstract nouns as symbols or intimations of a god-like experience: thus, words such as *love, care, justice, peace, reconciliation* becomes descriptors that sidestep any sense of God as agent; hence the abstract nouns offer the desired spiritual responses to the subjectivist.

In this quadrant, the additive "spirituality" becomes a patina overlaying materialist convictions about self-directed lives. Many, however, use the word as a way of expressing their sense that there is another agency beyond the material that cannot be discounted. Amid the unraveling, growing numbers of people turn to this language to express the conviction that there is another source of agency, but they don't know how to name that agency, or how to connect with it in any practical sense. Their struggle should be expected. In a time of unraveling, it is normal for people to act in contradictory and confused ways; they are wrestling with the awareness of disruption, struggling to give it language, and tentatively testing alternatives. As citizens across the West seek to reconnect with that other agent, modernity's wager hasn't totally eradicated the memory of this agent, but the capacities to discern where God might be present are atrophied.

---

14. White, *End of Protest*, 91–93.

People still have a restless memory of God's reality. What is generative about this quadrant is the complexity of ferment it contains. While a spiritual subjectivity can be one more round of privileging the Self, it is also a place where a fermenting and bubbling is happening. It is where the intimations of another agent can be experienced. It can be a space where the disruptive Spirit is gestating something new.

Theurgism

White labels the fourth quadrant *theurgism*, the belief that some form of supernatural revelation from the nonnatural, nonmaterial realm drives the forces of change in persons and structures. White makes his contention after reflecting on Occupy as an illustration of a movement for change. His conclusion is that revolution requires divine intervention. While a strange proposal within the frame of the modern West, it has a well-established history within recent movements of Western thought.[15] In European political history over the last several centuries is this underlying expectation that a religious or mystical irruption would revolutionize the world—a reality too often neglected or elided out of the intellectual story of the modern West.

White's proposal is not new. It lies within a tradition of messianic-religious expectations that have been far more than the ravings of extremists or marginal sectarians. White's label for this quadrant is less than helpful. It proposes an admixture of neo-paganism few would identify with or readily accept. Further, the label hides or dismisses important work about the nature of change by both Christian and Jewish thinkers in the twentieth century. The notion that a transcendent agency is at the core of fundamental change is not the raving of marginal people, but lies at the heart of the Western tradition, even if that tradition has been dismissed or marginalized. We propose that a more helpful name for this quadrant is "Modernity's Void"—to indicate this absence of perspective and the overarching materialist reading of the modern West. Even in the unraveling of the West, the overarching conviction about the sources of social transformation remains naturalistic and materialistic. There is little sense that any agency outside the individual or the structures of social systems can bring change.

---

15. See, for example, Lilla's descriptions of Franz Rosenzweig and Eric Vogelin in *The Shipwrecked Mind* (New York: New York Review of Books, 2016).

Diagram 3 adapts White's diagram to visualize the basis for the refounding being proposed.

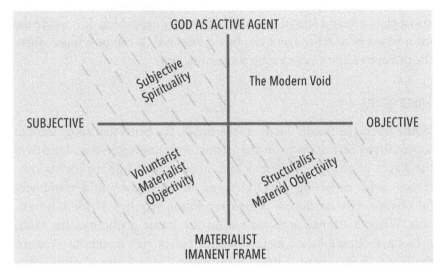

Diagram 3

The poles of the vertical axis are renamed as the Materialist Imanent Frame and God as Active Agent. The poles of the horizontal axis remain the same. The dashed lines across three of the quadrants are used to suggest that they all fall within the interpretive framework of Rieff's Third Culture, Taylor's immanent frame, and modernity's wager.[16] The quadrants are also renamed:

- **Upper Right Quadrant: The Modern Void.** Within modernity's wager there is no objective sense of God's agency except, perhaps, within the world of private, inner, personal experience. It is this perspective that still colonizes the ways Euro-tribal churches function.

- **Upper Left Quadrant: Subjective Spirituality.** There is agency outside of the Self—a spiritual force of some sort—but such a sense is vague and inchoate, more feeling than lived practice. The most profound challenge for refounding of the churches involves engaging those who sense an Other but don't have the language to give voice or form to this sense.

---

16. See Charles Taylor, *A Secular Age* (Cambridge, MA: Belknap Press, 2007).

- ▪ Bottom Left Quadrant: Voluntarist Materialist Objectivity.
  The power to act to change the world lies in the autonomous Self, along with hosts of other such selves. It is part of the core narrative of modern, liberal democracy. As such, it represents a narrative that has become increasingly difficult to sustain.

- ▪ Bottom Right Quadrant: Structuralist Materialist Objectivity.
  Forces involved in a complex interaction of structures are what bring about change. Change isn't the result of autonomous human actions. Rather, human actions are themselves caught up in a function of complex social and structural dynamics beyond the scope, or venue, of voluntarist actions. Objective research and extensive data gathering into the objective forces shaping a society can be critical means by which societies make informed decisions about the kinds of actions that need to be taken in response to social forces. Emphasis is placed on the processes of rationalization as the primary method of understanding the dynamics of change.

The lines across quadrants 2–4 propose that the overarching narrative of the West remains firmly within a materialist-naturalist framework whether of the voluntarist or structuralist kind. Quadrant 1, the Modern Void, is what that term states: an empty space. God's agency remains a distant memory, but it doesn't, however, affect the workings of modern life. The Christian life is recognized as a realm that remains important for some in terms of private, personal, inner sustenance, but little more. At the same time, quadrant 2 suggests that something else is happening in late modernity as the wager unravels. There is this emerging ferment as growing numbers of people, while dropping out of the formal denominational systems of the Euro-tribal churches, seek that Other, the forgotten Agent, but who yet don't have a language with which to give voice to this search beyond the tepid, amorphous word *spiritual*. It is here to which the churches must turn their refounding attentions. Louis Dupre expresses well the nature of this engagement:

> No program of theological renewal can by itself achieve a religious restoration. To be effective a theological vision requires a recognition of the sacred. Is the modern mind still capable of such a recognition? Its fundamental

attitude directly conflicts with the conditions necessary for it. First, some kind of moral conversion has to become indispensable. The immediate question is not whether we confess a religious faith, or whether we live in conformity with certain religious norms, but whether we are of a disposition to accept any kind of theoretical or practical direction coming from a source other than the mind itself. Such a disposition demands that we be prepared to abandon the conquering, self-sufficient state of mind characteristic of late modernity. I still believe in the necessity of what I wrote at an earlier occasion: "What is needed is a conversion to an attitude in which existing is more than taking, acting more than making, meaning more than functions. . . . What is needed most of all is an attitude in which transcendence *can be recognized again.*"[17]

Refounding in Liminal Spaces

When you wish to discover the new unexpected actors that have more recently popped up and which are not yet *bona fide* members of "society," you have to travel somewhere else and with very different kinds of gear. . . . [T]here is as much difference . . . between learning how to drive on an already existing freeway and exploring for the first time the bumpy territory in which a road has been planned against the wishes of many local communities.[18]

Rieff and White provide clues as to why fundamental change has been so difficult and point in the direction of refounding. As Dupre suggests, the direction calls for the recognition of God's agency in the world. This calls for something far different than the congregations, denominations, and leaders the Euro-tribal churches formed within modernity's wager. The primary metaphors we are proposing for shaping this refounding are unraveling and fermenting/bubbling. Several convictions flow from these metaphors:

---

17. Louis Dupre, *Religion and the Rise of Modern Culture*, 117, italics in original.
18. Bruno Latour, *Reassembling the Social: An Introduction to Actor-Network-Theory* (Oxford: Oxford University Press, 2007), 22–23.

- Unraveling suggests the West and its Euro-tribal churches are in a liminal place;

- Notions of reforming are not capable or addressing this crisis of liminality;

- The situation is no longer that of reforming but refounding.

Refounding is a huge idea akin to the language of transformation. Almost a decade ago, a young African American named Barack Obama became the president of the United States. His election was shaped by a nation hungry for change, ready to embrace this man's brilliant rhetorical imagination. Expectations were high not only among his own citizens but across the world. Without disparaging the desire and imagination of Obama, it is fair to say that at the end of his presidency it was clear that transformation had not occurred. On the contrary, complex forces of reaction had been let loose around the world. It seemed as if, in the tug of war around the question of how change occurs, it was not the voluntarist but the structuralist side that prevailed. The underlying forces and structures of modern societies proved too powerful to be transformed by the emotive appeals of "Yes, we can."

The notion of refounding can be an empty slogan as people become ever more jaded about the possibility of significant change. It becomes hard to believe that human aspiration can make a difference in reshaping/transforming the world. It seems, sometimes, there are forces beyond human hope or imagination that thwart our efforts to transform this world. In the context of this realism, we must ask how we can refound the churches in ways that are not shaped by romanticism about another time or idealism that fails to take into account the blunt realities of the principalities and powers. How can a refounding be more than the naïve imaginations of modern people caught in their beliefs in progress, or the narcissistic conviction that we, as self-actualizing selves, can refound the church by thinking right, believing right, doing justice in the right way, and employing ourselves more arduously? Refounding requires radically different agenda from new pharisaisms.

Mark Lilla states: "To live a modern life anywhere in the world today, subject to perpetual social and technological change, is to experience the psychological equivalent of permanent revolution."[19] As the unraveling unfolds something else is happening—a bottom-up, edge-in, bubbling,

---

19. Lilla, *Shipwrecked Mind*, xiv.

calling forth something yet to be named. This is where God's Spirit is already ahead in the refounding of social and religious life. A focus on reforming existing systems, in Latour's words, won't provide the "gear." While the unraveling disorients established systems, the fermenting and bubbling point to where we might trace the unexpected ways of God.

Between the unraveling and the bubbling is the space of tension, a liminal, yet-to-be-comprehended space that cannot be managed within existing frameworks. Liminal space is the space between the recognition that our familiar vocabulary no longer accounts for where we are, and the awareness that we don't yet have language or practices that describes our situation. In liminal space there is no return, no reforming. It is genuinely about a refounding. The liminal[20] is a disruptive space wherein established stories don't make sense for its members. It has several movements:

Stable Cultural Consensus. Societies create stories about themselves to explain how they were founded, the values and commitments that make them who they are, and the means of being successful within a culture. These stories provide people with the means of identifying with each other, knowing how to operate in the world, and distinguishing themselves from others. These can be family, ethnic, racial, national, and religious stories or, more likely, a combination of such stories.

Early Christians, for example, figured out how to thrive in the relatively hostile environments of the Roman Empire during their first four hundred years by framing a story of their origins and creating practices for living together within the Empire.[21] A group thrives when its stories, liturgies, and practices assist members to make sense of and navigate their world. In America, for example, the "American Dream" once provided people with a story about themselves. For a good part of the modern period, the story of modernity's wager gave identity and purpose to citizens of Western liberal democracies.

---

20. A simple definition is: "the condition of being on a threshold or at the beginning of a process" (Webster). The framework of liminality was initially applied to the Euro-tribal churches a number of years ago in Alan J. Roxburgh, *The Missionary Congregation, Leadership and Liminality* (Harrisburg, PA: Trinity Press International, 1997) and has subsequently entered into mainstream discussions about the church in its late modern context. The fact that most writers using liminality in relationship to Euro-tribal churches see it as a way of proposing reformations suggests a lack of understanding about the nature of liminality. Liminality in the context of the changes occurring to the churches in the West was also discussed in Alan Roxburgh, *Missional Map-Making* (San Francisco, CA: Jossey Bass, 2010). See also Gerald A. Arbuckle, *Earthing the Gospel* (Maryknoll, NY: Orbis Press, 1990).
21. See, for example, Kreider, *Patient Ferment*.

Unraveling of Core Stories. At some point these long-established stories lose their capacity to provide their members with the stability and meaning to navigate a changing world. When this loss of a group's ability to make sense of a changing environment occurs, two things happen:

First, the group's relationship with its environment becomes tenuous and disruptive. Today, this is observed, for example, in a growing anxiety about a shrinking middle class within which the American Dream has become an illusion. It is illustrated in the powerful reactions of those who voted in favor of Brexit, as a majority sensed that the official story about an equal nation serving all was untrue. In late modernity, increasing numbers of middle-class people hoped that by working harder and longer they could maintain a sense of economic security, but now there is a growing concern that all their effort is only leaving them behind. Young people have assumed a story about adulthood and education that offers them social and financial freedom. Yet they graduate with degrees and find no jobs. As they move in with their parents, or share rental housing with other young adults, they hold a deepening anxiety that their presumed story of middle-class life in a liberal democracy is untenable.

Second, the internal cohesion of a group unravels as members stop believing its stories. The established stories, structures, skills, and leadership of institutions have lost their capacity to hold people's loyalty not because what they are doing has not changed or has not been updated, but because their narratives about life have lost their ability to hold people in the midst of the unraveling. This can be observed in the "Gones" and "Dones" leaving the Euro-tribal churches. People cry out for political, social, economic, and religious change, but the elites themselves have lost the capacity to listen or act differently or step outside their own preconceptions.

Liminal Space: The Experience of Failed Stories and Systems. As the unraveling continues, the gap between people's experiences and the claims of established organizations deepens. People lose faith in the capacity of these systems to provide direction. Everyday life makes less and less sense in terms of established narratives. People feel more and more cast upon themselves with few systems of support. This breakdown can be experienced as chaos or gradual loss. The result is an environment of disorientation, anxiety, and rising resentment. As the stories upon which people have built their hopes fail, and they have yet to discern where to find alternative support in a world that makes less sense, they live in liminal space—and a great deal is happening:

- **Anger and blame.** We deal with anxiety and disorientation by looking for people or systems to blame. Scapegoating and resentment grows.

- **Fix and Reform.** Leaders still believe adjustments will fix or reform things. Established strategic, analytic, and "visioning" skills try to name the problem, propose a different future, and initiate action. The narrative of reform carries the presumption that existing know-how can make things right again, but it cannot be accomplished in liminal space. As Ulrich Beck stated, in the liminal "the accepted, accumulated side effects of billions of habitual actions have rendered the existing social and political institutional arrangements obsolete. . . . [T]he narrative of the controllability of the world has become a fiction."[22]

- **Communitas.** After multiple attempts at reform, fixing, and trying to go home again, the awareness comes that existing hierarchies and elites no longer have answers. As this recognition grows, people start coming together outside existing roles and structures to test new pathways. This is what is happening now to the Euro-tribal denominations as people leave at a rapidly increasing pace. As Victor Turner states: "Liminality here breaks, as it were, the cake of custom and enfranchises speculation."[23] Rather than overarching strategies directed from established centers, institutions, and elites, something radically different must take place. Liminality requires a refounding. Such a refounding doesn't mean everything is a blank sheet or there are no hints of direction. Nor does it mean that we must abandon the existing structures to which we already belong. The Christian life offers orienting practices for how we live in liminal space.

The Liminal Dynamic

This mixture of unraveling, fermenting, bubbling, and liminal space creates a tension between the desires to reform/fix and to risk/test. The

---

22. Ulrich Beck, *The Metamorphosis of the World* (Cambridge: Polity Press, 2016), 49.
23. Victor Turner, *The Forest of Symbols* (Ithaca, NY: Cornell University Press, 1967), 106.

fermenting and bubbling are offstage from public discourse. Another dynamic continues. Existing experts, elites, and professions redouble their efforts to make their systems work. As, for example, the environment enters more a critical state, there is an increasing conviction that technology will fix the problem, rather than force people to make the hard choices, which will require major changes in values and practices among people. Denominational systems continue looking for ways to reorganize, restructure, or reform. They continue to search for new ways of restating the essence of their originating ecclesiologies.

Reformation and Rationalization

In liminal space the language of reformation misdirects. Even in the new millennium, it remains difficult for the Euro-tribal churches to talk about the unraveling without the reformation being their default lens. The picture that lives inside these churches, a picture they seem unable to get outside of because it is so embedded in their language world, books of order, and constitutions remains that of the sixteenth-century Euro-tribal reformations. The five hundredth anniversary of Luther's precipitating event was in 2017, and amidst such celebration it seems impossible to imagine alternatives. As important as those European reformations have been, they can no longer address what is happening to the churches of the modern West. Reform language keeps pressing us to make "The Reformation" the standard for responding to our crisis. Euro-tribal churches seem unable to get outside this picture.

This reform narrative carries the belief that we have a basis from which to rationally assess what has happened to the churches and, on that basis, propose manageable, strategic actions. At heart, this is a repeat of the processes of rationalization that have powered modernity.[24] Rationalization,

---

24. An elemental drive in the early part of the Enlightenment, particularly following the Thirty Years War and the Peace of Westphalia, was, among elites, a profound fear of the ordinary and everyday wherein uneducated people were driven by primitive passions that had produced the decimation of the Thirty Years War. Part of the agenda of the Enlightenment, along with the way the nation-state gets formed, is to produce nonlocal structures of rationality that removed the passions and ignorance of the ordinary and everyday. This is no small factor in our loss of the local as places of creativity and emergent life (see Stephen Toulmin, *Cosmopolis: The Hidden Agenda of Modernity* [Chicago: University of Chicago Press, 1992]). See also Zygmunt Bauman and Tim May, *Thinking Sociologically*, 2nd ed. (Oxford: Blackwell, 2001), 175ff. They observe about the application of rationalization to society: "Once applied to . . . the organization of the society at large—rational analysis can serve to limit choices or diminish the range of means from which individuals may draw in order to pursue ends."

as a sociological term, describes a process of early modernity where local, diverse customs and traditions that had shaped people's actions for millennia were replaced by a radically different set of methods we now consider normative. Rationalization, as a method, stands over against local customs or the specific practices groups used to direct their lives.

In the early part of the Industrial Revolution, for example, people in different areas of England operated on a schedule that was shaped by the movement of the sun and measured on sundials, which was problematic when one wanted to rationalize how people used time. Rationalization was necessary to manage the transportation of produce and raw materials. The standardized clock placed everyone on the same time scale and, in so doing, removed the impediment of local time zones. Local, everyday life was gradually eradicated, making way for a rationalized ordering of everyone's daily life. State bureaucracies did a similar thing by rationalizing in areas like law, education, and medicine across a whole country. The customs and habits of the local and everyday became unimportant, as almost everything in society was rationalized—the measure of efficiency, the management of outcomes, and the ability to get as close to certainty as possible. Traditional forms of local and everyday life dissolved.

One of the more disturbing examples of rationalization was its application by Frederick Winslow Taylor to industrial work forces in the time-management systems.[25] His underlying conviction was that the control and management of people and environments were crucial for a successful society. That which cannot be managed becomes a source of fear and reaction.[26] This is not to say such processes are inherently wrong. Rationalization has given us immensely good things. The point here is that these are now the deep defaults out of which we operate and, as such, often preclude our ability to see what is at stake in the liminal spaces of our unraveling. One might say that the current movement of globalization is an example of this rationalization process. Part of the resentment toward globalization is the sense that the rights of national and local populations to choose their own ways of life are undermined in the name of some abstract ideal of global economic efficiency. This reaction is visible in Brexit, as well as the way

25. Frederick W. Taylor, *The Principles of Scientific Management*. Kindle edition, first published in 1911.
26. See the sociologist Zygmunt Bauman's assessment of this characteristic of rationalization in modernity in his haunting analysis of the Holocaust in *Modernity and the Holocaust* (1989; Malden, MA: Polity Press, 2006).

Wallonia, a tiny province in Belgium, stood against a major EU treaty with Canada in 2016.

Processes of rationalization are embedded in the normative, professionalized hub-spoke structures and bureaucracies of Protestant denominations. They thrived into the last third of twentieth century when their structures and institutions began to unravel. In the face of the unraveling, processes of rationalization increased in attempts to fix the problem. The primary means of understanding the unraveling was the existing narrative of rationalized control.

Applying methods of rationalization in liminal space leave us inside established worlds of expertise with the default assumption that with the right studies, methods, and organizational strategies, it is still possible to manage the unraveling. Denominations still pour huge amounts of energy and resources into such rationalizing processes through studies, data gathering, or the creation of new labels to propose ways of reforming themselves. One major US denomination, as late as 2017, has embarked on a nation-wide process of writing a new mission statement. Their conviction remains that rationalizing processes still give them the power to reform and renew in the unraveling. Such default methods cause organizations to reproduce (reform, renew, retool, restructure) existing norms, roles, habits, and practices using different language. Reform and restructure are no longer tenable.

Refounding in the Ferment of Unraveling and Bubbling

Beyond the reach of rationalization technique is a refounding that reformations cannot comprehend. The language of refounding invites us to step outside this picture that holds us captive. As Latour states, when you want to discover the new unexpected actors who don't fit into the rationalized models of existing systems, you have to travel somewhere else and with very different kinds of gear. One must not drive along well-mapped highways but enter, as if for the first time, a bumpy off-road trail that current systems resist or reject.

Refounding is an invitation to see the unraveling from a different perspective. It calls us to pay attention to the Spirit's movements from the edges, from the side effects of life in the local rather than from principles laid out in the sixteenth century or our current operating manuals. Such paying attention is a huge quest. In Beck's language, "We are all prisoners of a language world that conserves the old certainties . . . and makes us blind to the new diversity of options."[27] Christian life in the West is being refounded by the Spirit, but it is happening off to the side, coming in through the back door. The unraveling creates a fermenting and bubbling involving a thousand small effects among ordinary people trying to step outside the failed promises of the modern because they sense that another future is being formed.

There's no guarantee that Protestant denominations will discern this or join the Spirit. For the most part, the leaders of denominations still don't know how to enter and participate in the liminal spaces, so they don't connect with the fermenting. The movements of refounding are not visible to those who dwell in the narratives of management, control, and reformation. In liminality, longings for predictability, continuity, and control generate a reactionary nostalgia for reformation. As Lilla notes:

> To live a modern life anywhere in the world today, subject to perpetual social and technological change, is to experience the psychological equivalent of permanent revolution. . . . Anxiety in the face of this process is now a universal experience, which is why anti-modern reactionary ideas attract adherents around the world who share little except their sense of historical betrayal. Every major social transformation leaves behind a fresh Eden that can serve as the object of somebody's nostalgia. And the reactionaries of our time have discovered that nostalgia can be a powerful political motivator, perhaps even more powerful than hope. Hopes can be disappointed. Nostalgia is irrefutable.[28]

There is no going home or making the previous dispensation central; nostalgia won't help.

In a social landscape shaped by rationalization and bureaucratization, people become less actors and more responders, less the shapers of a culture and more commodities or consumers inside a life organized by the state and capitalism. This has led to the presumption that the ways we now act in society are set; all we can do is reproduce existing habits and practices. While the reflexive reproduction of social life is important for the stability of a society, it is not the whole story. Amid the unraveling

---

27. Beck, *Metamorphosis of the World*, 31.
28. See Lilla, *Shipwrecked Mind*, xiv.

we can do more than reproduce what exists. We can act. In our acting, a different future ferments. In our acting, the refounding is discerned. The question is: what kind of acting is required of Christian communities inside modernity's wager?

8

Metaphors for Liminal Spaces

Introduction

Our context is rife with metaphors picturing the situation of the churches. Metaphors construct worlds. They connect and transfer meaning from one context to another. Metaphors both guide and express our desires. They are, therefore, more than just useful images or ideas. They are powerful shapers of our actions. Metaphors propose mental and emotional maps to guide us through our place and time. In the business world, for example, there is a plethora of metaphors to describe the nature of business and styles of leadership: a jazz ensemble, a working colony of bees, getting on a balcony and looking at the dance floor, and functioning as nimble units like the US Marines in Iraq. Metaphors can be powerful catalysts for change as they are turned into strategies for action. Therefore, it is important to be as self-critical as possible about the ones we use. The challenge of appropriating metaphors lies in the temptation to convert them into neat models or solutions that give direction along a pathway that the metaphor has made clear, distinct, discernable, and explainable. Metaphors, therefore, are tricky. They can beguile and misguide when they become so elegantly congruent and expressive of one's own emotional context.

A metaphor is not intended to serve as a model or template. When it is used in such a way, it can misguide. A metaphor is an evocative invitation onto a road of discovery, not the predefined shape of the journey or its ending. When it becomes more than an evocative invitation, it occludes our capacity to live in the ambiguous, liminal spaces of our time. Arguably, this is happening with the current use of biblical metaphors as leaders seek to name and manage the unraveling of our times, or create solutions to the ferment of our times through programs and strategies.

There is a tendency to assume that the guiding metaphors for our time are located in scripture, which is to assume that certain biblical metaphors can serve as guiding models. Metaphors such as exile, exodus, and diaspora are being used in this way. But is this pervasive assumption of there being a "biblical" metaphor to guide us in our liminal space helpful? What if there aren't any biblical metaphors describing our current reality?

This chapter explores metaphors currently in use to understand what has been happening to the Euro-tribal churches. It looks at where they are helpful and in what ways they limit or misguide our evaluations of our situation. On both sides of the Atlantic, Christian life is in a space of flux that is unraveling long-established assumptions, expectations, and images about the place of the Euro-tribal churches. This is compelling churches to search for language and images to make sense of what is happening to them. They are appropriating differing biblical metaphors that aren't helpful in describing the contextual and historical realities of the churches.

Metaphors Locating the Euro-Tribal Churches

Exile

This popular metaphor seeks to make strong connections between the situation of exiles from Judea and contemporary churches. According to the metaphor, like Judah in 587 BCE, the Euro-tribal churches have been taken into exile; they are into a modern Babylon. Therefore, understanding how exilic Israel addressed Babylon (Jer. 29) will provide direction for how the Church should behave today.

Old Testament exile language is picked up in the New Testament to describe the situation of early Christians. First Peter 1 describes Christians as being "exiles of the Dispersion"[1] spread across Asia and the Mediterranean basin. The metaphor does not refer to a psychological state of loss or anxiety, but the concrete reality of what was happening to people who identified themselves as Christians as the gospel moved across the known world. The idea of exile in this text is akin to that of the diaspora Jews living post-exile. Parallels with the current experience of the Euro-tribal churches are not there. The primary experience of exile is of being separated from

---

1. The Jewish diaspora wasn't a metaphor but a long-established fact of Jewish life that shaped the realities of early Christians. It is fairly clear, for example, that a majority of the converts at Pentecost were diaspora Jews attending the festival or living in Jerusalem before they died. In this sense, the notion of diaspora was an actual description of social reality for many involved in this Jesus movement.

social, and to some extent political, power and influence. But we have not moved to another physical land, only to the unfamiliar territory of being seen as completely irrelevant to our contemporary world.

Exile metaphors appeal to the contemporary psychological experience of a particular age group of Christians who are no longer in the generational majority. Exile proposes a pervasive sense in the Euro-tribal churches that their forms of Christian life have been ripped away; they feel as if their world has been taken from them. They are experiencing grief, loss, anger, confusion, and resentment. Their questions feel like those of the Babylonian captives: "How can we sing the LORD's song in a strange land?" (Ps. 137:4) These older generations of Euro-tribals feel resentful about their situation (Ps. 137:9), which contributes to the conviction that the Babylonian exilic community parallels their experiences. The exhortation in Jeremiah 29 to dwell in the place to which they were sent and to seek the good of Babylon appeals to those trying to address the situation of the churches. The problem is that the people of the Euro-tribal churches haven't been sent anywhere against their will and are not dwelling in some strange land. Many other things may be happening, but this metaphor does not describe their reality.

While psychologically appealing, exile has no material relationship to the situation of the Euro-tribal churches. The people of these churches are members of the dominant cultures. They are, overall, middle-class, white-collar, and have been very well situated inside the sociocultural reality of the globalized West. Their members run corporations, sit on town and city councils, run businesses, and teach in schools. The metaphor appeals to the pyscho-dynamics of late modernity with its focus on the inner experiences of the self. It appeals to the experiences of unraveling.

As a metaphor, exile draws people into their feelings of loss, disorientation, and anger, but it fails to offer a realistic assessment of their situation. The idea of exile also appeals to an older, Baby Boomer, white, middle-class need for models that will provide strategies for fixing her or his situation. Exile offers a template appealing to a default reaction for finding a "way out" with biblical solutions. In 1 Peter 1, Christians are identified as exiles. But that is precisely who they were; it was a description of their reality. The popular use of this metaphor is another form of the wager. Its appeal lies in the reassertion of a human control that occludes the need to listen to the Spirit. It closes off the liminal space with proposed solutions. Where liminal practice invites the difficult work of awakening, listening, and discerning, the metaphor of exile closes off these avenues.

Resident Alien

Introduced in the early 1990s by Stanley Hauerwas and William Willimon,[2] this metaphor struck a chord in North American churches. It offered a vision for how the American churches were feeling about themselves and proposed how they might recover their vitality. They needed to learn how to become aliens in their own culture. The presenting conviction was that these churches were in "Constantinian" captivity, shaped by the norms of the nation-state and consumer capitalism rather than the countercultural ethos of the gospel. The churches, therefore, needed to become a sociopolitical society within the existing society, shaped by the politics and practices of the gospel.

These images certainly struck a chord for many in the churches. It made clear that the churches were to be an alternative social reality within North American culture. Numerous life-giving experiments in forming churches shaped by the imagination of resident aliens have characterized the period since the book's publication.[3] The metaphor has remained evocative for Christians who are trying to come to terms with the unraveling of Western life. Notions of a non-Constantinian form of church took hold and became an important pointer for those seeking to imagine the character of the church today. John Howard Yoder's writings on this theme have provided an important framing for many seeking to grasp what it means to be the Church in this unraveling.[4]

On balance, resident alien is a helpful, evocative metaphor that prompts the churches to reimagine their life. Yet, though the Constantinian critique is important, is it a sufficient descriptor to express the current situation of the churches? Today, is there any sense of a "Constantinian" captivity? Doesn't this language now misdirect? It may have made some sense to a Boomer generation with memories of high church attendance and, to some degree, still affected by the imagination of their parent's generation where God and country were the dominant forms of self-understanding. The generations since have little or no memory of that story. They live in a different world. This metaphor pointed to a political and social captivity of the once-dominant Euro-tribal churches. At the same time, does

---

2. Stanley Hauerwas and William Willimon, *Resident Aliens: Life in the Christian Colony* (Nashville, TN: Abingdon Press, 1990).

3. See William Stringfellow's earlier book, *An Ethic for Christians and Other Aliens in a Strange Land* (Waco, TX: Word Books, 1973), that made a similar argument to Hauerwas and Willimon. Even as far back as the early 1970s, he saw growing numbers of Christians feeling like they were aliens in their own country.

4. See John Howard Yoder, *A Royal Priesthood* (Independence, MO: Herald Press, 1998).

it sufficiently critique the default of these churches to reconceive themselves continually within the European reformations of the sixteenth and seventeenth centuries? It is not only a "Constantinian" imagination that makes little sense today, but also a "Reformation" imagination. The ways in which the metaphor of resident alien is conceived may not be sufficient for the refounding required.

Journey

A biblical image that stands out as a hopeful metaphor is journey. Abram and Sarai are the paradigmatic couple in whom is embedded an imagination for journeying in liminal space. Old and without generativity, they set out on a journey in which they birthed a future. With the whole modern West in upheaval, we are already on a journey. People sense the ground shifting, sign markers disappearing, and the ending of a time and place that once made sense. The journey metaphor is congruent with our current experience. It is an image within which Euro-tribal churches might see themselves within God's purposes, even as they have been rendered powerless. An Abram and Sarai–like journey moves past notions of return and fixing. It invites us into a space of trusting God, though we can't know the details of the journey; a place where we must improvise within the drama of God's agency.

The challenge of the journey metaphor is in getting clear about what it does and does not mean for the churches. It has to be held in tension with other metaphors. Journey is about picking up and moving away from somewhere. This has great appeal to a largely rootless culture with little investment in the local. We will be emphasizing the importance of being rooted. Yet, at the same time, there is a journey to be made which, like Abram and Sarai's, involves a letting go of control and power, a setting aside of the need to know outcomes and define destinations. Thus, this important image of a journey like that of Abram and Sarai has to be held in tension with this call to be rooted, to embrace the call to stability we will discuss later. For the Euro-tribal churches, this story of Abram and Sarai's journey must be held in tension with the Benedictine call to stability. As contradictory as this may sound, the counterintuitive journey is not one of moving away but becoming rooted. The Abram/Sarai journey is the willingness to live inside a way of life wherein one cannot know or control the outcomes or destinations. The journey that modern Western Euro-tribals have been on is one moving away from stability into the limitless freedom to go anywhere and be anything. The journey to which God's Spirit is inviting us is back into the local and everyday.

Diaspora

Diaspora is a metaphor that grows out of the exile experience. Following the Babylonian captivity, a majority of the Jewish exiles did not return to Israel but spread out to form diaspora communities across the world. The same thing occurred again after the destruction of Jerusalem in the seventies, when all Jews were expelled and were dispersed across the world.

Diaspora, as an image of the modern church, is picked up by Walter Brueggemann. He recognizes it as a more helpful metaphor than exile. In his introduction of the book *The Church in Exile*, Brueggemann states:

> Midway through his exegesis, however, there is a notable shift of gears that Beach does not acknowledge—a shift that is, in my judgment, altogether commendable. By consideration of the narratives of Esther, Jonah and Daniel, Beach takes up texts that are in fact from the subsequent period of Diaspora of Israel and not from the usual period of exile. The sequel from exile to Diaspora here is a critical one, one that many interpreters, including this commentator, are making. The difference is that the theme of "exile" leads to an expectation of a return home to normalcy.[5]

Brueggemann makes helpful connections between communities living in a situation of diaspora and the practices of hope, imagination, and missional living. However, there is a more realistic use of diaspora language in the growing presence across the West of migrant, refugee Christians from other continents. Euro-tribal Christians have not yet connected well enough with this diaspora to listen and receive from their experiences. Perhaps the value of diaspora as a metaphor with the Euro-tribal churches is in the invitation to listen to and learn from this diaspora in their midst. This is an important element in a refounding process. These diaspora Christians bring words from outside. The liminal challenge for the Euro-tribal churches is to enter a space of humility and reception wherein they can receive from these diasporas by sitting at their tables and receiving their hospitality.

Diaspora expresses the psychological feeling of the Euro-tribal churches but doesn't bear the weight of their concrete reality. Brueggemann states:

---

5. Walter Brueggemann, "Introduction," in Lee J. Beach, *The Church in Exile* (Downers Grove, IL: InterVarstityPress, 2015), 11–12.

By contrast "Diaspora" is a practice of life and faith among those who are far from home, who settle in new contexts that become home, with no serious expectation of returning to an old normalcy. The matter is decisive for getting on with ministry. "Exile" might be a hope for recovery for the way the church used to be, whereas "Diaspora" is a recognition that there will not be any return home and there will not be a recovery of any old normalcy.[6]

Materially, the Euro-tribal churches are not far from home. They are not in a diaspora situation. This is not being picky. Irrespective of psychological and emotional experiences, these churches must confront the material reality of their situation. It is not diaspora. These churches are not migrants settling in new contexts. The symbols and geographies in which they have dwelt for generations surround them. The embodied, unavoidable fact is that their "home" is the context of their situation. That reality can't be imagined away without misdirecting the situation, which is partly why the Euro-tribal churches continue to propose actions out of the default that there can, or will, be return or recovery. Most books and proposals coming forward are still about return and recovery because these metaphors of exile and diaspora lie deep in their imagination.

Diaspora does describe immigrant communities coming into the West.[7] As such, it connotes an experience of dispossession, dispersion, and scattering. These are not the characteristics of the Euro-tribal churches. Diaspora is increasingly connected with globalization in much religious and nonreligious literature around issues of development. It describes the very real current upheavals of peoples that are creating unprecedented global diasporas of political and economic refugees. This is the context in which the language of diaspora needs to used, rather than being applied to the Euro-tribal churches.

---

6. Brueggemann, "Introduction," *Church in Exile*, 12.

7. The metaphor is used in books describing the experience of migrant groups to the West. See, for example, Luther Jeom O. Kim, *Doing Diaspora Missiology: Toward "Diaspora Mission Church"—Rediscovery of Diaspora for the Renewal of the Church and Mission in a Secular Era* (Eugene, OR: Wipf & Stock, 2016). See also Jared Looney, *Crossroads of the Nations: Diaspora, Globalization, and Evangelism* (Skyforest, CA: Urban Loft Publishers, 2015).

Where Should Our Imagination and Energy Be Directed?

The above metaphors tend to weight the focus and energy of people in the Euro-tribal churches in a certain direction. That may not be the intention in their usage, but, nevertheless, they hold a certain posture toward the culture of the late modern West. This posture can be justified and has a good deal of legitimacy. The question here is one of discernment. In the context of the unraveling, where is the Spirit inviting God's people to locate their primary imagination and energy? These metaphors compel their users to see the central challenge to be addressed as something negative. They support an undercurrent that puts the Euro-tribal churches in the position of being cultural victims. The churches inside these metaphors have cultivated a passive-aggressive stance toward late modern culture. These metaphors carry within them indications of the stances the churches should take over and against this culture, as well as point to where their energies should be directed. If one is in exile, for example, then some other group or structure has caused it and one's energies should go toward how to resist or come apart from that group or structure. One's desires are continually being pressed toward an over-and-against posture. That desire, once embodied, determines the kinds of stories (theologies, practices, structures) one embraces to shape identity.

These metaphors, on balance, turn our imagination toward an over-and-against stance more than any other. As such, they misdirect how the Euro-tribal churches should address the question: how, in the context of the unraveling, do we discern where the Spirit is inviting God's people to locate their primary imagination and energy? These metaphors do not provide a helpful rendering of where we find ourselves in the unraveling of late modernity. Today, we stand at the end of modernity's wager without any viable alternatives to fill the vacuum of anxiety and resentment. This is not to say that the modern West has somehow been all bad and negative. It has been glorious in many ways, providing life-giving gifts on a global scale. The unraveling story is not about the fact of modernity's multiple gifts, but that the premises of life that have been so central to that modernity are unraveling.

There is anger in the land as more and more people feel at risk or are sold short by the promises of modernity. We can blame immigrants, the incursion of other religions into the West, or the loss of some moral basis from a secularized culture. We can be drawn back into nostalgia myths, but they, like the metaphors discussed above, cloud the possibility of a

Christian imagination to turn its energies to a far different story within the modern West.

Another story is present that invites different metaphors. While elites and institutional leaders continue to pour huge amounts of energy into shoring up modernity's wager, something far more hopeful is afoot. Amid the unraveling is a diffuse, holy desire still working to find language—a rising of faint memory showing up increasingly in, for example, White's quadrants. Here is where the Spirit is at work. It is time to lay aside metaphors like exile, diaspora, or exodus and to embrace the ferment and bubbling of God's Spirit all around us. These are the metaphors that offer missiological hope for the refounding of God's people and the refounding of Western societies.

Fermentation and Bubbling[8]

Unraveling proposes that what is happening to the Euro-tribal churches is the work of the Spirit; unravelling is about God's agency not simply sociohistorical events. If the Spirit is at the heart of the unravelling, then what we might be experiencing is the agency of God. This shifts the focus from the inward-focused experiences of the Euro-tribal churches outward toward discerning ways of joining with God.

Fermenting and bubbling may appear strange as primary metaphors for engaging modernity's wager and the crisis of the churches. Fermentation is an evocative image. It involves the active breaking down of substances to produce a new element, as in hops producing beer or grapes producing wine. Bubbling refers to the work of that change occurring beneath the surface. Fermenting carries within it the notion of something being formed out of sight, away from expected places, beneath the assumed places of power and knowledge. This fermentation is now bubbling up from beneath with an unexpected energy.

The richness of these metaphors is that they communicate that something has been fermenting out of public view for a long time before its effects are seen in a bubbling which is, at first, hardly noticeable but then starts to be noticed in many diverse places. We find these metaphors inviting and compelling. The Mennonite theologian Alan Kreider uses the fermenting image to describe the formation of the church in its first

---

8. We are grateful to the recent work of Alan Kreider in his book, *The Patient Ferment of the Early Church: The Improbable Rise of Christianity in the Roman Empire* (Grand Rapids, MI: Baker Academic, 2016).

three hundred years. We believe these are metaphors that reconnect us more helpfully with the agency of God and the uncontrollable, irruptive power of the Spirit. Kreider describes the bubbling in the early churches as something that "was not susceptible to human control, and its pace could not be sped up. But in the ferment there was a bubbling energy—a bottom-up inner life—that had immense potential."[9] He writes:

> Fermentation is an intriguing process. It is gradual. Except for a stray bubble that emerges now and then, nothing seems to be happening. Until late in its operations, it is unimpressive. And yet it has a cumulative power that creates and transforms. As Michael Pollan, who writes insightfully about food, observes, "A ferment generates its own energy from within. It not only seems alive, it is alive. And most of this living takes place at a scale inaccessible to us without a microscope."[10]

A bubbling fermentation describes what the Spirit is doing today. These are metaphors of opportunity and hope for the Euro-tribal churches. But such opportunity and hope will require a refounding. Kreider's observations are important. His argument about the early churches is that they formed and grew in the midst of a "patient ferment." He stresses the critical nature of this patience. We are grateful for his insights. He is pressing against the devouring urgency so present in the modern world and the churches—the urgency to strategize and determine outcomes so embedded in modernity's wager and the fundamental conviction that it is all up to us. In the modern imagination, God's agency is little more than the backup battery for human agency.

At the same time, fermentation does not necessarily need to take a long time. Beer, for example, was once the preferred beverage of the West. Long before the marketing of wine, beer was the drink of choice. Excellent beer can be fermented and produced within three to four days. We say this not to deny Kreider's argument, but to suggest that in the modern West and for the Euro-tribal churches the process of fermentation has been going on for quite some time already. A bubbling from beneath is breaking the surface all over the place. The Spirit is acting. It is time for the churches to recognize and participate in the fermentation of refounding.

---

9. Kreider, *Patient Ferment*, 3.
10. Kreider, *Patient Ferment*, 73.

The metaphors of ferment and bubbling imaginatively describe the possibility and processes of refounding. As in the early church, so the Spirit is working today. The book of Acts is the drama of the Spirit's fermenting and bubbling that took the church to places its leaders never imagined. The bubbling of the Spirit removes the possibility of managers and elites crafting their designs and strategies. Bubbling, as a metaphor, describes what is happening from below—what is unseeable by those who need to control outcomes. It comes from the bottom up, from the outside in. God's power is working in the ordinariness of the everyday to remake the world.

Chris Hedges[11] argues that change occurs in a society when intolerable gaps develop between ordinary people and the reigning narratives of the state, its economics, and its elites. Such gaps produce revolts. These gaps of expectation and hope are driven by a sense that the state, the elites, and the social and economic institutions have lost touch with life on the ground for ordinary people and the common good. At these points, bubbling and fermenting emerges from below and from the edges to produce the elements of massive change. This reality is being played out across the United States and Europe. It is also being played out in the Euro-tribal churches.

The French Jesuit Michel De Certeau[12] investigated the social upheavals in Paris that in 1968 came close to a revolution that could have toppled the French government. His report proposed that professional analysts and elites missed the bubbling and fermenting just under the surface in the everyday life of factory workers and ordinary citizens who felt they had no control over their economic lives.[13] These people had lost a sense that the state and the economy had any concern for the common good. In response, and out of the sight of professional analysis and rationalized data-gathering studies, such people were continually testing how to bypass the established codes of existing institutions, elites, and hierarchies. Their continuous testing was not an organized strategy of the few

---

11. Chris Hedges, *The Wages of Rebellion: The Moral Imperative of Revolt* (Toronto: Knopf Canada, 2015).

12. Michel De Certeau, *The Practice of Everyday Life* (Berkeley: University of California Press, 1984).

13. In a similar way one could argue that the professional classes failed to see the revolt of the ordinary that was present in Trump's election or the Brexit vote (see, for example, Arlie Russell Hochschild, *Strangers in Their Own Land* (New York: New Press, 2016). One can even go back to the 2008 financial collapse when Alan Greenspan the then chair of the US Federal Reserve and, at that time, one of the most listened-to leaders around matters of economies and financing stated, in retrospect, that he never saw the financial crisis coming.

leading the many. It was an unorganized, unpredictable bubbling that signaled deep change.

In 1968 that bubbling broke the surface of public awareness as workers took to the streets of Paris. The elites were taken by surprise because they had no framework within which to place what was happening, just as currently these same elites struggle to explain Brexit or Trump or the pushback to their agendas from ordinary people. Because their frameworks tended toward their own kind, the elites reported that the eruptions on the streets were led by students from the universities. The students, however, were joining the eruptions of the factory workers who poured their frustrations and resentments out onto the streets. Ordinary people felt increasingly disconnected from power elites and their institutions. Below the thresholds of visibility, a ferment was bubbling; something was at work that, at first, had neither language nor direction.

This bubbling of change can be enormously mixed and complex. It is, initially, composed of inexpressible feelings, unorganized texts of resistance, pieces and fragments of varying stories. When taken together, they become intertwined, weaving together into something that is not planned, and becoming a myriad of ways of saying "no" to existing forms of life, structures, institutions, and the interpretations of meaning and place provided by elites. While this bubbling moves in multiple and often contradictory directions—some reactive, some xenophobic—the metaphors of fermenting and bubbling also offer hopeful pointers to what the Spirit is up to across the modern West. They invite Christians to discernment. They suggest an imagination within which the Euro-tribal churches can be refounded.

9

The Christian Vocation in the Fermenting and Bubbling

". . . adapted themselves to the dominant paradigm, and consequently no longer had any paradigm or ideas of their own that they could have confidence in. They mistrusted their own ideas and so capitulated to those of their opponents" (Robert Misik).[1]

"For though we live in the world, do not wage war as the world does. The weapons we fight with are not the weapons of the world. On the contrary they have divine power to demolish strongholds." (2 Cor. 10:3–4, NIV)

Introduction

The vocation of the Euro-tribal churches is to fuel an insurrection against the dominant lie of modernity's wager. They can live into that vocation to the extent that they create spaces wherein God's people hear, practice, recapitulate, and engage the invitation to awaken to God's agency in the world rather than continue their current preoccupation of trying to fix themselves. God's story, to be clear, is not about creating spaces, or liturgies, for modern Selves to find refuge for a time; nor is it some kind of therapeutic or "spiritual and not religious" healing for battered selves. These roads are simply means of making God useful to the dominant story of the Self. The gospel of Jesus Christ involves the overcoming of the modern Self as the center of meaning within the world. The required insurrection is nothing less than the ending of the Self-centered story

---

1. Robert Misik, "The Courage to Be Audacious," in *The Great Regression,* ed. Heinrich Geiselberger (Cambridge, MA: Polity Books, 2017), 123.

and the re-entering of the Body that is the extended, communal body of Christ in the midst of the local. Here is where the refounding begins. Within this frame lie clues to the Christian vocation in the fermenting and bubbling.

The French anthropologist and sociologist Bruno Latour, himself a Christian, argues that even in these early decades of the twenty-first century, we are "in a history utterly different from that of the twentieth century."[2] The stage upon which we now stand as Christians, as compared with the once great Euro-tribal churches, is not the one that shaped either these churches or the modern West in the twentieth century. Yet our approaches remain largely those of the past century. We seem to have little capacity to understand the extent of the changes that are occurring, though they have been gestating since the beginning of the modern age. The confidence that formed the modern West has all but gone. The unraveling of modernity's wager continues apace. More effort at strategies built around the primacy of human energy will change nothing. In this liminal space, we all find ourselves in a place where "there's no longer a home, not for anyone. . . . Everyone's going to have to move."[3] The Euro-tribal churches cannot enter the fermenting by retrenching or staying where they are. The good news is that God is sending new teachers and mentors, for example, African Christians who are immigrants into the UK and Hispanic Christians who are being made to feel like aliens in the United States. We can also look toward resurgent First Nations peoples in the Americas.

The wager's promise was that everyone would increasingly benefit from the largesse of state, the power of the economy, and the development of the Self. This illusion continues to find new fuel in the promises of globalization, or the latest ways to increase "personal performance," to "cultivate happiness and . . . success."[4] The obscenity of these claims is their blindness to how infinitely small a percentage of humanity could possibly take advantage of these hopelessly glib promises. Rather than the promised happiness, what we have is an expanding sense of anxiety and

---

2. Bruno Latour, "Europe as Refuge," in Geiselberger, *Great Regression*, 79.
3. Latour, "Europe as Refuge," 79. This reality provides clues as to the missiological imagination that must form the churches again. This imagination will be found in the Augustinian sense of another city, which implicates us all in the profound, disorienting tension of being all to a place but also on a journey to this other city. This is a tension experienced by so many Christians who are migrants, such as Africans in the UK and Hispanics in the USA. It has not been the experience of the Euro-tribals.
4. Newspaper full page ad in the *Globe and Mail*, Saturday, September 9, 2017, "Personal Performance Summit," 8.

precariousness among growing majorities who face increasingly attenuated lives because of the failed promises of globalization and neo-liberal economics. As Latour observes, "[T]here's no longer a planet able to fulfill the dreams of globalization."[5] We cannot go home again.[6]

The Euro-tribal churches of Europe and North America were built on the promise of dominance—a center-periphery world in which they were the primary drivers and beneficiaries. That story is over. It cannot be resuscitated. Latour's question must be addressed by the churches: "Are you going to keep nursing dreams of escape, or are you going to search for a land in which you and your children might live. . . . [T]here is no planet for globalization and we are going to . . . need to learn to change the entire way" we live.[7]

Continuing attempts to fix our churches, denominations, and particular kinds of ethnic enclaves fail to grasp the challenges before us. It is the failure of the wager, especially in terms of its manifestations in neoliberal globalization and the centrality of the Self. We are all in the same liminal space—a thick, mixed humus—which, just like the huge migrations now reshaping our global habitation, requires us to leave what have been our "homes" as Euro-tribal Christians. The ferment of the Spirit calls for us to enter a kind of journey, like Abram and Sarai.

This ferment cannot be engaged by reforming homogenized, ethnic, racial, and cultural enclaves. These efforts fail to grasp the location of the Spirit's ferment. This refounding invites us to discern forms of Christian life that cross the growing ethnic, racial, ideological, and economic divides. The church's vocation is to demonstrate what is involved in such a common life. A society worth living must have some kind of picture of how we can live together. Such a picture has been obliterated in the wager but might be rediscovered in the ferment in so many ways. The Euro-tribal churches will need to leave the home they have built for themselves since the European reformations and be willing to risk so much of themselves in entering the ferment. In this sense they are at a place of needing to become like Abram and Sarai.[8]

---

5. Latour, "Europe as Refuge," 79.
6. See also Gut Standing, *The Corruption of Capitalism: Why Rentiers Thrive and Work Does Not Pay* (London: Biteback Books, 2017)
7. Latour, "Europe as Refuge," 80.
8. There is a whole other level of ferment that must be noted here that is being brought into the sphere of public discussion by African American, Hispanic, and Indigenous theologians. It is critical for these Christians to bring this ferment into the consciousness and discussion of the Euro-tribal churches. This is the whole question of colonization, "Whiteness," and Christian identity. For an excellent introduction and framing of this critical element of the

The call for this refounding is not because there is something so precious about either the Euro-tribal churches of the West that they must be continued, but because this West and these churches are the places where God's Spirit has formed us and now calls us to the vocation of refounding. Without redemptive social structures, people are left rootless and at the whim of powers that do not seek their good. The One who cried out that all things are being made new is the One who now calls Christians to turn from their need to fix and reform their churches and join the movement of refounding to the glory of God. This is the longing of the One who rose from the dead to make all things new, break down the walls of hostility, and bring all things together as Lord.

We live in the decaying elements of a world that can no longer hold itself together and leaves its citizens to their own fragile selves. We are witnessing a widening loss of faith in the systems of life upon which modernity's wager was based. We live in societies where citizens recognize that if they fall, they will not be caught by the state, their work, their church, or their neighbor. Some of the broad political turmoil that has resulted from the unraveling of modernity's story involves a reinvigorating of the desire for the state to help its citizens. In the UK the supporters of Jeremy Corbyn and the political left he represents are hearing a story of how the state is going to save them. But even this form of response is, itself, a testimony to our primary point regarding the erosion of the promise. There seem to be no alternatives on the horizon. We have been raised in a narrative of progress that claims if something fails there's a solution just around the corner. This myth is failing. People feel fragile and exposed because the horizons don't seem to suggest alternatives. There is fear that pensions will fail, and that hospitals won't have the funds to keep going. In this great unraveling experts and elites don't know what to do.[9]

An example of these fears and the reactions to them can be seen in the UK debate arising from the Grenfall tragedy in London where a substandard high-rise housing burned down, killing a significant number of residents and throwing the survivors at the mercy of local governments that seemed unable to respond. These events have had a profound impact

ferment, see the Fuller Theological Seminary Missiological lectures delivered by Dr. Will Jennings titled: *Can White People be Saved?* November 2, 2017. (This lecture is available as a YouTube video.)

9. See, for example, the recent book by the former governor of the Bank of England, Marvin King, *The End of Alchemy* (New York: Norton, 2016) who acknowledged that we have entered an era of great economic uncertainty that is frightening in its implications. See also Wolfgang Streeck, *How Will Capitalism End?* (London: Verso, 2016).

on UK news reporters who were confronted with the extent to which the victims of the fire were deeply hostile to the media because, in the midst of a gross human tragedy, they saw the survivors as objects for a story—a form of entertainment. The residents were angry with the media, and the confrontation shook up the reporters because that is not how they understood themselves.

The German economist Wolfgang Streeck sees contemporary societies at a place where their systems of social support are critically weakened. Citizens are feeling vulnerable in a world where we are left to our individual ends with few collective capacities to form alternative ways of living and supporting one another. He sees us having entered a liminal interregnum,

> a period of great uncertainty that looks more and more like a world left to individual opportunism of collectively incapacitated individualized individuals as they struggle to protect themselves from looming accidents and structural pressures on their social and economic status. The social world of the post-capitalist interregnum has cleared away the supporting role of government, state, unions, clubs . . . and so forth. There is, therefore, now a deepening sense of vulnerability in which at any time, anyone can be hit. . . . Society, having lost its ability to provide effective, proven templates for social existence, individuals only have themselves to rely on while social order relies upon the weakest possible mode of social integration.[10]

Christian Life in the Ferment—Pilgrims among the "Hills" of Modernity

The persistence of Christian life will mean both its capacity to resist and to cultivate practices that confront the unraveling when there is no predicting of where the unraveling is going. There is no blueprint for a different future except the persistent remembering of an agency and order that must, again, direct our lives. For Rieff, the reality of God's agency has been systematically removed by the elites within modernity's wager. But the wager doesn't go all the way down. In everyday life all kinds of

---

10. Interview with Wolfgang Streeck, *Ideas* (podcast), CBC Canada, February 9, 2017.

people still inhabit a faint memory of that other story that the high places of modernity had believed erased.[11] While we live in a politics whose morality is shaped by the demands of a global marketplace, where governments lose their legitimacy and disillusioned and resentful citizens are thrown upon themselves, that is not the only story. We live in the brilliance of Augustine's saeculum[12] wherein the God who bodily raised Jesus from the dead has declared a new creation that cannot be erased or relegated to places of usefulness. Within the unraveling is a bubbling and ferment within which the Spirit of Jesus is actively inculcating and prompting a refounding.

The ferment and bubbling of the Spirit are images of hope and expectancy. Far more is happening in the unraveling than the dystopian fears that currently shape conversation and fill the media.[13] This other story of new creation actualized in Christ, in the reality of the saeculum among us, invites the churches to rediscover their vocation. A picture of what is needed for this refounding to happen is given us in Psalm 121, a psalm of ascent. The Euro-tribal churches are being invited to become migrants and pilgrims of this God to take us beyond ethnic and affinity enclaves into neighborhoods. Psalm 121 is a pilgrim song for those joining the ferment of God's future.

Pilgrim songs were recited on the journey to Jerusalem to celebrate festivals and remember Israel's founding stories. As pilgrims ascended toward Jerusalem, they saw all about them the signs of compromise with Canaanite culture, the Canaanite gods enshrined over the city. The first line of the song includes a question: "I lift up my eyes to the mountains—where does my help come from?" (121:1, NIV). Seeing the Canaanite high places produced a sense of dread. Everywhere the pilgrims looked, the hills cried out with the overwhelming presence of Canaan's gods declaring that the story shaping the world was that of fate, of life dependent on placating fickle gods. Was there no other story, no other form of help for a

---

11. Streeck is blunt around some of the current myths energizing Western governments or offering hope to citizens. He states that the "idea that we can tame capitalism into a more equitable, social justice frame is a utopian ideal" (*Ideas*).

12. For Augustine, the *saeculum* was a time—the time between the ascension of Christ and his return—not a space (i.e., Augustine would not think of a "secular state" in any modern sense). For him we are encompassed in a creation that is always and everywhere filled with God's order and agency. This is part of the great refounding now required for the Euro-tribal churches.

13. See, for example, the recent upsurge in people buying George Orwell's *1984* as well as more recent novels such as Michel Houellebecq, *Submission* (London: Farrar, Straus and Giroux, 2015), John Feffer, *SplinterLands*, (Chicago: Haymarket Books, 2016), and Mohsin Hamid, *Exit West* (New York: Riverhead Books, 2017).

pilgrim searching for another land? The pilgrims broke out into confession, affirmation, and hope. Behind the hills and Jerusalem's lamentable life is another picture, a different frame:

> My help comes from the LORD,
>> the Maker of heaven and earth.
> [3]He will not let your foot slip—
>> he who watches over you will not slumber
> [4]indeed, he who watches over Israel
>> will neither slumber nor sleep.
> [5]The LORD watches over you—
>> the LORD is your shade at your right hand;
> [6]the sun will not harm you by day,
>> nor the moon by night.
> [7]The LORD will keep you from all harm—
>> he will watch over your life;
> [8]the LORD will watch over your coming and going
>> both now and forevermore. (NIV)

Amid the unraveling is this other story. It is not about a remnant or a faithful minority holding on, but of God's remaking the world. The narrative of hope for the Euro-tribal churches is that God is at work in the refounding of society. There is no withdrawal into enclaves of faith, but there is an invitation confidently to reorient ourselves from the "hills" toward the agent who is fermenting and bubbling a new creation.

The beginning of this refounding is the recovery of the conviction that God is the primary agent amid the unraveling who is already fermenting and bubbling a different future. The unraveling is not the story of what is happening. The proposals that follow are not about how God might be useful in some movement of social change. They are not, primarily, a reaffirmation of the local in the face of rationalizing, homogenizing, bureaucratic forces. Proposing such would simply be continuing a narrative of God's usefulness. Neither are these following proposals an accounting of why a neoliberal, global consumer society must be replaced by a more communitarian economics.[14] Nor, finally, are they about how to replace rampant individualism with a new sense of a commons. All of those

---

14. See Peter Block and Walter Brueggemann, *An Other Kingdom: Departing the Consumer Culture* (Hoboken, NJ: Wiley, 2016).

challenges need to be addressed, but they are neither the reason for nor the source of our proposals. Rather, our proposals are rooted in the confession that God is agent among us and, therefore, our primary calling is to be a people who discern where God is at work and join with the Spirit in refounding. Christian life must now be reoriented around the confession that God is the primary agent among us. The challenges of globalization and neo-liberalism, of consumer capitalism, of restoring the Commons, of forming communities that resist the homogenizing, rationalizing powers of the state are critical but to the extent they're the primary drivers of our actions, we remain inside modernity's wager. There is no hopeful future for either the West or Christian life in that direction.

How do we join the Spirit's fermenting to discern God's agency in our contexts? It involves the cultivation of practices rooted in the everyday life of the local. This, in turn, requires that we turn away from questions of how to fix our churches and turn to discerning God's actions in our neighborhoods. Current forms of church life are antithetical to such living. Joining the ferment of the Spirit requires a Christian life deliberately shaped around practices.

Practices and Desire

A practice is a set of habits that shape the ways we live our everyday lives together. Many of our friends rise early each day to go to the gym. That's a practice. Some stop at the local coffee shop midmorning for a coffee. That's a practice. Practices are habits that become embedded in our lives. When they do, they shape not just our behaviors but how we see our world. Recently, one of us decided to live without a vehicle, which meant walking everywhere or travelling by bus. It changed the rhythms of life and opened our eyes to a world we could not see from a car. This, too, is a practice of life. Practices are rhythms of life that orient our desires.

This interrelationship between practices and desires is important. Across the Euro-tribal churches there is an upsurge of movements focused on fixing, improving, and reforming.[15] Church planting, for example, is resurgent in North America, but anecdotal observations are that most church planting is shaped by the practices of affinity group gatherings

---

15. See Alan J. Roxburgh in *Joining God, Remaking Church, Changing the World: The New Shape of the Church in Our Time* (New York: Morehouse Publishing, 2015) and *Structured for Mission* (Downers Grove, IL: InterVarsity Press, 2016) for further discussion of these dynamics in congregations and denominational systems.

just like the existing patterns of Protestant churches. In other words, the underlying desires driving these movements remains fixated in finding new forms of making the church work among people who are essentially the same in terms of economics, social class, and ethnicity. As such, they do not challenge the underlying practices of congregating with one's tribe. We need practices that reorient and school our desires in different directions.

Desires are formed through repetition. One of us wanted to improve his capacities in running. He assumed that would involve some strengthening exercises and new training techniques. To his surprise, his trainer didn't go in these directions. She watched him run and then showed him how his feet splayed to the sides rather than land squarely in the middle of the foot and heel. As counterintuitive as it felt at the time, Alan found himself repeating, on a daily basis, ways of walking that caused his feet to land in the middle of the foot and heel. It was hard work and required a great deal of attention because, over many years, Alan had embodied a particular way of walking. His body's desire was to keep returning to long-established patterns. His new practice reshaped the "wiring" of his body so that it would desire this new pattern as the natural rhythm of walking and running. Such repatterning is no simple task.

We take for granted many of our everyday practices that direct our desires. They are, therefore, hidden from our self-understanding. We are usually unaware of these practices because they are second nature. One of us was raised in a setting where the safest way to function was to be quiet as much as possible and find places, at home or in the classroom, near to but apart from others. Later in life, married and with children of his own, he realized that these patterns were still embodied in him as he came home and involuntarily sought out spaces to be physically with himself or in his own head. Changing these patterns took a several years of intentionally practicing new habits.

The personal and social practices that pattern our lives range from the simple and innocuous to the complex and transforming. They can be life-giving or destructive. North Americans, for example, have taken on a practice that only came into existence in the 1950s but is now so embodied in their personal and social life that it's taken as normal. If there is need to go somewhere—even to the store up the street—we automatically drive. The car is so deeply embodied in our lives that we don't think about its use. It's just what we do. If someone suggests we walk to the store, our inner response shows how much this practice shapes our desire. We resist. It feels like we are wasting time by walking rather than driving.

Several years ago, Alan's family moved about a mile into another neighborhood where they could purchase a large multifamily house. For the previous twenty years, Alan had gone to a specific coffee shop in the previous neighborhood. He had spent hours in that coffee shop reading books, meeting friends, and drinking some of the best coffee in Vancouver. On cold, rainy days there were always a couple of favorite corners where he sat. After the move, Alan would get into his car and drive back to the old coffee shop. It was out of walking range, but over and over, Alan's desire led him back. Twenty years of a simple practice shaped his desire and oriented his love to the old familiar smells, the chairs and tables, and the people he recognized.

To dwell in his new neighborhood, each time Alan packs a bag with books and heads out the door he has to choose, in the face of the old desire, not to get in a car. This is a discipline in reorienting his love. The old coffee shop is a wonderful place, but to participate in the refounding of Christian life he must dwell in his neighborhood and find a new coffee shop. Practices shape what we desire. It's true for all of us. But the unraveling of our communities and the ferment of the Spirit calls us to re-school our desire in new practices.

It may sound strange and wrongheaded to propose that a refounding practice is to belong to a church community in your neighborhood. It is hard to imagine not driving five or ten miles on Sundays to be with the affinity group we meet with every Sunday, to sit in the same pew we have been in for years, or to serve on the same committee. These practices shape our desires, our habits, and, therefore, our loves. Once we are formed inside a practice, especially church practices, we find biblical or theological rationales to support them. Most of our church practices are not based in biblical or theological convictions.

Things as simple as clergy, preaching, pews, worship bands, and organs might be good in themselves, but they come from specific social contexts that we have come to love and, thus, justify as essential elements of being God's people. Our argument is that in the unraveling of modernity's wager and the Spirit's ferment breaking out before us, Christians are being called to be schooled in practices that will look quite different from those of the churches formed in modernity. What are the practices that orient our desires around becoming communities of God's people that are sign, foretaste, and witness of how God is remaking all of life? What sort of practices propel us into the fermenting and bubbling of the Spirit?

The answers begin in the recognition that God, in richness, abundance, and grace, is already acting. There is already a fermenting and bubbling of something new. As people across the West lose faith in its dominant stories, they long for alternative ways of forming common life. This longing is the prevenient work of the Spirit of Jesus. In this fermenting and bubbling lie the signs of God's agency in the unraveling. We need practices for joining with God. Such practices are those that call us out of affinity enclaves into our neighborhoods. These are practices that give us the capacities to discern in multiple expressions of the bubbling where the Spirit is gestating this resurgent hunger for God. Rather than the fear and timidity pervading our churches with their minimalist sense of what is possible, we need an imagination like the psalmist's, who looked beyond hills populated with myths and stories denying the reality of Yahweh to see the One who is the maker of heaven and earth. We need practices that refound ourselves around Paul's doxological announcement that we live in the time of the open secret: Jesus Christ is reweaving the torn, shattered fabric of creation and human community.

This story is more than a set of ideas or confessions articulated once or twice a month on a Sunday morning. It cannot be circumscribed within feelings derived from worship bands, heart-pulling dramas, stirring sermons, or video presentations. This gospel story calls for a people shaped by practices that run counter to the wager. The next chapter proposes such practices without presuming a type or model of church. There's no bias in terms of form, style, or size. Refounding gospel communities are expressed in the cathedral and around the table of a home, by ten and ten thousand people.

10

Practices for Refounding

Introduction

This chapter argues for the refounding of communities of Christian life rooted in the local. The remaking of Christian community is a much more difficult art than is often imagined. The discussion in chapter 9 about the relationship between practices and desires indicates how difficult a journey it is going to be. We do not want to pretend that this is some kind of six steps to refounding the churches. The kinds of practices proposed here are radical even as they are profoundly simple. They call for nothing less than the conversion of the Euro-tribal church's imagination and desires.

These practices propose the undoing of the churches we have constructed through the twentieth century. The existing notions of clergy and their training that have characterized Protestantism in the modern West have no future. There is no way around the fact that the proposal for refounding calls for a radical change in the practices and desires of God's people. The practices proposed here are directed toward this remaking of Christian community in the West. They are not presented as a new form of spiritual direction for individuals. They are intended to undergird the remaking of Christian social life for the sake of the societies within which we live.

Being God's People: Practicing Parish Rather than Congregation

Any discussion of refounding must return to Newbigin's seminal claim that the congregation is the hermeneutic of the gospel.[1] This is a citation

---

1. See Lesslie Newbigin, *The Gospel in a Pluralist Society* (Grand Rapids, MI: Eerdmans, 1989), chapter 18.

from *The Gospel in a Pluralist Society* that is continually referenced in terms of the mission of the church in the West. Instinctively, this language of congregation continues to make sense to most people because it is almost the only language they know to describe coming together as God's people. This is a significant challenge for the movement of refounding.

It makes sense to most Christians that if there is to be any hope of something happening in the Euro-tribal churches, it will happen at the local level, which, by default, means congregation. The shared, common life of a people together in a specific context as a community of worship and common witness will be the basis of this refounding. While there's usually little argument around this, it represents a huge challenge in terms of the habits, practices, desires, and loves that shape congregational life in modernity. Newbigin's intention in using the word *congregation* has been misunderstood and misused. He introduces it toward the end of *The Gospel in Pluralist Society* to propose that the primary witness and explanation of God's refounding all creation in Jesus Christ is the presence of a people who practice gospel life in the place where they live. But, in our context, the use of the word *congregation* confuses Newbigin's intention and obscures what is involved in the refounding because of its sociocultural use across the modern West. Any refounding will need either to depart from the language of congregation or significantly redefine it.

Newbigin's statement raises important interpretive questions. What does it mean to form communities of God's people in modernity, where the conviction is that life can be lived well without God? How do we confront the broad reality wherein practically all God-talk is actually about the Self and its actualization? What kind of Christian community both resists modernity and cultivates an alternative story to that of the sovereign state with its promise to provide us with all the security we need? What does such a community look like in a time when the sovereign Self is conceived as the center of meaning? If globalized capitalism is the bearer of the good things in life, what is the place of such a community? A refounding of the Church requires the formation of local communities that practice a counterstory.

Such a refounding cannot be done in present forms of congregational life. Language is never simple or neutral. Words are complex pictures loaded with cultural meanings that shape how we see the world. Words used with a specific meaning in one period of time are used in another with their meaning fundamentally changed. An example is the word *network*. A generation ago, television was controlled by a series of networks (ABC, CBS, NBC in the US; BBC, ITV and SKY in the UK; CBC and CTV in Canada). These limited, monopolistic media corporations determined what people watched. Network signified control through a certain style of messaging represented in iconic personalities interpreting events and supplying meaning to their audiences. The use of network today bears very little resemblance to that earlier understanding.

Congregations

The word *congregation* is the common usage to describe a gathering of Christians. What does its usage suggest? I go to a shopping mall and congregate with strangers to whom I owe nothing. The people in the mall make no claim on my time, money, or life. One attends a concert or sports event, congregating with thousands of cheering, screaming fans. We might form emotional bonds with the people about us in our common enthusiasm, but once the game, play, or concert is over, we are strangers again with no claim on one another's lives. To congregate is to gather or assemble. When this is the primary descriptor of church, we can too easily come to see church as a gathering or an assembly where something happens, where goods are offered for consumption, or where a concert or event is performed for us.

The language of congregation fortifies a dominant perception that church is primarily a place where people gather to receive certain kinds of goods and where certain things happen. While there are components of being God's people that the language of congregation captures, it cannot bear the weight of what is involved in being a community of God's people in a context of refounding. It is, however, the primary language used today to describe the church. The idea of congregation determines our perception of being God's people, and it fails to shape not only the kind of dwelling in the local that is required for refounding, but also the kind of Christian community such dwelling demands.

The word *congregation* is used in both Old and New Testaments, where it usually refers to an assembly of Israel. But what must be understood is that there is no one-to-one parity between its use in Old and New Testaments and our current usage. The types of societies described in the scriptures knew nothing of associational cultures. They lived in close proximity to one another and were covenanted groups shaped by the primary frame of God's agency among them. The word *congregation* was also used in the fifteenth century when Benedictine reforms created congregations of monks.[2] Again, the challenge is that these sources of congregation describe forms of society that no longer exist.

The current meaning of congregation must be understood in the context of modern social forms. In this context, congregation can't bear the freight of the refounding. The challenge of finding recoverable, usable language in the refounding of the church lies in the character of modern societies and the ways in which they have totally changed the meaning of words. The word *congregation* means something different from what it did in the scriptures or fifteenth-century Europe. We need to get at this difference first, to grasp why we need to stop using the word and, second, to stop practicing the habits of being God's people embedded in the notion of congregation.

When Matthew addressed the congregation of Israel concerning Jesus, he began with a genealogy (Matt. 1:1–17). When God addressed Moses out of the burning bush, it was with, "I am the God of your father, the God of Abraham, the God of Isaac, and the God of Jacob" (Exod. 3:6). In both cases, identity was defined in terms of God's covenant and relationality with a specific group of others across generations. Within this identity lay obligations to one another that were not contractual but rooted in covenant. Identity, role, and purpose were located within these covenantal relationships of obligation.

When people congregated, they did so inside this imagination. Their identity within a community was more a "we" than a "me." It was not a social contract or personal decision to associate with certain people like themselves for as long as it was meaningful or convenient. While it has not been that long since this kind of social life existed within the wider society, it hardly exists in modern Western societies.[3] Today, our churches reflect our fundamental values as associations formed around the individual, the social contract, and the primacy of affiliation over covenant and obligation. The common self-understanding of persons in most

---

2. It occurs once in the NT (Acts 13:43), where it is a synonym for synagogue. It is not used to describe the identity or form of early Christian communities. In the Old Testament it referred to Israel as the holy people of God when they were all assembled together.

3. As we shall point out, it is present again across the West through the increasing immigration of peoples from the global South as well as in North America, our terribly slow awakening to the presence of First Nations people on whose lands we now live after hundreds of years of colonization. A critical refounding practice that will need to be taken up is how the Euro-tribal churches might learn to listen to these various peoples as gifts of grace and life, receiving from them and being midwifed by them back into lives of covenant and accountability.

Protestant congregations is a reflexivity shaped by a search for a congregation that fits our style, meets our children's needs, or provides the kind of experiences that augment and expand our spirituality and growth.

Low commitment and low levels of belonging characterize associational societies. Congregating is a voluntary act, a brief contract for a season that carries little or no obligation to the others who also happen to be congregating in that specific place at that moment in time. This is why it became easy, in the latter half of the twentieth century, to create congregations that were, for all intents and purposes, full-service shopping malls or concert halls. Clergy were formed by this imagination. They have been trained to lead associational communities of individuals who establish social contracts to congregate for a period of time then disperse.

The Euro-tribal churches cannot be refounded around this imagination. The bubbling and fermenting of the Spirit requires something far different. It calls for a deep dwelling in the local over a long period of time that involves schooling in new practices. This schooling needs new language and new imagination.

Refounding and the Parish

Some words have not yet been so thoroughly colonized by the contractual, associational imagination of modernity, even if their meanings have become weak, lost, or truncated. *Parish* is one such word.[4] It is an important refounding word. Originally, it wasn't a religious or church word, but a political word designating a certain kind of organized territory. That meaning can still be detected in the way, for example, Louisiana is divided into parishes. The term has to do with where people dwell; it is about one's living space, one's neighborhood. Originally, it described the place where people dwelt with others and, often, among people who were not like them. It carries the sense of place where one sojourns with neighbors.

We are not proposing parish as a refounding word in the sense of the current usage as an ecclesiastical division within a denominational structure, although even that language still carries with it the sense of

---

4. There are now movements that seek to reframe church life within this notion of *parish*. See, for example, Paul Sparks, Tim Soerens, and Dwight Friesen, *The New Parish* (Downers Grove, IL: InterVarsityPress, 2014), as well as the "New Parish Conference" held yearly by *Together in Mission* in Birmingham, UK. Without using the language of *parish*, Christopher Smith and John Pattison's *Slow Church: Cultivating Community in the Patient Way of Jesus* (Downers Grove, IL: IVP Books, 2014) makes the same argument. For a reflective study of the development and meaning of the idea of *parish*, see Andrew Rumsey, *Parish: An Anglican Theology of Place* (London: SCM Press, 2017).

a geographical place of belonging. In Anglicanism and Catholicism, a diocese is divided into parishes, and a collection of proximate parishes is known as a deanery. In its current usage, however, parish has become largely an administrative structure within an overall organizational framework. What is lost in this organizational and administrative usage is this more substantive understanding as the place where a people dwell and worship. In fact, the majority of members of most current parish churches do not live in the parish and do not know the people in the community around the church building. Most members drive in from somewhere else and their clergy, shamefully, are in the same situation, driving into the parish just like someone drives to their job across town. Parish churches in modernity function as congregations, which is a sad commentary on the depth of commodification within the Euro-tribal churches. It's not only that the automobile determines the ways of being God's people but that, like almost all other jobs in consumer capitalism, clergy placement is an issue of a job assignment that has no bearing on the actual place to which clergy are assigned. Too many Protestant congregations are an agglomeration, a congregating of affinity and ethnically based groups whose members drive distances to be with one another without any sense of the communities they either drive out of or into to meet with one another.

In the midst of this modern colonization, church as parish offers a picture of the minimum requisite for refounding. Communities of God's people, at a most basic level, become parishes, not congregations. This means churches are comprised of Christians living in the same geographical neighborhood. They are communities of people who dwell together in a small geographical area. Refounding requires the recovery of the parish as a beginning point.

To state it as simply as possible: parish means that the church community to which I belong is one that lies within the bounds of my neighborhood. We practice being God's people together as we live in and among the people of our neighborhood and community. If God's Spirit is already ahead of us in the bubbling and fermenting, then it becomes essential to be a people of God who learn to dwell in our neighborhoods. Without this dwelling there can be no discerning together the work of the Spirit in the bubbling. The recovery of parish is essential.

The radical nature of this proposal suggests the extent to which the Euro-tribal churches have ceased to comprehend the nature of gospel life and the competing desires that struggle for ascendancy in our troubled time.

The wager of modernity is characterized by the desire to assert and fulfill one's self in terms of personal identity with its freedom to choose what one consumes. Current forms of congregational life support and deepen these desires, making God useful to one's ends. A refounding church is guided by desires that challenge the current desire of state, capital, and Self. As Augustine emphasized, the church is to be the primary public form of human community as it worships and dwells with the people among whom it lives. Today, this has to mean parish, not congregation.

If the church, in the language of Newbigin, has the vocation of being the sign, witness, and foretaste of where all creation is moving—if it is to be the "hermeneutic of the gospel"[5]—it can't do that within current associational forms of congregational life built around affinity and individual identity. The practices of refounding invite parish in an imaginative not administrative sense. Amid a growing recognition of the critical need to reweave the fabric of social life in the West,[6] the Christian story has become faint and weak because it has lost touch with the agency of God in the local, everyday life of neighborhoods. The fact that some can argue that in a networked world of dispersed life the old notions of neighborhood are irrelevant is testimony to the depth of colonization and the deep misunderstanding of Christian practices. Within this fundamental refounding practice of the parish there are then a series of other practices that continue to deepen a community's life in the local, direct their common desires toward discerning God's reality in the local, and open them to all those dwelling with them in the local.

Communities of God's People Formed around the Daily Office

Some practices of the parish call on us to build personal rhythms that, when practiced as a norm within the community, form a way of life that gets expressed in its context. One of these is a practice that has long informed Christian life: the Daily Office. The Office is comprised of specific times each day when Christians turn aside from whatever they are doing to engage in a brief period of prayer, scripture, and liturgy. It continually reminds us that God is the primary agent and maker of our lives and of our world. It is a practice that provides the basis for being a people

---

5. Newbigin, *Gospel in a Pluralist Society*, chapter 18.
6. See, for example, William T. Cavanaugh, *Church as Field Hospital: The Church's Engagement with a Wounded World* (Grand Rapids: Eerdmans, 2016), Luke Bretherton, *Christianity & Contemporary Politics* (Malden, MA: Wiley-Blackwell, 2010), and Nicholas Sagovsky and Peter McGrail, eds., *Together for the Common Good* (London: SCM Press, 2015).

who are listening for God's presence and discerning God's actions. The act of stopping to wait before God in prayer and scripture orients our lives around an agency radically different from modernity's wager. The Daily Office forms us in the conviction that this is God's world and we are God's people. In keeping the Office, we are telling one another that the future of the world, the shaping of a common good, and the discernment of life in liminal spaces are dependent upon our awakening to God's actions in the world.

The Office is foundational to our awakening. There are numerous examples of how the Office is kept across Christian traditions. The Northumbria Community, for example, begins its Morning Office in this way:

> In the name of the Father, and of the Son,
> and the Holy Spirit. Amen
>
> **Opening sentences**
> One thing I have asked of the Lord,
> this is what I seek:
> that I may dwell in the house of the Lord
> all the days of my life;
> to behold the beauty of the Lord
> and to seek Him in His temple.
>
> . . .
>
> **Declaration of faith**
> To whom shall we go?
> You have the words of eternal life,
> and we have believed and have come to know
> that You are the Holy One of God,[7]

In reciting these words at the beginning of each day, our imagination is oriented in a particular direction. We confess, with thousands of others, our desire for God's ordering. This kind of liturgy expresses the intention to have our whole self formed by God's life. Such an intention comes from the recognition that here is the only place where one finds the source of hope for oneself and the world. It is a confession, which, when recited each day, becomes a revolutionary counternarrative to modernity's wager.

---

7. See https://www.northumbriacommunity.org/offices/morning-prayer.

A simple, yet difficult step in the refounding lies in recognizing the need to practice the Daily Office. The Office doesn't have a grand goal. It doesn't have the appearance of a strategy for remaking the world and, therefore, may not appeal to those who still need power and control. There are no statistical measurements, no dashboards, for assessing progress or success. Practicing the Office involves laying down the need for such markers. It is about living in liminal space with trust and hope. The Office is the basis for and precursor to the practice of discernment, which is about attending to God's agency in our everyday lives. Whether in a huge church or at a table gathering, we propose that this practice become a central rhythm of life and of belonging.

Being communities of God's people in local contexts—parishes—is an essential refounding practice. What does this mean in deeply individualistic cultures? We have said that it means being communities of God's people in the places where we live—in our neighborhoods. Overall, this means letting go of congregations that are drive-in affinity groups and becoming people of God in the places where we dwell.[8] In these communities we invite one another to be shaped by the simple practice of the Daily Office.

Practicing Stability: Inhabiting the Local[9]

The practices proposed here are intended to be simple, ordinary activities that reconnect us to the everyday rhythms of our neighborhood and community. At the same time, it would be wrong not to recognize they are demanding and counterintuitive. They represent a way of life largely lost to Christians in the modern West. The refounding is about ordinary life rerooted in the local. It's not about heroics or extraordinary people who single-handedly save the world. These practices are not about some Star Trek–like journey of "going where none have gone before." Such

---

8. We know that those who live in rural contexts need to do some driving, but the principle is the same—where do we join together as a worshiping community connected to the place where we dwell and engaged with all of God's people rather than affinity and tribal groups?

9. In naming this practice, we are well aware of the massive barriers to this stability. In North America and the UK, migrants and new peoples from across the world find themselves in increasingly vulnerable situations where they don't have the ability to choose stability no matter how much they might long for this sense of place after so much displacement. If those who are not migrants and immigrants in a strange land fail to recognize this, this practice of stability can become another elitist choice that only the rich and powerful can choose, a luxury of the white Euro-tribals in the land. This would be a tragedy of immense proportions. In this context, see chapter 11 below where we engage this question of the migrant and the refounding of the Church.

romantic ideals are for the movies, but not the refounding of the Church. The practices we are proposing go in the opposite direction: invested in the local, shaped by the ordinary, and formed in neighborhoods.[10] Along with being in the parish and being shaped by the Daily Office, there are other practices that will shape this refounding.

Stability is about the decision to embrace the vocation of remaining in one place and choosing not to move about from place to place. It is rooted in a long Christian tradition. This practice calls us to a radical counter-narrative to the ways of modern life that keep insisting people overcome any claims to places of stability and permanence. Refounding requires a commitment to stability in the local. Global capitalism and the technological revolutions propose that since we now have digital interconnectivity with others, across the street and around the world, our relationships are not primarily in the local. The local is old-fashioned and not progressive. But numerous observers contest these claims. They argue that, in fact, we are captive to a life that is producing the opposite of belonging and connectivity.

Marc Dunkelman in *Vanishing Neighborhoods* argues that the net result of both capitalism and technology is a diminution of belonging, public space, and the intermediary social structures of neighborhoods. Michael Harris in *The End of Absence* chronicles the loss of the ability in many of the emerging generations to live in those spaces of absence so essential for creativity and the formation of social imagination.[11] William Cavanagh in *Church as Field Hospital* writes: "We talk of the 'global economy' increasing interaction among people, but the reality is of increasing detachment from the material world and from each other." Graham Ward in *The Politics of Discipleship* makes much the same point when he states that the "Internet itself is a vehicle for radical displacement and transportation. . . . [I]n the face of the Internet, the physical body is just a node in an infinitely extensive matrix."[12]

---

10. There are so many excellent materials being produced today around this question of practices in ordinary life. Within the bubbling and fermenting of the Spirit among us we are being gifted with the stories of how everyday people are practicing the parish in their own contexts. Of the many books there are some wonderful recent ones that are worth a lot of attention. See, for example, Tish Harrison Warren, *The Liturgy of the Ordinary: Sacred Practices in Everyday Life* (Downers Grove, IL: InterVarsity Press, 2016).

11. Michael Harris, *The End of Absence: Reclaiming What We've Lost in a World of Constant Connection* (New York: Penguin/Current, 2014). Harris rightly suggests that living "in the real maelstrom of change, however, means blindness. But this much we know: Just as every technology is an invitation to enhance some part of our lives, it's also, necessarily, an invitation to be drawn away from something else" (21).

12. Cavanagh, *Church as Field Hospital*, 52, and Graham Ward, *The Politics of Discipleship*:

The deeper crisis is that we seem, like those in Plato's cave, to be caught inside the wager to the extent that there appears to be no alternatives. There is an inevitability in people. We know something is radically amiss, but what is there to do? "Progress is inevitable" seems to be the confession that must be confronted with a different understanding of how life is formed. This is part of the missiological challenge for the Euro-tribal churches. In this narrative of the inevitability of modern progress lies a profound loss of the sense that our situation is one that demands we, as Christians, demonstrate another way of human thriving shaped around God's ordering and agency. It still appears that when the Euro-tribal churches look up unto the hills, they see the inevitability of modern progress within which all they can do is make a God useful or an ameliorating spiritual resource.

God has been domesticated as a servant to a way of life that has lost any sense of dwelling together across differences in the local. Stability, or the practice of remaining, is not some optional form of life for the uber-Christian. It is not a weird, inappropriate demand of religious zealots out of touch with the real world. It is the way that makes possible the rediscovery of how to discern and respond to God's agency. In the absence of stability, we lose a proper sense of human agency because we increasingly feel ourselves captive in a nexus of forces over which we feel we have no control. When we look up to the hills, it is with the sense that there is nothing but the inevitabilities of a technological, globalized modernity and its wager. The practice of stability is the place from which we see our situation and discover ways of shaping a common life in the local. The practice of stability provides us with a place from which to see, listen to, and dwell with the people around us.

But stability is not the current situation of the churches. Embodied in us—in our thoughts, physical habits, muscles and sinews, and coursing through our blood—are narratives that tell us that stability is naive, and out of touch with a globalized, networked world where place is irrelevant and impractical. The stories and habits embodied in us precede and shape our rational knowledge. Our most significant stories, moments, and experiences dwell in our bodies—literally, in our bones, sinews, muscles, nerves, and organs. Our bodies carry, express, and recapitulate our habituated practices and beliefs about who we are and how we are to act in the world. This means we are not hopelessly caught in a nexus shaped by

---

Becoming Postmaterial Citizens (Grand Rapids, MI: Baker, 2009), 100–104.

the powers of modernity's wager. We have God-given capacities to take on new practices that can transform how we are embodied in the world and, therefore, our picture of how the world works, of what's important and how we act. The practice of stability is one such revolutionary action that within a local gathering of God's people—a parish—can refound the Church and life in the West.

Guest More Than Host

The refounding of the Euro-tribal churches must recognize that these communities have been shaped in narratives of dominance and power, but they cannot grasp the meaning of this fermenting within their status and places of power. The practices of life in the parish, stability, and the Daily Office create the conditions for another practice—learning to become guests rather than hosts.

Such a refounding practice requires explanation. If God is fermenting another future, then we need to understand how God is an agent in the world. This section takes a specific angle to this question. The way God is present and, therefore, loves the world, is expressed in the Old Testament in Israel, God's people, and, in the New Testament, in Jesus. The Euro-tribal churches can discern the practice of love in relationality in the ways God is acting in Israel and Jesus. In both instances God is agent in the form of guest rather than host. By any measure, this is a radical reorientation for most Euro-tribal churches that will amount to their refounding.

In a recent interview, George Steiner, regarded as one of the most significant Jewish thinkers of the twentieth century, described something of what it meant to be Israel, God's people, in the Old Testament.[13] In describing Israel's character, Steiner points out that "for several thousand years, approximately from the time of the fall of the First Temple in Jerusalem, Jews did not have the wherewithal to mistreat, or torture, or expropriate anyone or anything in the world."[14] Israel was without power or control. It was not to behave like the other nations for whom power and control were primary ends. He then describes the present-day reality for Israel as a nation like other nations, contesting for power and control. In this he reflects on what he perceives to be the Jews' mission. His

---

13. Laure Adler, "You Really Need to Read This Terrific Interview with George Steiner," *Forward*, March 27, 2017, http://forward.com/culture/367139/you-really-need-to-read-this-terrific-interview-with-george-steiner.
14. Adler, "You Really Need to Read."

understanding comes directly from an understanding of Israel as God's people in the Old Testament:

> But today, Israel must necessarily . . . behave like the rest of so-called normal humanity. . . . [B]y becoming a people like others, the Israelis have forfeited that nobility. . . . Israel is a nation between nations, armed to the teeth. And when I look from the top of a wall at the long line of Palestinian workers trying to get to their daily jobs, standing in blistering heat, I can't help seeing the humiliation of those human beings in that line, and I say to myself, "It's too high a price to pay." To which Israel answers: "Be quiet, you fool! Come here! Live with us! Share our danger! We are the only country that will welcome your children if they have to flee. So what right do you have to be so morally superior?" And I have no response. To be able to respond, I would have to be there, on the street corner, giving my absurd spiel, living the daily risks there. Because I don't do that, I can only explain what I perceive as the Jew's mission: to be the guest of humanity. And, even more paradoxical (which places the mark of Cain on my forehead), what convinced me was something Heidegger said: "We are the guests of life." . . . [W]hoever is thrown into life has a duty to that life, an obligation to behave as a guest. . . . In the Diaspora, I believe the task of the Jew is to learn to be the guest of other men and women.[15]

Is it the case that the primary way God is present in the world is as a guest? The Euro-tribal churches who have drunk so deeply of power and control must become guests in their own places to discern the Spirit's ferment. To be a guest is not to be in control, not to be in power, and not to determine the terms and conditions of what it means to dwell in a place. In the unravelling of the dominant Western narrative, a primary element of the refounding requires our becoming guests rather than hosts. This is a radical turning of tables; it is a profound change of imagination. What does it mean for a community of God's people in a local context to ask the question of how they become guests in their own communities, seeing their neighbors as hosts? This posture of not being in power

---

15. Adler, "You Really Need to Read."

or the place of control, of being a guest in another's place, enabled Israel to discern the purposes of God in the world. It was as they broke that relationship and asked for a king of their own that they lost the capacity to love the other.

The New Testament descriptions of God coming among us in Jesus bring us into the same reality: Jesus's being with us was as a guest without power. In the birth narratives this vulnerable God is present. In the kenotic hymn of Philippians[16] is the recognition that he who was equal with God did not take equality as something to be grasped and held onto, but Jesus let go of that power coming all the way down to the vulnerable place, not just of guest but slave. What kind of Euro-tribal Christian communities can be the sign, witness, and foretaste of God's fermenting in the West? They will be communities that are becoming guests rather than hosts in their own contexts in order to discern the ferment of the Spirit in the other.

We propose that a continuing practice of local communities of God's people in the parish is to ask one another how they can act as guests in their community. How do we dwell in our communities in such a way that the other is host? How do we dwell with the other in ways that we no longer have the power or control? This practice cannot be picked up from a book or weekend training; it's not a five-step package. On the contrary, it is an awkward journey of learning on the way where the pathways and outcomes are unclear. Our conviction is that we cannot discern the Spirit's fermenting without embracing the posture of guest, not host.

The question of what all this might look like is not easily answered because it is a journey into a counterintuitive world. A recent book by the American author Suzy Hansen helps us to see how we might go about this journey. She writes her book from Turkey, where she lived for some nine years. Her title tells a significant part of her story. She is an American living in a post-American world in another country. She is struggling with the question of identity: what do we become when the identity that has guided us for so long and appeared as the primary truth about the world is upended by the other? She describes her book in this way:

> This is a book about an American living abroad in the era of American decline. When Baldwin, or Ernest Hemmingway, or Henry James wrote from abroad, America had not yet achieved its full imperial status. The 1960s ushered in a golden era of global intellectual

---

16. Philippians 2:5–11.

engagement—Robert Stone, Gore Vidal, Paul Theroux, Joan Didion, Mary McCarthy, among others—but even that would paradoxically fade in the age of globalization. As America, growing more powerful abroad, turned more inward-looking at home, so, too, did the going-abroad books, so many of them celebrating the transformation of one's self, and extolling a conception of the world as a meditation and wellness center for the spiritually challenged. . . . I would never have admitted it, or thought to say it, but looking back, I know that deep in my consciousness I thought that America was at the end of some evolutionary spectrum of civilization, and everyone else was trying to catch up. . . . How could I, as an American, understand a foreign people, when unconsciously I did not extend the most basic faith to other people that I extended to myself? This was a limitation that was beyond racism, beyond prejudice, and beyond ignorance. This was a kind of nationalism so insidious that I had not known to call it nationalism; this was self-delusion so complete that I could not see where it began and ended, could not root it out or destroy it.[17]

In a parallel way, Euro-tribal churches, still live in this consciousness of Western Christian nationalism even while living increasingly in a post-Christian world. It is this delusion that continually embeds us in the assumption that we are hosts—that we have the answers and the fixes. What does this mean when Western Christians, much like Americans, have lived for several centuries in a world in which they were the empire, a world that is effectively over?

As a young adult, Suzy won a scholarship that took her from her home in New York to Istanbul, Turkey. Ostensibly, the two-year scholarship allowed her to understand more deeply the life and effects of Islam among the people of Turkey. She had grown up in a small, conservative, mostly white small town on the Jersey shore. She had developed, as a budding, educated journalist, a standard progressive, liberal outlook on life and on America's role in the world. When she settled into a journalism job in New York, she never imagined she would leave that city or her role as a reporter. Her story is not primarily about Turkey or Islam, but her

17. Suzy Hansen, *Notes on a Foreign Country: An American Abroad in a Post-American World* (New York: Farrar, Straus and Giroux, 2017), 21–23.

own awakening as an American in what she describes as a post-American world. Her discoveries involving self-awareness and the narratives that had formed her provide important insights for Euro-tribal Christians coming to understand how they view themselves and how they actually engage a post-Christian world. This kind of awakening lies behind the recognition that only by becoming guests, rather than hosts, can we Euro-tribals discern the fermenting of God among us.

Hansen, as an American with her given stories of American generosity and American exceptionalism, was awakening to the reality that the world outside North America had altogether different narratives about America and who she was as an American. These narratives of the other represented nothing she had ever encountered or imagined growing up on the Jersey shore, being educated in university, or working as a journalist in New York. They turned her world upside down. Her recognition was that there "simply was no way for the American mind, perhaps the *white* American mind, to imagine these things."[18] African American theologian Willie Jennings makes much the same point in his book *The Christian Imagination*[19] when he describes the European–North American Christian imagination as one that makes all other stories a subset of its own. It was the Euro-tribal, North American white story that became the central story through which all other stories were read, which meant that it became practically impossible for the Euro-tribals to hear the stories of others for themselves. In every encounter the Euro-tribal assumes the role of host; everyone else assumes the role of the guest who needs to fit into the primary Euro-tribal story.

Hansen points to this reality when, after a period of time in a Turkish town where there had been a mining disaster, she realized that "the resilience of my own innocence was the most terrifying" as she sought to hear the stories of these Turkish villagers. She came into this situation with her own strong sense of what life should look like, but in Turkey, as she encountered the other in their own contexts, she "began to feel that the entire foundation of my consciousness was a lie."[20] As an American shaped inside a narrative of exceptionalism, she was slowly coming to terms with a different reality which involved a

---

18. Hansen, *Notes on a Foreign Country*, 19 (italics in original).
19. Willie James Jennings, *Christian Imagination* (New Haven, CT: Yale University Press, 2010).
20. Hansen, *Notes on a Foreign Country*, 11.

newly recognized ignorance. . . . You cannot grow up in the second half of the twentieth century in the United States of America and live abroad in the twenty-first and not feel it all the time. . . . [I]f I learned something about America in Turkey—or later in Egypt or Greece or Afghanistan or Iran—it felt like disruption. My brain experienced the acquisition of such knowledge like a cavity filling: something drilled out, something shoved in, and afterward, a persistent, dull ache and a tooth that would never be the same.[21]

The pervasive story of Euro-tribal Christians is that we have been hosts within an empire. The embedded practices of empire still lie deep in our imagination. It crops up all the time in discussions about the Church, in the means of "reaching" specific "people groups," in figuring out how to meet the needs of people or help those not like us. All of this is the language of a host who assumes empire or, at least, the ownership of the reigning story. It is these perspectives and their habits that remain the primary ways in which the Euro-tribals continue to try and comprehend the unraveling. But the challenge is to embrace practices in which we become guests not hosts, which means letting go of the stories of primacy and the assumption that we have the answers and the means for fixing and meeting the needs of others so they can fit better into our story. We must seek ways of becoming like Jesus, who chose to be guest rather than host.

Hansen continually returns to the writing of James Baldwin, the African American writer who lived in Istanbul for several years and wrote about his experience as a black man living in America at the midpoint of the last century. He was keenly aware, in an almost prophetic way, that Western hegemony and empire was coming to an end and that this ending was a hard journey for white people. When one has been used to having all reality defined from one's own perspective, the result is confusion, anger, and reaction. This is the situation of the Euro-tribal churches. The loss of place requires a radical revision of identity. Hansen's story also illustrates the difficulty of this practice in our parish contexts. She was able to listen and discern a ferment because she left her own world; she stepped outside her own tribal story and learned to dwell, as a guest, with the other. This is what made all the difference in the world. But such an awakening does not require this uprooting from the stability of place and the

---

21. Hansen, *Notes on a Foreign Country*, 15.

normativeness of the parish. As two authors living on two different continents in two very different cities (Vancouver and Birmingham), we live in neighborhood contexts comprised of the nations. We no longer need to travel far afield to dwell among the other. The invitation, right in our own neighborhoods, is first, to see the other among us and, second, to cultivate a posture of becoming a host to these peoples in order to listen to them and enter their worlds.

Practices That Resist the Privatization of Christian Life

The gospel forms a people who are more than, and other than, the sum total of the individuals who happen to choose a particular worship location. It is Newbigin's framing that lies beneath so much of what has been written in this book, namely, that it is, finally, a community of God's people practicing Christian life together who are the hermeneutic of the gospel. At one level this is an obvious statement. But, at this moment, it is also a crisis of imagination that is undermining the very possibility of refounding. Multiple books are being published describing the emergence of new categories of Christians who are simply finished with the forms of Euro-tribal churches they have experienced, whether in established traditions or in new forms of house and simple church. There is now a deeply settled sense that the forms of church present across the West are irrelevant to the levels of unraveling that people are experiencing.[22]

There is an emerging conviction that an individual's personal spiritual life no longer requires the discipline or commitment to established agencies of common life; religion can now be found in everyday life without the need for the rituals and liturgies of a Christian community. It is not that there is an either-or dichotomy between religious life within the bounds of a Christian community and religious life experienced in everyday life, but that there is an increasing option for the later and an abandoning of the former. Everywhere we turn across North America and Europe, we encounter people across generations who are opting out of what they call "church" and trying to find religious life in other ways.

It was a painful moment for one of us to listen to a friend who is on the

---

22. There are a plethora of books and magazine articles on these issues. Any Google check of the words *Dones* and *Gones* will take one into the conversations around these issues. Some examples would be: Elizabeth Drescher, *Choosing Our Religion: The Spiritual Lives of America's Nones* (Oxford: Oxford University Press, 2016), and Linda A. Mercadante, *Belief Without Borders: Inside the Minds of the Spiritual but Not Religious* (Oxford: Oxford University Press, 2014).

staff of a denomination describe how increasingly she comes away from her Sunday worship more tired and discouraged than when she entered. She is now questioning why she is expending that kind of energy. She is in her early fifties and has been a faithful worshiper all her life. It is not that she is going through some crisis of faith. She is finding her church to be an exhausting experience disconnected from her everyday life. Attending church is killing her desire to worship. She doesn't represent a trickle, some small proportion of people. She is representative of a huge number of Christians.

To engage the refounding challenge before us, there must be a commitment to resisting this understandable response to the irrelevance of Euro-tribal life. The practices outlined above offer some ways of engaging in this resistance, but they are all empty of their power to refound without the concrete reality of Christians who are being formed as a worshiping people coming together faithfully to practice a liturgical life. This common life in the parish will involve practices that have formed the church since its beginning. Some of the most critical are:

Eucharistic Community as the Embodiment of God's Agency

Worship and sacrament are central practices that form us as a people of place, stability, and fidelity. The primary demonstration of the confession that Jesus is Lord is a local community of God's people regularly formed and fed around a eucharistic life. It is not possible to sustain life in the parish without a deep commitment to being a community formed around the Eucharist.[23] This means a commitment to the practice of gathering together to celebrate a liturgy of the Eucharist. To say this does not imply the need for a certain kind of building, or even an ordained minister or priest, but that there has to be a regular gathering of Christians in a local area to celebrate and be continually formed around the Eucharist.

What we are pressing into here, in terms of practice, are two things. First, the centrality of the Eucharist in the refounding of the church. This is locating the primary activity of worship not in the Reformation emphasis on the preached Word, wherein the primary focus has become the trained clergyperson who preaches and everything else is either preparation for or response to the preaching event. While recognizing the

---

23. Various communities and traditions use different language. For some this focal liturgy of the church is called the "communion" or the "Lord's Supper." The point here is not to debate this language but to emphasize its centrality in forming a people of God in a parish.

place of the Word in worship, which is already centrally established in most Eucharistic liturgies, our argument is that the notions of Word and preaching that have come from the traditions of the European reformations will not create the possibility of refounding. The Eucharistic liturgies present the best possibility for a worship of refounding today. Second, despite all the good reasons given and experienced regarding the irrelevance of current worship life in the face of the unraveling of the West, there can be no refounding apart from the regular coming together of Christians around the Eucharistic liturgy. This is not the to argue for or present a framing of this central liturgy.

Perhaps one of the most eloquent descriptions of this in terms of the life of the church and its missiological witness within a community is present in the writing of an Orthodox theologian, Alexander Schmemann.[24] His argument is that we cannot participate in our worlds as God's people, as guests in the name of Jesus, without participating in the life of a eucharistic community that is shaped around a common table, the symbols of bread and wine, and the recognition that we can only be encountered by God through this gathering as a community wrought by this table. This is the table that continually draws us back into the confession that our life together is utterly dependent upon the God who meets us in Jesus Christ, that this is God's world not ours to make and impose, and that this God who meets us in the table is present for the life of the world. Without this regular practice together, we have no witness to the world and we lose the understanding of how God is the primary agent among us. The refounding requires a eucharistic people gathering together regularly in the parish.

Common Meals

A way to resist the privatization of life is the practice of a common meal together as a community of God's people. Quite simply, rather than setting up church programs based on age and interest, or putting people in house groups—as has been the practice of many churches since the late 1960s—why not encourage people in the parish regularly to plan a common meal together in one another's homes? The common meal was once a core element of Christian life in the early life of the church. There is a history to be explored as to why and how the life of people of God was redirected from a common meal gathering to one of formal "service" led by professional,

---

24. Alexander Schmemann, *For the Life of the World: Sacraments and Orthodoxy* (Crestwood, NY: St. Vladimir's Seminary Press, 1988).

"ordained" leaders. The common meal gathers people across generations around a table where they can share their life in the community. This is already starting to happen in many places as Christians in local communities gather to share a meal, practice dwelling in the Word around a text, and then interact around the question, "Where have you seen God at work in the neighborhood this week?" These simple practices invite prayer and discernment about how to join with what they see God doing. Others gather around the meal, practice dwelling, and then do a simple form of the Ignatian Examen by sharing responses to simple questions: Where have you been aware of God's presence this week? What have been moments of gratitude? What are places where you seek prayer? There are myriad ways of shaping a common meal that will regularly form a group of God's people in a common life together in the neighborhood.

Hospitality

We've written a lot about the growing levels of isolation, fear, and anxiety in our communities. One of the simplest practices for local communities of God's people to engage their neighborhoods is to practice hospitality. This is, fundamentally, about slowing down our lives to connect with those who live in our community. It can be done in so many different ways, from sitting with someone in the coffee shop to being attentive to who is in line at the store to inviting them over for some front porch conversation or a simple meal together. In all our experience of working with Protestant churches, we know that these simple practices have become daunting challenges to most Christians because they have lost touch with their communities. But testing some simple ways of becoming hospitable in the neighborhood is a way of reorienting our energies and attentions away from our affinity groups and church programs and back into local communities and neighborhoods.

It will be in regaining this simple practice of dwelling with our neighbor that we will learn how to discern what God is doing. That is part of the meaning of Acts 16 where Paul and his companions receive their Macedonian call from a man.[25] They head off to Philippi where they must have searched out a synagogue because that was the normal way they went about their work as God's agents. They had a map and a plan for how

---

25. The text in Acts 16 is careful to point out that Paul's vision came from a "man" of Macedonia because the direction of Luke's story is the encounter with Lydia. In the context of the time, it would have been a radically disorienting experience for these disciples to have imagined that God's Spirit was directing them to a woman, albeit, a Gentile woman even though she was a God-fearer.

they would go about being God's agents, but the Spirit was still preventing them from practicing their normal life. There was no synagogue. As a result, on the Sabbath they went outside the gate of Philippi in the expectation they would find a "place of prayer," which meant a gathering of Jewish men. They didn't find that either. Outside the gate they, somehow, engaged a group of women and, in the midst of them, Lydia. There is a great deal going on in this story, but one of the primary points is that the hospitality of Lydia broke the patterns and habits of the disciples. In this disruptive encounter, they discovered a way of being church that had not been in the imagination of Paul and his group. Their understanding and practice of church emerged from them accepting her hospitality and, therein, discovering a whole other way of being God's people. Hospitality is an essential practice of the refounding. It is about an attitude of generosity, of sharing, and of being with the other. Hospitality is a practice that represents the gift of God among the people of our community. It is about a table that is generously shared, that invites generous conversation and a generous opening of one to another. This kind of hospitality opens the space for our hearing what God is doing in our communities.

Public Good as Eschatological Practice

When institutions with established narratives unravel—whether nations, churches, or family structures—it is always the weakest that suffer the most. For the affluent and those who have made good in the prevailing environment, the effects of suffering are, at first, hidden away in statistics or distant neighborhoods. After a time, the suffering becomes more public, so that those who still have privilege and power begin to feel anxious about the situation. They fear that their rights, their lifestyles, and their prerogatives might be undermined. In these situations of unraveling when things are slowly falling apart, people retreat into affinity groups. They limit their attention to media that undergird their views of the world. They see God as a bulwark where they can retreat into their varied forms of personal spirituality that address their need for wellness and mindfulness, whether it be the embrace of ecstatic religious experience or the words of a leader who promises to make all things right again.

We fear that this is the reality now before the West: the terrible temptation to scapegoat the foreigner, the other, the migrant, and the reactive need to have some assurance that our particular form of the truth is the truth without exception. We are in the midst of a night that is being shaped by a deep fear and reaction to the other among us, a race to the lifeboats to protect our own. Such directions are antithetical to the refounding to which the Spirit is calling the Euro-tribal churches.

The truth of the matter is that the golden age experienced by the churches of North America immediately following the wars of the last century is over. The brief recovery of an attachment to faith experienced across Europe in the 1950s has similarly vanished. There is an unbearable truth that is still being processed within the collective consciousness of the Euro-tribal churches that their place of privilege was never going to be an eternal gift given by God to a special people; it was never secure and could never last. It existed for a brief period of time in the second half of the twentieth century and it is now doomed to disappear. This is one reason why we argue that a critical refounding practice for these churches is discovering how to act as guests in our own land. It is also why we have continually argued that the only hopeful location for this refounding is in the local and the everyday. As difficult and counterintuitive as it might appear now, the local and the everyday is the theater within which we will learn to improvise the refounding of social life in the West and, in so doing, refound the forms of gathered and lived life of God's people.

The practices we have outlined to this point are the concrete forms of refounding. For many they will appear utopian and unreasonable; for others they will seem utterly unattainable from where we stand right now. There will be a sigh of anxiety or denial from the ordained because these practices will undo their roles. The challenge here is that globalization and consumer capitalism have become such all-pervasive stories among us that we have forgotten that there have been and can be alternative stories. This is one of the core challenges that these five practices seek to address. They are forms of protest and disorientation that create the possibility for Euro-tribal Christians to awaken from modernity's wager, from the hills and high places of Mammon, to see that there is, truly and hopefully, another way to live, another way to be God's people for the sake of the world.

This leads us, for the moment, to a final practice: the call, in our parishes, to seek the common good of all who dwell with us in the local. Such a way of being in the parish as God's people is an anticipatory practice of the eschatological future God is already forming for the whole creation. Seeking the common good is not about a new way of giving charity. It is, in the words of Isaiah, the anticipation of the day when all the mountains and valleys of inequality and injustice will be levelled. This is why it is impossible to remain in our single-affinity, drive-to congregations as centers of our Christian life. Only by rooting in the parish can we turn our attention, humbly, as guests and hosts, to embracing and joining with the multiple others in our community to participate with them in seeking the common good of all who dwell with us.

This is not an act of the privileged seeking to help and meet the needs of the not-so-privileged. It is about partnering to discover together across community the message made clear to us in Jeremiah 29 where the prophet articulates God's purposes for the exiles in Babylon. They are to seek the good of the city to which they have been sent. They are to root down in that place, build houses, plant gardens, have children, and not try to return to some other place or time that seems to them more akin to who they are. As God's people in the parish, we do not re-create what we have done in congregations by creating localized affinity groups huddling together around our own in-house rituals. We work with others to discern how we seek the good of the neighborhood. Walter Brueggemann makes the connections between these practices we have outlined: "Eucharist is the great extravagant drama of the way in which the gospel of abundance overrides the claim of scarcity and invites to the common good. There is no doubt that the church's Eucharist is, among other things, simply a replay of the manna narrative in the book of Exodus."[26] He describes this practice of common good in these words:

> Persons living in a *system of anxiety and fear*—and con-
> sequently greed—have no time or energy for the common
> good. Defining anxiety focuses total attention on the self
> at the expense of the common good. *An immense act of
> generosity* is required in order to break the death grip
> of the system of fear, anxiety, and greed. Those who are
> immersed in such immense gifts of generosity are able to
> get their minds off themselves and can be *about the work
> of the neighborhood.* Children of such enormous abun-
> dance are able to receive new commandments that are
> about the well-being of the neighbor and not about the
> entitlements of the self.[27]

In the early part of twenty-first century, a congregation in Birmingham, England, sought to change what had been a fairly nonexistent conversation with their immediate community. Their first step was to engage the

---

26. Walter Brueggemann, *Journey to the Common Good* (Louisville, KY: Westminster John Knox Press, 2010), 32.
27. Brueggemann, *Journey*, 25–27.

neighborhood in a simple question. "What are the most important needs of this community?" represented the core ingredient of the conversation that a research team initiated. The community was fairly affluent and not an obviously needy community. The results were slightly surprising. The top two responses expressed the desire for a children's playground and a location to drink coffee or tea so that they could talk to friends and neighbors. It was not necessarily what the church had expected to hear, but since they had land available, they led the community in a fund-raising exercise to provide a children's playground and, shortly afterward, to open a community café adjacent to it. These were their first missional acts as a congregation that went beyond "Come to our worship services."

It was important that the conversation sought the discernment of the community. The congregation would almost certainly not have thought about a playground or a gathering place for coffee. Providing the space and also the leadership to raise the funds, but not actually giving the total gift to the community, transformed what had been a rather impoverished conversation with the community.

There are not many resources that help us to develop an imagination about engagement in the common good. Recently that has begun to change with the publication in the UK of Together for the Common Good.[28] In the foreword of this imaginative collection of essays, Rabbi Julia Neuberger offers an important distinction concerning what is involved in seeking the common good. She asks how people of God can engage the growing disparities of our communities now characterized by work with little pay, increased isolation in a social media world, and the inability to experience place as other than a stopping off space in the endless movement of a globalized capitalism. Her response is critical. She invites us to turn away from the modern, bourgeoisie notion of charity, which has become the dominant form of Christian response across middle-class congregations with their fund drives, volunteer charities, and means of helping people or meeting needs. Rather than being shaped by charity, she proposes the Old Testament practice of *tzedakah*, which means the ways in which God's ways of acting are to even up and reset the balance—a permanent form of the Jubilee year. Seeking the common good is about participating in the resetting of the balance in our communities, something we can only participate in if we dwell—and, thereby, worship—where we live.

---

28. Sagovsky and McGrail, *Together for the Common Good.*

Some elements of practicing the common good are helpfully laid out in this book. One simple act is finding out what is already happening in one's community. One of us discovered that the simple act of regularly going to the same barbershop on the main street immediately puts us in touch with the crosscurrents of life there. What we need to disavow is the abstractive actions of study documents or demographic surveys as the entry point into listening to what is happening. By giving time weekly to have conversations with different people in the community, we begin to get a picture of what is happening.

Anna Rowlands describes other continuing ways of attending to the common good. She proposes that as we engage with people in our community, we practice ways of speaking and acting that unite rather than separate people. This is especially important when we are talking with others about or across differences of tribes, or about immigrants and new people in our communities. Further, as we dwell in community, we must practice awareness about how we respond to differing groups of people. What are the inner verbal and bodily responses that have become default patterns? Are there ways we have stopped seeing some people? Do we value certain people or groups over others? Are there people whom we have deemed nonessential or a nuisance? As we practice this kind of attentiveness, what can emerge for communities of Christians in the neighborhood are possibilities for discerning new ways of building relationship with others in the community.

What are some ways to start developing and testing these new forms of social life across difference with those we might have written out of our lives? How, connecting with other practices, do we learn to be with them as guests rather than hosts, listening to their stories and entering their table lives? How is our practice and understanding of the Eucharistic gathering deepened, and how does this deepening offer us the possibility of discerning what God is up to in a fresh way? It will be in living out these practices and questions that it becomes possible to ask the eschatological question about who we are as a local community of God's people in this neighborhood. We can start to ask: given the new relationalities we are sharing in this community, given how we are hearing God around the Eucharist, what, therefore, in the light of God's eschatological future, is the common good for this community now?

We have outlined six practices of Christian life for the refounding of Euro-tribal churches as the sign, witness, and foretaste of God's future for all creation. These are practices that both require such a refounding and provide a pathway along which to discover such a refounding. There is no pretense that these are easy. Others will, undoubtedly, want to offer a parallel or different set of practices. So be it! The more we wrestle with these questions, the more we will learn from each other and, hopefully, discern the patterns of faithful life the Spirit is now gestating in the ferment.

We have written a great deal about the local. While we believe the local is the critical center for refounding, we do not want to offer one more magic bullet or solution-driven tactic that can, again, be programed into another fix for the churches, or the theme for the next round of conferences. The passion that drives us is radically different from that. We are convinced that in this night in which we dwell, God is at work. There is, already, in all kinds of ways among ordinary people in everyday life, hidden away from all the workshops and programs emanating from gurus and church structures, a fermenting and bubbling that invites our joining. This fermenting and bubbling of God's eschatological future is down on the ground in the local. That is why we see the local as so important: it is here that God is unraveling modernity's wager and gestating the future. Our instincts are that, as Euro-tribals, these six practices might guide us along a trail that will never be clear. Our conviction is also that, as Euro-tribals, we will never be able to embrace these practices or discern the road without a humble readiness to become learners and guests among those other Christians that God is bringing among us today—the migrant, the immigrant, the people who were in this land long before the colonizations began.

11

Missionaries in the New West

> Christianity should enjoy a worldwide boom in the new
> century, but the vast majority of believers will be neither
> white nor European, nor Euro-American.[1]

Introduction

A renewed concern for the common good has taken place against a
backdrop of huge change both in society and in the shape of the world
Church. In terms of society, the period immediately following the fall
of the Berlin Wall and the collapse of Communism in Eastern Europe,
sometimes called the "end of history," signaled a shift from industrial
societies to a globalized world of information technology. That shift has
interacted with late modernity's turn toward hyperindividualism.

At the same time, the world Church has been changing its shape in a
number of epoch-making ways. Philip Jenkins has spoken of the emergence of the "next Christendom" as a way of describing the shrinking of
the Church in the Northern Hemisphere and the rise of the Church in
the Southern Hemisphere. That southwards march, further complicated
by the resurgence of the Church in countries like Russia and by the emergence of an indigenous Church in Communist China, signals a shift in
what constitutes the mainstream of Christianity. As far as the Church is
concerned, these enormous social and religious developments are relatively recent, rapid, and little foreseen.

To some extent the surprise concerning these changes flowed from the
fact that theology was still dominated by Western minds and yet, on the
ground, something remarkable took place in the 1960s and 1970s outside

---

1. Philip Jenkins, *The Next Christendom: The Coming of Global Christianity* (Oxford: Oxford
University Press, 2007), 2.

of the Western world that was largely unnoticed and undocumented by the West. Christianity began to grow in many parts of Africa, South America, and Asia. This growth was all the more unexpected because, with some notable exceptions, it followed years of very little expansion in many of the same nations despite the presence of missionary activity for more than a hundred years. It is documented in some detail by Jenkins in *The Next Christendom.*

Many of the nations that adopted Christianity as the majority religion in their societies were also among the fastest growing nations on earth in terms of population growth. Nigeria, for example, which has seen astonishing growth among Christians of many denominations, is expected to be the third largest nation on earth in population terms by 2050, with only India and China having larger populations. Jenkins comments that the decision to hold the 1998 World Council of Churches Eighth Assembly in Harare, Zimbabwe, was symbolic of the journey of Christianity from the Northern Hemisphere to the Southern Hemisphere.[2] The First Assembly was in Amsterdam in 1948. In fact, an earlier recognition of the shift in the center of gravity of Christianity was noticeable in the holding of the Fifth Assembly in Nairobi in 1975.

Despite a very detailed examination of the growth of Christianity, Jenkins offers little in the way of an explanation for the facts that he so effectively presents. In some ways that is not surprising because at a local or national level, the factors that have led to this astonishing renewal of Christianity are complex and particular. Clearly the factors that have led to the growth of Christianity in China are markedly different than those in Nigeria or Brazil.

Three Themes from Growth Outside the West

"Revival" Movements

Despite the complexity of the picture, three major themes emerge that have a resonance for the situation of the Western world. First, those who have experienced Christianity in these vibrant growing churches of the South speak of a revival, not dissimilar in character and spirituality from the kind of revivals that so impacted the Great Britain and the United States in the eighteenth and nineteenth century. Sometimes the word *revival* is consciously evoked by such events as the vast tent meetings the

---

2. Jenkins, *Next Christendom*, 4.

evangelist Reinhard Bonke held in many African nations over the last few decades, or the huge December prayer meetings, sometimes numbering more than four million people, outside of Lagos.[3] But even when revival is not explicitly referenced, the spiritual temperature, confidence, verve, and energy that is present in these young churches clearly reflects the kind of growth that one associates with a revival culture and experience.

Pentecostal and "New Church" Movements

The twentieth century—and particularly the second half of the twentieth century—has seen the astonishing growth of the Pentecostal movement. In 1906 during a revival meeting in the church of William Seymour, an African American pastor based in Los Angeles, the Azusa Street out-pouring, as it is sometimes called, gave rise to the fastest-growing religious movement of all time. Arguably, it is also the fastest-growing movement of any kind, whether religious or social. Pentecostalism forms a much larger percentage of the total Christian community outside of the traditional heartlands of Christendom. It is estimated that 80 percent of Protestant Christianity in East Asia can be described as Pentecostal in some sense. Most scholars speak of three waves of Pentecostal expansion. Classical Pentecostalism, which gave rise to new and independent Pentecostal denominations, represented the only form of Pentecostal organizational expression until the 1950s. At that time, Pentecostalism was understood by sociologists of religion as the religion of the poor.[4] However, the second wave of Pentecostal expression in the charismatic movement broke that stereotype. At the same time, the Classical Pentecostal churches were experiencing rapid social mobility in common with earlier "redemption and lift" revival movements. The entry of the charismatic form of Pentecostalism into the historic denominations widened the impact of the Pentecostal movement, not just in the West where these movements began but, as we have commented, most notably in the various missionary churches in Africa, Asia, and South America.

The third wave (and the fourth, fifth, and more waves) was sometimes called, rather unimaginatively, "The New Churches." In common with

---

3. Jenkins, *Next Christendom*, 74. Jenkins refers to an event organized by the Redeemed Christian Church of God in 1998 numbering up to 2 million people but events since then have been much larger.
4. The Scandinavian scholar Nils Bloch-Hoell was the first to advance the theory of Pentecostalism as a religion of the poor in his book on the Pentecostal movement published in 1964. Nils Bloch-Hoell, *The Pentecostal Movement: Its Origin, Development and Distinctive Character* (Oslo: Universitetforlaget, 1964).

the first two waves of Pentecostal growth, these various expressions of Pentecostal encounter also quickly impacted the global South more than the Northern Hemisphere from which they sprang.

Allied to the southern growth of Pentecostalism were a whole variety of independent churches ranging from the Zionist churches in South Africa to the Kimbanguist movement in the Congo and the Celestial Church of Christ in West Africa. Although these very different churches were not technically part of the Pentecostal movement, they shared a number of commonalities, in particular their ability to contextualize Christianity and especially to recognize and develop indigenous leadership.

End of Colonialism

That brings us to the third factor in the growth of Christianity in the former mission fields outside of the Western world. The end of the colonial period, beginning in the 1950s, led to a significant reappraisal of missionary activity on the part of mainline Western churches, many of whom were all too conscious of the beginnings of their own decline. A loss of confidence at home was accompanied by a reassessment of mission abroad. The consequence of this reappraisal of a movement that originated at the beginning of the nineteenth century was the gradual withdrawal of missionaries from the mission field and the transfer of power and responsibility to national Christians. This process was inevitably complex and contentious. In some cases the mission boards were worried that national Christians were not ready for leadership. To a certain extent there were many cases where this was true because the dead hand of missionary leadership had resulted in many of the best leaders departing to begin independent churches. But in other cases it was a significant underestimation of what nationals could achieve.

The transfer of leadership led to a process of contextualization that was uncomfortable for many missionaries. To enter the First Presbyterian Church in Accra, Ghana, is to be transported into a scene straight from rural Surrey, United Kingdom. The church spire, the pews, the pipe organ, and that unique smell of floor polish that seems to belong only to ancient church buildings, create a slightly surreal experience. However, once the worship begins, replete with drums, clapping, shouting, and dancing, you can be sure that you are indeed in Africa. According to local Christians, all of these manifestations of African worship were forbidden by earlier generations of missionaries. Small wonder that so many competent African leaders departed to form their own churches. One might note a similar "departure" is well underway in the established Euro-tribal churches across Europe and North America.

An attitude of superiority toward the Christianity of the Southern Hemisphere still exists among the very Western leaders who lost confidence in the missionary enterprise. Philip Jenkins reports the comments of the retired Episcopalian Bishop Spong of Newark, New Jersey, in response to some decisions that he did not like at a Lambeth Conference in 1998 in this way:

> Spong professed himself appalled by the whole tone of Third World spirituality, with its "religious extremism": "I never expected to see the Anglican Communion, which prides itself on the place of reason in faith, descend to this level of irrational Pentecostal hysteria."[5]

Bishop Spong was correct in identifying African Anglicanism as imbued with a Pentecostal flavor and indeed the same could be said of almost all denominations in the Southern Hemisphere. The Roman Catholic Church has been deeply influenced by this remarkable spiritual movement in many of the lands in the global South. But perhaps more importantly for Spong and for all Christian leaders in the former mission-sending nations in the West, leadership in the emerging mission churches was now firmly in the hands of national Christians who now had the ability to translate Christianity in cultural terms in ways that even the most sensitive missionaries had usually failed to accomplish. The former ecclesial power of the mission-sending churches, reinforced with mission dollars and the implied threat of their withdrawal, was no longer enough to transmit the modernity of the West, so eagerly embraced by leaders like Spong. Cultural imperialism has been decisively ended and, in the process, the churches of the South have been freed to find their own voice, vitality, and vigorous growth.

Connected Themes

There is a curious connection between these three themes. The modern missionary movement sprang from a revival movement birthed in the "enthusiasm" of the Holiness movement.[6] This movement grew in par-

---

5. Jenkins, *Next Christendom*, 121.
6. The story is told that when John Wesley, then a member of the Church of England, approached Bishop Butler of Bristol to recount Wesley's conversion, the bishop responded, "Enthusiasm, sir, is a horrid thing; a very horrid thing indeed."

allel on both sides of the Atlantic from the middle of the eighteenth century, gathering strength throughout the nineteenth century.

The first missionaries expected to see the same kind of revival springing from a Holiness spirituality that had first impelled them to become missionaries. Although long delayed, that same seed finally came to life in the form of a revival spirituality in Africa, Asia, and Latin America. Pentecostalism as a movement was also a child of that same Holiness tradition and experience that emerged in Britain and North America with the preaching of people like John Wesley.

These early missionaries, in seeking converts, expected that some would emerge as leaders who would eventually take responsibility for their own churches and, possibly, come to the West as missionaries alongside the original sending churches. The originator of the modern Western missionary movement, William Carey (1761–1834), described this expectation as "the blessed reflex." Harvey Kwiyani, an African missiologist now teaching in Liverpool, United Kingdom, describes the origins of the early missionary movement, especially in terms of the involvement of lay people in mission:

> As these developments were taking place, there was expressed some expectation of the "blessed reflex" or "reflexive action," that at some time in the future Christians from the rest of the world would invigorate Western Christianity in one way or another. The term *blessed reflex* itself was used in the early nineteenth century by Western missionary leaders to talk about the hope of a time when the "sending" churches of the West would be challenged and renewed by the churches then springing up in Latin America, Africa, and Asia. The Western missionaries believed that the impulse that energized the missionary movement of the nineteenth century would create a reflex action in the rest of the world that would, in return, benefit the Western sending churches.[7]

It might have seemed incredulous to Christians living in the West at the beginning of the twentieth century that Carey and others should have entertained such ideas. First, because Christianity had undergone a dramatic transformation during the nineteenth century in terms of its

---

7. Harvey C. Kwiyani, *Sent Forth: African Missionary Work in the West* (Maryknoll, NY: Orbis Books, 2014), 70f.

numerical growth and societal position, and second because there was little sign of dramatic growth on the various mission fields after a hundred years of missionary activity. But that is to forget the somewhat perilous state of Christianity all across the Western world at the end of the eighteenth century. It is also to ignore the vision of the earliest missionaries for a church that would genuinely reflect the various cultures of the world without a presupposition of any Western superiority either in terms of culture or faith.

The Possibility for the Refounding of the Churches in the West

The potential for a much delayed "blessed reflex" has arrived at the end of the twentieth century and the beginning of the twenty-first century, nearly two hundred years after the first stirrings of the modern Protestant missionary movement. The arrival of this possibility has not arisen because of a simple missionary strategy, but more because of the convergence of two realities, one religious and one socioeconomic, that intermingle in interesting ways. We will look only at the first of these stories: the religious narrative.

It has become an accepted fact among missiologists that mission has ceased to be from the West to the rest and is now from everywhere to everywhere.[8] That is partly because of the growth of world Christianity so that there is now a viable Christian presence, seen or unseen, in almost every group of people on earth. But it is also because, at its heart, Christianity is a missionary faith. To fail to engage in evangelism, to spread the faith to new areas of the world, to see the conversion of new people groups, seems like an aberration of the very essence of the faith. Mission, to the West, is partly an overflowing of this revival and missionary zeal, a determination to see the whole world as legitimately an extension of the mission field on one's doorstep.

As part of that zeal for mission in general, many Christians from Asia, Africa, and Latin America express a sense of a debt of gratitude to be repaid. Many Africans are conscious of the cost of missions in terms of the early death of significant numbers of missionaries and their families, not so much as a result of persecution, though that sometimes happened, but

---

8. See, for example, Samuel Escobar, *The New Global Mission: The Gospel from Everywhere to Everyone* (Downers Grove, IL: InterVarsity Press, 2006), and Michael Nazir-Ali, *From Everywhere to Everywhere* (Eugene, OR: Wipf and Stock, 2009).

more from disease. Yet, no matter how many died, more still came—an astonishing commitment. Koreans often speak with gratitude of the death by persecution of the first missionary to bring the Bible to the attention of the Korean people. It is a complex story involving a Welsh Presbyterian Christian, Robert Jermain Thomas, who worked as a missionary for the London Missionary Society and distributed Bibles on behalf of the Scottish Bible Society. He was martyred at the age of twenty-seven, giving his last Bible to his executioner. His career was not an obvious success, but Korean Christians cite his endeavors as marking the beginning of the Protestant, and predominantly Presbyterian, churches in Korea. Koreans send many missionaries abroad and have a special and heartfelt commitment to mission among the declining Presbyterian community of Wales.

It is one thing to have a "debt of gratitude"; it is quite another to have the means to repay it. The Korean churches, partly because of their numerical growth, but also because of the growth of the Korean economy, have been able to fund missionary enterprises on a significant scale. It is also the case that some of the historic denominations, through their global communions or through missionary organizations such as the Council for World Mission or the Anglican's Church Missionary Society (CMS), have been able to engage in what is sometimes called, rather unattractively, "reverse mission." The idea of going forward in mission by being in reverse seems rather clumsy as a description, but the core idea of mission returning to the west is clear.

A number of African denominations and significant individual congregations have also been able to resource strategic missionary enterprises in the West. Some, such as the Church of Pentecost, the Celestial Church of Christ, and the Church of the Seraphim and Cherubim, are largely concerned for the provision of pastoral care for their members that have immigrated to the West. Others, such as Nairobi Chapel and the Christian Redeemed Church of God, have very clear and particular strategies through which to fulfill their sense of missionary calling. The leaders of Nairobi Chapel, a large and relatively wealthy congregation in suburban Nairobi, have a clear strategy at work in the West, not to establish more Nairobi Chapels but rather to seek out partnerships so that genuinely multinational congregations might emerge. Their approach is both thoughtful and imaginative. The Redeemed Christian Church of God has an entirely different strategy, which can be seen in Point Five of their mission statement: "We will plant churches within five minutes walking distance in every city and town of developing countries and within five minutes driving distance in every city and town of developed countries."[9] In order to accomplish this goal, the RCCG does not offer funds so much as a "parish" or a recognized territory to the ministers they either ordain or recognize.

Individual Christians from other lands, feeling a call to missions in the West are often required to be rather more entrepreneurial than those in the historic denominations or larger African ecclesial systems. Many arrive as individuals seeking to evangelize, church plant, or both. They come mostly from a strong sense of personal call that sometimes arrives in the form of visions, direction from a valued mentor or spiritual parent, or simply because of a growing internal conviction. One such person told me that he had come to Birmingham, England, because he had received a vision with the name Birmingham and England clearly present. He had to look Birmingham up on a map because he had never heard of it and did not know exactly where it was. There are many such individual accounts of call followed by action.

Large numbers of those who arrive in the West, thinking of themselves as Christians, have almost certainly not come to engage in mission but to earn a living. They are what is rather unattractively called "economic immigrants." That could mean business people sometimes employed by international companies, professionals such as doctors and other workers in the health system, or manual workers simply looking to improve their standard of living. The accounts of many of these immigrants are that they began to take their sometimes rather nominal faith much more seriously when they arrived in the West. They had imagined the West to be thoroughly Christian in its make-up and their experience of the reality was something of a rude awakening. What happened to the West, they wonder, and what might happen to my children?

In seeking solace and meaning in the welcoming company of fellow believers in congregations full of people that they understand, enjoying the living worship, and believing that their children now have a sound moral environment, their attention turns to God's purpose in bringing them to Western climes. It was not the invisible hand of the market that brought them, they conclude, but the ever-present purpose of God. The idea of mission to the West brings meaning to their sojourn.

However Christians arrive, whether as part of a sending body, as individual Christian missionary entrepreneurs, or as "economic migrants,"

---

9. Mandate of the Redeemed Christian Church of God, http://www.rccguk.church/mandate/.

regardless of ethnicity or denominational affiliation, the result is usually the same. Christians from other lands end up gathering a group of existing Christians from their home country and another ethnically specific congregation is created. Large numbers of such congregations have been launched. Since 1990, the most vigorous of the African denominations, the RCCG, has planted close to one thousand congregations in the United Kingdom. Although the sometimes transitory reality of black majority churches (BMCs) makes it hard to be certain about numbers, it is likely that at any particular time, around three thousand such churches are present in the UK.

The hope and rationale of the evangelists is also often the same. The argument runs that it is necessary to build a solid base of worshippers from which to evangelize. Once that has happened, then it might be possible to reach out to the surrounding white population with the message of the gospel. When such congregations fail to reach out to the indigenous white British population, or even when some white people are converted but decline to remain in such a setting, preferring to worship in white majority churches, the conclusion is drawn that white people are either resistant to the gospel or that they are fundamentally racist in their attitude toward black leadership, or both. One can have some sympathy with such a view. Harvey Kwiyani writes:

> For most people in the West, even well-wishing Christian leaders, to be black is still to be suspicious. To be an African black is even worse. Afe Adogame once noted that in many Western cities, a typical African on the street is first greeted with suspicion, perceived as a criminal, refugee, or a beggar until proved otherwise. Unfortunately, a typical African Christian in a Western church is also greeted with suspicion, perceived as a potential criminal, refugee, or beggar, and more often than not, he or she cannot prove otherwise. Many African Christians in the West have to face this reality every day in their lives and ministries.[10]

That is not to say that all BMC churches have an initial missionary focus. There are many, especially those who worship in the language most commonly used in their homeland, who recognize white English people are very unlikely to learn Amharic or the Congolese version of French in

---

10. Kwiyani, *Sent Forth*, 175f.

order to be part of their fellowship. More importantly, the pastoral life of such churches is usually directed toward addressing the very specific needs of recently arrived nationals, some of whom may be living as illegal immigrants.

The Challenge of Forming Intercultural/Multiracial Churches

Behind the immediacy of the necessity to meet the obvious practical needs of their flock, there exists a deeper desire to address the urgent missionary situation of the West. That desire is partly driven by a deep sadness generated by the declining indigenous churches they see around them. How could mission-sending nations have come to this? There is also a more pressing agenda for these churches—especially but not exclusively, those who worship in languages from outside the West: they are aware that unless something changes, they will not be able to retain the loyalty of their own children and grandchildren, many of whom do not identify with their parents' culture and language. They observe this, in the UK, for example, in what happened to West Indian congregations comprised of immigrants from the 1950s onward. These congregations were shaped around the needs of the immigrants who did not feel welcome or at home in white majority churches. These once vibrant churches are now in severe decline, having failed to retain their children and grandchildren born and raised in Britain. The outcome of this complex story serves as a warning to the newer churches that do not wish to become single-generation churches.

Beyond these warning signs, they are also aware that their children have evangelistic opportunities among their friends in the very diverse, multi-ethnic communities of the changing European and North American cities that were not open to first-generation immigrants. Having given their initial energy to planting among their own peoples, some of these communities are looking for support, advice, and partnership from indigenous Christians. But how likely is it that such partnerships might be forged? This is not and will not be an easy matter. Kwiyani observes:

> To imagine God's Spirit at work in this cultural diversity, and to imagine that God might be up to something in bringing Christians from around the world to Western cities, requires that we confront racial discrimination in all its forms. It is the single most significant factor in the missionary impact of non-Westerners—or minority

> Christians—in the West. The main problem, at least
> to me, is that racial discrimination seems to have been
> accepted as a reality against which we can do nothing.[11]

He is absolutely correct to acknowledge the seriousness of racism. There
are, however, other factors at work in forging genuinely intercultural and
interracial partnerships in mission in the West.

Euro-Tribal Churches Embracing the Gift of Immigrant Christians

First, it needs to be acknowledged that the astonishing revival fueling the
growth of the Christian church around the world since the latter half of
the twentieth century is an amazing gift for which we, in the West, ought
to be profoundly grateful. Moreover, to witness the arrival of literally millions of Christians in the West—the "blessed reflex"—finally arriving, is
an immense gift of the Spirit and a precious partnership that is lost at our
peril. Many of the largest churches in most Western European cities are
now composed of Christians from other continents. Some of these congregations form vibrant communities of faith and action. Alongside the
undoubted racism in the West, which needs to be confronted, there is the
challenge, beyond embracing of the other, to build multi/cross-cultural
local communities of God's people. This is a huge task—an inherently
difficult undertaking. How might we of the once majority, Euro-tribal
churches see the presence of so many Christians from other continents?
Harvey Kwiyani, again, helps us to see a way forward. He suggests that
African Christianity, for example, has the potential to invigorate British
Christianity:

> Even though many of these non-Western churches are
> patronized by non-Westerners almost exclusively and are
> unable to evangelize beyond their own fellow nationals,
> there is evidence that their presence is actually invigo-
> rating British Christianity. For instance, whenever people
> talk about Christianity in London today, they have to
> consider African and Caribbean Christians, both in Pen-
> tecostal churches and in mainline churches. Indeed, a
> small number of Christians in the city account for over
> 60% of church attendance. . . . It is the argument of this

---

11. Kwiyani, *Sent Forth*, 177.

> short book that a proper engagement between British
> and the non-Western Christians resident in Britain will
> enrich British Christianity and hopefully, help it redis-
> cover its missional impulses to re-evangelize Britain.[12]

This is a wonderful aspiration and one which the authors of this book would like to see extended beyond the shores of Britain, to every Western land. However, there are some serious issues that need to be faced if that is to become possible.

For Kwiyani the three most common responses to cultural diversity in the West are:

First, the hope of assimilation has been a dominant theme in the USA. The idea is that the newcomer will quickly learn English and become American in culture and aspiration. The "old country" can be remembered in terms of heritage and fond memory, but, as a living entity, is abandoned at the border.

Second, the idea of cultural pluralism is that the dominant culture determines the "norm," but other cultures coexist alongside the mainstream culture provided that they agree to accept that the dominant culture determines what takes place in the public domain.

Third, the concept of multiculturalism seeks to create a society where many cultures exist side-by-side, enriching one another without one culture exercising dominance. Eventually, it is presumed, what emerges is a new common culture created by and shared by all.

Within the Christian world, a degree of assimilation has taken place and Christians from other lands are making a contribution to the various British and North American church systems they have joined. It is questionable whether they are able to bring the best of their cultural contribution to such an arrangement. The dominant culture creates the framework in which that contribution might be made. More often than not, the results are long periods of cultural pluralism expressed as ethnic segregation. Christians exist in silos, recognizing one another but divided not just by race, language, and culture but also by denominational structures. We are not proposing such assimilation. On the contrary, we are arguing that these movements of immigrant Christians into the West is

---

12. Harvey Kwiyani, *Mission-Shaped Church in a Multicultural World* (Cambridge: Grove Books, 2017), 14.

the work of the Spirit inviting the once dominant churches of the West to discover the way of refounding by becoming the "guest" of the migrant, the other, rather than the "host."

The idea of multiculturalism's ability to function in a broader society where competing narratives are potentially on a collision course is questionable. Multiculturalism is itself part of a narrative that could be described as somewhat insidious because it pretends to be neutral ground. But to do so, it functionally denies the spaces for surfacing the history of ideas, values, and convictions that lead to its own creation. A Christian multiculturalism is, however, a much more fecund possibility. It invites the possibility of not just connecting creatively with Christians from the "blessed reflex," but creating a much more dynamic community of God's people in the West that moves beyond siloed people groups. This is not an easy path to tread. Again, Kwiyani:

> I have heard countless people say that British Christians prayed for revival, and they could not recognize it when it came because it was black. This is very true. Revival has come, but it looks like the messy migration of African and Caribbean Christians to Britain and thus it does not look like revival at all.[13]

How will Western Christians recognize and connect with the extraordinary gift of the Spirit in the refounding of the Church, namely, that millions of Christians are being brought to the West? The reality of migration is hardly new. Christian immigration to escape persecution, find places of socioeconomic safety, and to worship freely is deeply embedded in Christian imagination. Whether it be the settlement of Huguenots in Britain or the Puritans in New England, stories of immigration have been normative for Christian life. Perhaps the more recent form of what we have called Euro-tribal churches in North America serving specific ethnicities and expanding largely to meet the needs of those ethnic communities is more aberration than norm? In similar fashion, most denominations in the UK have had strong ethnic and class identification until very recently. The unraveling of these narratives and the Spirit's ferment in the migration movements that bring the "other" to the West is, potentially, the most critical gift of refounding the Spirit is giving to the churches.

---

13. Kwiyani, *Mission-Shaped Church*, 19f.

We are not advocating contentment with a cultural pluralism that means existing side-by-side, meeting the needs of specific tribal communities, even if there are a variety of ethnic congregations within a single denomination. This imagination fails to see what the Spirit wants to call into being with the gift of immigrant communities to the West. At the moment, the immigrants joining existing congregations and denominations help boosts numbers, increase financial resources, and assist the need for ministerial candidates specifically and leadership more generally. But this very process of assimilation buries the very gift that immigrant Christians bring to the West. It's not about assimilation to the existing sociocultural systems of the existent denominations; it's about their being with and becoming a "guest"—which is the opposite of assimilation.

This gift of the immigrant Christian might best be expressed by using a different lens. Many of the authors' students are from Africa, Asia, and Latin America.[14] It is fascinating to listen to their accounts of God encounters in their daily lives. A Brazilian female student explained how God seemed to turn up so often in her daily life: "When I leave home each morning I take hold of the conviction that nothing that happens to me each day, that even my meetings with people, my conversations, nothing is purely a chance event. My expectation is that God is involved in every conversation and my spiritual ear is attuned to what God is doing and saying." This lens of awareness and sensitivity to the Spirit of God is refreshing and, of course, many of us in Western churches can admit it is conspicuously absent in our daily lives. How much have we potentially missed of God's present activity?

As we listen carefully to the lived experience of our brothers and sisters from other continents, it becomes obvious that God's agency is primary for them. Yet strangely their activity in mission can easily look at though they place an emphasis on human action and so it's easy to conclude that their perspective is not really different from that of Western Christians. But it is one thing for us to be active on God's behalf with God as a distant spectator and quite another to see God as primary with us as believers being graciously invited into God's activity. Our struggle is transformed from total responsibility for mission and the rescuing of the Church toward one in which we are constantly seeking to join with God's presence in mission.

---

14. These students are from ForMission College, Birmingham, UK.

If the refounding of the Euro-tribal churches is not about new strategies but a transformed attentiveness to God's agency in our contexts, then it will be as we join with these immigrant Christians to learn from them about how to know and expect God in these ways. This refounding experience calls upon us to become guests rather than hosts in discerning the agency of God.

The lens that is still central in the Christian life of so many Christians from other continents still sees God as the primary agent in life. It is the activity of God that provides the lens through which life is viewed. The idea that God is simply useful for our own needs or that we are left to our own actions as Christians is understood as a form of madness from which one might need to be delivered. The centrality of the primacy of God is something so far from the everyday experience of Western Christians that it is a difficult reality to convey. Perhaps only in the telling of stories can one gain a sense of what is at stake here.

One such story comes from Smyrna—not the Smyrna that is one of the seven churches in Revelation, but Smyrna, Tennessee. For a long time the congregation of All Saints Episcopal Church in Smyrna had experienced a decline in numbers and an aging of its members. They were struggling financially. Then they learned there was a crack in the foundation that ran the length of the building. Symbolically and practically it looked as though there was no choice but to close the church. The witness of All Saints was going to come at an end. The bishop had sent an able priest there to assess the situation. The Rev. Michael Spurlock loved the people, but could see no alternative but closure. Then he received an unexpected phone call from a refugee from the Karen people who lived in Myanmar who announced that he and his fellow refugees were Anglicans and had been trying to find a Church of England congregation. They found it difficult to locate Church of England buildings in America and then discovered that Episcopalians were part of the same communion. His inquiries led him to Michael Spurlock. Could the church help him and his fellow refugees—a group of around sixty people?

Spurlock wanted to know what they needed and found the answer was just about everything. They needed money, employment, housing, help in dealing with filling out government forms, and, most of all, a community for worship. It was not an easy request for a cash-starved congregation at the point of closure to address. Michael Spurlock phoned the bishop, who was very quick to advise him to help in whatever ways were needed. That was the appropriate Christian response and the diocese would help. The congregation was struggling for cash, but it did have sixty-four acres of land. Michael wondered what the Karen refugees could offer in response. The answer was that they were farmers and were especially gifted at market gardening. In particular, they knew how to grow some Asian vegetables that could sell for a good price.

Over a period of time, the Karen people earned a living for themselves and produced enough money to solve the financial problems of the church. Their community more than doubled the size of the congregation and brought new life to the church. After a period of time, white Americans recognized that something special was happening to All Saints, something that they too wanted to be part of. The church is now growing, but not just because of the Karen refugees. They brought numbers, but more importantly they brought a new sense of the agency of God: God brought them to Smyrna, God provided for them; the primacy of their faith in God shone through. That different lens produced among the white members of the congregation a sense of the immediacy of the presence of God, of the need to place God at the center of their community life, of their dedication in seeking guidance from God, all resulted in the resurrection of All Saints. The Karen people exemplified what so many immigrants bring with them to the West: a conviction that God is alive and active. God desires us to live in community and within that community to demonstrate hospitality and generosity—the life in fact of the kingdom.

Summary

It is hard for those of us living in the West to see the extent to which the radical individualism of our culture has converted us to a way of life that has undermined faith and all too often reduced our worshipping communities to places that are intended to meet our needs. And, if we feel that a congregation is not meeting our needs, then all too often the response is to join the throng of those who explore the next great church in town. Perhaps the greatest gift of the immigrant communities in our midst is to allow us to see ourselves through their eyes. Not the eyes of judgment, but the eyes that help us grasp the extent to which our culture has evangelized us rather than the reverse. That will take a huge amount of humility on the part of Western Christians. We are not noted for such humility; we are still convinced that we are to be hosts meeting the needs and helping the other. The Spirit, in the unraveling, is creating a different space. The ferment for refounding is located in the dual invitation of the Spirit—our call to the risky space of guests and the immigrant gift of experiencing God's agency. We need to say, not "Join us and we will accept you," but rather, "Come and change us so that together, as part of a changed church, we can locate the purpose of God for our land. Give us new eyes that we might see again the kingdom."

12

Gospel and Culture:
Living between Two Ages

This final chapter was written in Advent, a time of preparation for the great festival of Christmas. The previous chapter reflected on our need for both change and humility. Meditating on those themes in Advent causes us to wonder how much has changed in the period since the 1960s and how much humility has been both necessary and experienced since then.

In the 1960s, and to some extent in the 1970s and even the 1980s, it was not uncommon for clergy, particularly in the established Church, to become frustrated at seeing churches full at Christmas, only for parishioners to disappear for the rest of the year. Occasionally, a vicar would harangue the congregation about their lack of commitment. Sometimes those remarks would be widely reported in the press. The familiar joke in the UK was that the abbreviation C of E did not mean Church of England, but Christmas and Easter.

From our present perspective it is difficult to imagine any clergyperson engaging in such a public haranguing, but it reflects the extent to which the relationship between church and the public square has changed. The expectation that we should see, or can see, our community or parish as owing a duty to the Church has evaporated. And yet, strangely, the longings for a connection with the Christian story have not disappeared but are being expressed in different forms. In the same period that vicars were metaphorically wagging their fingers at their Christmas congregations, a small group of Christians from a number of churches in the neighborhood where one of us lives gathered on Christmas Eve to sing carols on the local village green. They probably numbered no more than thirty people; some of them were my family members.

That simple act of worship became a community tradition and various customs attached themselves to the event. In recent years some five thousand people from the community have attended. No publicity has ever been issued; no great attractions are involved. An offering is taken for local charities and carols are sung to the carillon that is part of the school overlooking the green. We are in a curious period of transition, we might even say of reinvention and reimaging of the relationship between Christianity and culture. Humility and openness are vital in such a time as this.

When Paradigms Change

The temptation induced by the challenge of change is to find ways of making minimal adjustments in response. As early as the late 1950s, and certainly by the beginning of the 1960s, the church was being challenged to become more relevant to the needs of the modern age. That theme, which had been pursued through the pages of publications like *The Modern Churchman*[1] since the early part of the twentieth century, surfaced in the popular media through publications such as John Robinson's book *Honest to God.*[2]

Bishop Robinson's book hit the headlines partly because he was a bishop in the established Church, partly because he had a gift for a memorable phrase, and partly because he highlighted a central dilemma for the Church of his time. The themes and approach were to be echoed much later by Bishop Spong in the American Episcopal Church. Could the relevance and, therefore, the position of the church in society be rescued by demythologizing core elements of doctrine? Or was this simply an accommodation to the prevailing culture of the Enlightenment that paradoxically demonstrated the utter irrelevance of the Christian faith and the Church?

The position of the "modernists" or "liberals" within the historic churches was lampooned in the much later BBC comedy *Yes, Prime Minister.* In one episode, Sir Humphrey Appleby, a senior civil servant, discusses with the Prime Minister the appointment of a new bishop who is something of a "modernist":

Prime Minister: What's a modernist in the Church of England?

Sir Humphrey: Ah; well, the word *modernist* is code for nonbeliever.

Prime Minister: You mean an atheist?

---

1. *The Modern Churchman* (Oxford: Oxford-Blackwell, Liverpool University Press).
2. John A. T. Robinson, *Honest to God* (London: SCM Press, 1963).

Sir Humphrey: No, no Prime Minister. An atheist clergyman couldn't continue to draw his stipend, so when they stop believing in God they call themselves modernists.

Prime Minister: How could the Church of England suggest an atheist as bishop of Bury St Edmunds?

Sir Humphrey: The Church of England is primarily a social organization, not a religious one.

Prime Minister: Is it?

Sir Humphrey: It's part of the rich social fabric of this country. So bishops need to be the sort of chaps who speak properly, know which knife and fork to use. The sort of people one can look up to. . . . The church is run by theologians

Prime Minister: How do you mean?

Sir Humphrey: Well, theology is a device for enabling agnostics to stay within the Church.

Prime Minister: I don't want Canon Stanford. What am I to do?

Sir Humphrey: Well, you could turn both candidates down, but that would be exceptional and not advised.

Prime Minister: Even though one wants to get God out of the Church of England and the other wants to get the Queen out?

Sir Humphrey: The Queen is inseparable from the Church of England.

Prime Minister: What about God?

Sir Humphrey: I think he is what is called an optional extra.[3]

If liberal theology was likely to fail precisely because it became too closely entwined with the culture that it was called to critique, the position of those who were either more mainstream or evangelical was also to look for ways of "fixing" the problem. That fix was often expressed in terms of the search for a better program or, even worse, by reorganizing church structures to make them more efficient and, by extension, more relevant. The news that a particular church was growing and had found a way of communicating with unbelievers was often followed by an expedition to the inevitable conference or training course that followed. We could describe the embracing of programs in this simplistic way: as a tactic with which to confront change. That kind of tactic is simply the

---

3. Extract from a BBC television show found at: https://www.facebook.com/BritishComedy/videos/1967023973514898/?q=yes%20mr%20prime%20minister.

management of decline, not leadership that addresses the fundamental reality of the situation.

Very often, though not always, those initiatives came from North America. These various programs rarely found fertile soil outside of the remarkable situation and circumstances from which they sprang and almost never took root in the soil of Europe.

The Process of Refounding

It would be very easy to read the pages of this book and conclude that our fundamental message is that programs and structural change within the church are of no value. That is not the message we intend to convey. Rather we are claiming that programs and structural change are useful tools in our hands when we understand the bigger paradigm change that is taking place. In short, we cannot fix the present structures; we require a process of refounding.

But refounding takes time and we cannot simply abandon the structures we have while we discover the paradigm that is emerging but which is not yet clearly discernable. Furthermore, that which is emerging from within the ferment of change will not be clear or discernible for some time to come. That necessarily means that leadership, as compared with management, requires enormous courage in this period of transition. There are few certainties and even fewer guidebooks. Leading between paradigms is risky, uncertain, and difficult, but that is the leadership task now.

Leadership of this kind requires an understanding of the importance of symbols, hope, partnership, and experimentation. The former bishop of London Richard Chartres, who recently retired following twenty years as bishop, reflected on his period of leadership in a recent Lambeth Lecture. He began by noting that at the beginning of his time as bishop the diocese had been in decline for a long time:

> The decline in the active membership of the Church of England as a whole in the last quarter of the twentieth century was mirrored and exaggerated in London. Many of the congregations were aging and found it difficult to engage the young people who were flooding into the capital from other parts of the UK and from abroad. At the same time the disproportionate rise in London house prices made flight from the capital increasingly alluring

for many of the people who had been the backbone of the
church in the post-war period.

The parish of which I became vicar in 1984 was an extreme case study
of these general trends. St Stephen's Rochester Row in the mid-1980s had
already experienced twenty years of decline. At the beginning of the social
revolution in the 1960s, there had been about 550 members on the elec-
toral roll and an assistant staff of 6 curates and 4 nuns. There was even
a daughter church, St John's, the result of a 1950s church plant. By the
time I arrived as the Reverend Mr. Ichabod—"the glory has departed"—
there was an average Sunday attendance of 40, no assistant staff, and the
daughter church had been turned into the HQ of the London Diocesan
Fund.[4]

His desire was to arrest that decline and, if possible, to see growth take
place. He considered that to be the legitimate role of a bishop. From his
perspective, decline was not inevitable, and he did not intend to spend
his time managing it. Early on, Richard Chartres recognized that the
widespread closure of church buildings had produced a powerful visible
symbol of decline of the church:

> Buildings were seen as a burden, and it certainly remains
> true that an established but largely dis-endowed church
> carries a disproportionate share of the responsibility for
> maintaining an architectural and cultural heritage which
> regulatory bodies rightly insist belongs to the whole com-
> munity. In London the landscape is littered by churches
> in prime sites which were abandoned during these
> years—St. Paul's Essex Rd, St. Columba's Mare Street,
> Holy Trinity Mile End, and many more. Often sold to
> less careful owners, their decrepitude continues to be
> powerful propaganda for the idea that we are "at the sag-
> ging end and chapter's close" of the Church of England
> story in London.[5]

Symbols are important in signifying fundamental change. The commitment of the diocese to look for partners who could stop more church
closures by effectively replanting congregations into buildings that were

---

4. Richard Chartres, Lambeth Lecture, September 30, 2015, 1, www.archbishopofcanterbury.
org/speaking-and-writing/speeches/bishop-london-delivers-lambeth-lecture-church-growth-
capital.
5. Chartes, Lambeth Lecture, 2.

about to close was a significant indicator that change was both possible and actual. In that lecture, Bishop Chartres outlined other significant initiatives he undertook. Some related to the reorganization of structures with the intent of allowing decisions to be taken more effectively and to allow those with the appropriate gifts to be placed in key posts. The introduction of key staff, together with the location of new financial resource brought some hope to a depressing situation.

But possibly the most important contribution of the bishop flowed from an element of permission-giving to those who were engaged in effective ministry of one kind or another. Not the least of his permission-giving led to the establishment of a new training system for leaders within the diocese, a system that has now been extended to other dioceses as similar initiatives have developed elsewhere.

One consequence of what Bishop Chartres calls "vision-led" leadership, as compared with "problem-led" leadership, has been to envisage the creation of one hundred new worshipping communities within the diocese between the years of 2015 and 2020. It is likely that this goal will be achieved. It is important to acknowledge that this is not so much a "church planting program," though indeed at one level that is precisely what it is, but rather it is a consequence of something more fundamental—the decision to trust and enable the local. The processes for enabling action within the Church of England are themselves worthy of a different conversation, but for our purposes it is only necessary to note that they took place with the diocese of London.

Programs flow from an appreciation of the need for experiment around mission. They are a means of achieving an end, but the desire and vision for the end comes first. In short, you don't adopt programs to solve problems, you develop programs to express vision. In other words, there are some things that we can do. We are not helpless in the face of huge paradigm shifts in our culture. But what we do must flow from a set of imaginaries that begins with the idea that God is the agent, not us. And here we have a problem because the very declaration that there are things we can do can suggest that we are the agent and not God. The idea that we can "fix" things begins with the thinking that we are very much the agent. It is in addressing this conundrum that we are helped by the global church immigrating to the West. Our Christian brothers and sisters from other continents are certainly not passive in the cause of mission. They reflect an activism that is birthed in a deep and lived conviction that God is the agent. They may not have a plan when they arrive in the West, but they are convinced that God is already up to something and that they are called to be active participants. Discerning how to join with God begins by listening to God in prayer, in fasting, and in fervent worship. Responding to the ferment of the Spirit means making mistakes, experiencing opposition and failure, but ultimately God's purposes will prevail.

The Importance of Practices in the Discerning and Joining

Chapter 10 explored the importance of practices. The same conundrum about programs applies to the adoption of the practices that we outlined. First, we are not saying that practices are "in" and programs are "out." Second, we are not saying that adopting a pattern of spiritual practices is a kind of program. But, even more importantly, we recognize that simply requiring that people engage in certain spiritual practices is no more likely to produce a new kind of life for the people of God than assembling body parts produces a human being.

These practices are an inheritance from the riches of the past and, as such, are to be rediscovered, encountered, and adapted. They are not a rigid framework. They can only guide us in this refounding if we are hungry to discern God's agency ahead of us and we have a desire to work with them over time. Understanding the centrality of experiencing God becomes crucial in seeing how our actions flow from a strong sense that God is indeed the agent and not simply the approver of our plans from afar.

The Place of Planting

It could also be thought that this book is critical of church planting, seeing such efforts as just one more program that tries to fix what is fundamentally broken, as if more of something can somehow make it work again. While, overall, approaches to church planting are deeply flawed, the practice is not something that we are opposed to. We are not so much concerned with planting the church within an existing imagination, but with discovering forms of Christian life that join with God's ferment in the communities where we live, and the forming of new imagination about what God might be doing all across the Western world. There is no easy way to overcome this poverty of language. For the time being, we can work with that language while patiently seeking new communities of faith to develop.

In Europe there is a huge amount of church planting taking place.[6] Not only is the scale of such planting beginning to reshape what constitutes the mainstream in European church life, but sufficient numbers of historic denominations are now participating in church planting to significant effect. The Church of England, to offer one example of such a trend, has two strategic approaches to this issue. One is Fresh Expressions of Church, about which much has been written. The second is a newer initiative that flows from the appointment of a "bishop for church planting"—technically the restitution of the bishopric of Islington, gifted by the diocese of London to the Church of England nationally. This unusual development has been accompanied by a wider plan to plant "resource" churches, similar to that of Holy Trinity Brompton, though contextualized to meet local contexts. The concept is to plant at least one such resource church in every diocese with at least one bishop speaking about following the first such plant with a least three more in their diocese. There are ambitious plans to double the number of worshippers in Anglican churches over the next twenty years.

The importance of these developments is not just the issue of numbers or even the fact that initiatives on this scale were probably unthinkable even ten years ago. It is more that within this church-planting activity resides a degree of creativity and experimentation that allows the new to be birthed in a creative dialogue with the cultural paradigm that has emerged in late modernity.

Some twenty years ago, Martin Robinson wrote about "new church planting"[7] and was taken to task by those who said that the term *new* was redundant because all church plants were, by definition, new. Martin responded with the reflection that his own denomination had embarked on "old church planting" and these efforts had mostly failed. In other words, beginning churches that reflected the style, structure, and culture of existing church life without taking account of the culture that we were trying to connect with would, and did, fail. We needed to give planters considerable freedom to contextualize, to plant churches that were indeed *new*, or—to use another term—*fresh* expressions of church.

---

6. One initiative has drawn together primarily younger leaders from at least thirty European nations in a series of learning conferences and learning communities. It is called simply the National Church Planting process. It is not a program so much as a mutual coaching system, which leverages leadership from the different nations by exchanging stories and offering a certain amount of teaching.

7. Martin Robinson and Stuart Christine, *Planting Tomorrow's Churches Today: A Comphrensive Handbook* (Speldhurst, Kent: Monarch, 1992).

That is precisely what we can see happening in many situations, particularly in Europe. While it is difficult to describe in abstract terms what this means, the following is one example of what this might look like in a setting where the church is disconnected from the life of those who often care deeply that it exists but can't easily see that it has much to say to their lives. This is not just a question of relevance. The disconnect goes much deeper than this.

Reimagining Church and Mission in the Scottish Borders

Those with a passion for mission, whether in the form of evangelism, church revitalization, church renewal, or church planting, often comment that the rural scene is both different and often passed by. The failure to take the needs of the rural situation seriously is mirrored in secular as well as ecclesiastical life. From broadband to banks and housing to health, the needs of the rural scene are distinct and often unaddressed.

Like the inner city, the church in the rural situation is in difficulty, though for very different reasons. How does one engage in mission in a situation where people are asking spiritual questions, are often deeply conservative in their social attitudes, and yet are disconnected from the historic or inherited modes of church?

Alistair and Ruth Birkett arrived in the border region of Scotland, very close to the boundary with England, for family reasons. Ruth's family maintained a home there and, for a period at least, they needed help. Alistair and Ruth had been involved in ministry for some years, but now that kind of leadership was placed on the back burner for a time. They attended the local Church of Scotland, but they did not seek to engage in a leadership role. After a time, the perceptive minister of one of the local parish churches suggested that they might consider becoming involved in a new program that the Church of Scotland was pioneering through their "Emerging Ministries" fund. The fund financed Alistair and Ruth to engage in mission of an experimental kind for a five-year period.

The first year was to be one of listening to the community. What was God up to in this neighborhood? That was not an easy discipline for Alistair, who was something of an activist and could easily frame what he might do in this situation. The point of the year of listening was to ask questions and to gain a sense of the spiritual journeys of the people. As they built relationships, they were able to ask, "What would a spiritual journey look like for you?"

Year two saw Alistair and Ruth initiating a gathering: the Gateway Gathering. It responded to the descriptors of spiritual journeys that people had shared with them. The time, the place, the frequency, and the content reflected what they had learned in the listening process.

This experiment is now almost seven years old and a Gateway Fellowship has developed alongside the Gathering. The purpose of the Fellowship meetings is to address the spiritual questions that adults in the Gathering are asking. In practice it acts as a discipleship process.

At this stage there is an expectation, and the beginnings of a plan, to replicate the Gateway expression of church beyond the initial neighborhood to other parts of the border region. It is not particularly important to talk about numbers at this stage, but two points are worth noticing. First, there are more people involved in the Gateway structure than are involved in the two local parish churches nearby. Second, these are mostly younger families who have not previously connected with the existing churches. In other words, new ground is being broken, new people contacted, and notably people from a generation not able to relate to the existing church structures.

As you might imagine, some of those in the existing churches want to know when those who attend the Gateway gatherings are going to come to the parish church, or "proper church," as they see it. While that will probably not happen, still this new generation of growing believers might yet turn out to be the new church as the existing church continues to fade away. What that might look like in detail has yet to be addressed.

Despite the reluctance of many outside the church to attend the existing structures, the connection with the Church of Scotland was vital for Alistair in terms of gaining acceptance from those to whom he was speaking. The historic Church may not be attractive but still has social credibility. In some ways, we might describe this experiment as "the same yet different." It is the same in the sense that the kind of spiritual issues and practical activities are not so distinct from that of lively and growing churches in any age. It is different in that this is shaped around the concerns and questions of those who are in a conversation about spiritual issues. It is their journey that is being listened to. At a deeper level, Alistair and Ruth have taken the time, and been given the space, to discover what the God of mission has been in their community and have sought to shape the life of a Christian community around that.

Something's in the Air

No matter what the Church does in terms of experiment and innovation, it is not likely to make much difference unless there is a degree of receptivity in the culture. There is evidence of an unraveling of modernity's wager across Western societies. This unraveling isn't a uniform phenomenon across all nations and social groups. The strange entanglement of evangelicals with the radical right in America illustrates the challenges. The polarization of society in many Western nations between the extremes of the political right and left makes it even more difficult to read what is taking place.

As social and cultural paradigms break down, the Euro-tribal churches are beginning to experiment. Our contention is that this experiment mostly remains within the "fix and make work again" paradigm. There is yet to be confronted the challenge of refounding. What still lies before these churches is the challenge of either continuing to fix or the risky journey of joining with the God who is already active ahead of them in their neighborhoods and communities. The question of there being any kind of future for the Euro-tribal churches will not be addressed by how they reform themselves five hundred years after the great European reformations, but how they will be refounded. It will be a fragile, and provisional refounding, but it is a refounding that may yet be the hopeful remaking of these historic churches in the West.

Lightning Source UK Ltd.
Milton Keynes UK
UKHW020825051218
333492UK00007B/234/P